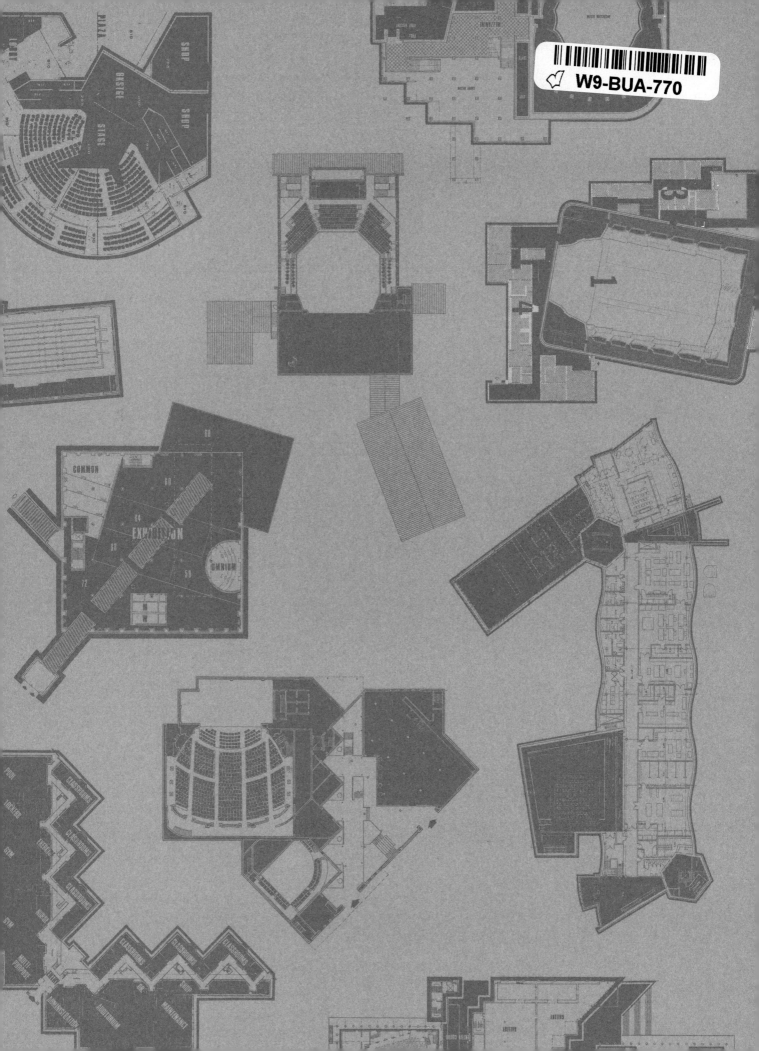

HARDY HOLZMAN PFEIFFER ASSOCIATES
BUILDINGS AND PROJECTS 1967–1992

PREFACE BY MICHAEL SORKIN

INTRODUCTION AND INTERVIEW BY MILDRED F. SCHMERTZ

BUILDING DESCRIPTIONS BY NICHOLAS POLITES

RIZZOLI
NEW YORK

First published in the United States of
America in 1992 by
Rizzoli International Publications, Inc.
300 Park Avenue South
New York, N.Y. 10010

Library of Congress Cataloging-in-
Publication Data
Hardy Holzman Pfeiffer Associates:
buildings and projects, 1967-1992 /
preface by Michael Sorkin; introduction
by Mildred F. Schmertz; building
descriptions by Nicholas Polites.
p.   cm.
Includes bibliographical references.
ISBN 0-8478-1480-7
ISBN 0-8478-1483-1 (pbk.)
1. Hardy Holzman Pfeiffer Associates.
2. Architecture, Modern—20th century—
United States. I. Schmertz, Mildred F.
NA737.H29A4 1992   91-29480
720'.92'2—dc20   CIP

Designed by Abigail Sturges
Edited by Kate Norment

Printed and bound in Singapore

Front cover: Robert O. Anderson Building,
Los Angeles County Museum of Art.
Back cover: Pingry School.

ACKNOWLEDGMENTS

This publication celebrates twenty-five years of making architecture. It is also the celebration of the many talented and dedicated associates, staff, consultants, and other professionals with whom we have shared the past quarter century.

In the preparation of this volume special thanks are due to David Morton of Rizzoli, graphic designer Abigail Sturges, and editor Kate Norment. Without their patience and insight the work could not have been realized in this form.

To our fellow professionals Michael Sorkin and Mildred F. Schmertz, who have written eloquently and honestly about what we do, we are most grateful. Special thanks go to Nicholas Polites for the concise presentation of many complex issues and ideas expressed in the Buildings and Interiors section of this monograph.

We also extend our appreciation to Eric Uhlfelder for preparing the extensive Catalogue of Work, and to certain staff members, both past and present, who have made substantial contributions to this monograph—notably Manjit Kingra, Miry Park, Christopher Perry, Christopher Lovi, Isabelle Matteson, and Ron Albinson. Their top-notch modelmaking, drawing, rendering, photography, writing, editing, and coordination gives us great pride.

Finally, we would like to recognize the special participation and unusual dedication of Donald Billinkoff and Leslie Fredette. They have been the steadfast shepherds of an unruly flock.

Hugh Hardy
Malcolm Holzman
Norman Pfeiffer

CONTENTS

PREFACE
Michael Sorkin

In an interview a few years ago, Hugh Hardy offered the following: "We've always avoided saying 'These are the principles we believe in.' A manifesto can be liberating because it gives you a cause. On the other hand, it is restricting because everything you do has to be the proof of it."

In today's vexed architectural climate, where predigested authority is constantly grafted to work to certify what is often no more than an architect's whimsy, this disavowal is bracing indeed. And yet, Hardy protests too much: the beautiful work he, Malcolm Holzman, and Norman Pfeiffer have built over a period of what is now more than twenty-five years can hardly be called unprincipled. However light the touch, theirs is no easy virtue, no mix 'n' match aesthetic of anything goes. Hardy, Holzman, and Pfeiffer's rich production is united by an overriding principle that is at once authoritative and ineffable: the standard of their taste.

And their taste is impeccable. Instead of attempting to deconstruct their own intentions, Hardy, Holzman, and Pfeiffer simply and eloquently state them: the work is always about what they like and never about what they think they ought to like. Theirs is architecture that seeks to give pleasure, not a didactic architecture that pummels us with yet another tale about the human condition or the bad news of the new age. HHPA offers a salve, not a commentary, architecture full of exuberance and wit—graceful, charming, ingratiating, and amazingly stylish.

Hardy, Holzman, and Pfeiffer have from the first grappled with the endemic condition of postmodernity: the loss of happy agreement about what goes with what. Of course, this moment of adjudication is also the primal scene of taste. The strength of HHPA's work emerges in their willingness to confront the competing claims of the maelstrom of objects and in the suave and assured ways they make forms and materials companionable. Eschewing both the ironics of pop eclecticism and the forced juxtaposition of fashionable disorder, HHPA counterposes in the service of a feeling of new continuities. Their sense of composition is abiding. From the beginning HHPA's work has been distinguished by great strength in plan (their beautifully graphic, black-and-white, just short of collagist plans are among the representational glories of the sixties and seventies), and the satisfying sense of unity in their work derives to a great degree from the sure pursuit of this underlying generator.

HHPA's special affinity for concert halls, theaters, and art galleries is hardly an accident. The partners see architecture as a performing art—not a setting exactly, but a collaborator. Whether modulating light, shaping reverberation, or pulling audiences into a theatric gyre, their architecture is continuous with the spectacle it enhances. While their means are ever innovative and ingenious, these are architects completely comfortable with old truths, with the idea that an encounter with a building should always provide a sense of well-being.

In their early projects HHPA were closely identified with the off-the-shelf look of the sixties and seventies, those exposed steel joists and lime-green ducts. Limber magicians of the limited budget, they broke away from the parsimonious moralism that had given so much modern architecture a bad name. The early work of these postfunctionalist flower children was well and simply built but gloriously loose in its love of color and pattern, in its genuinely relaxed character, in its sense of pleasure. As their commissions, with time, have grown in scope and in budget, in the possibility of richer materiality and larger reach, it has been HHPA's genius to have sacrificed none of the funk and none of the fun of the early days.

The work has evolved not simply in terms of a greater complexity of means but toward a greater expressive complexity as well. The palette is both richer and subtler and the spirit of invention more encompassing and more refined. The new images are indelible, from the striking weave of the Hult Center's ceiling to the eerie, calculated decay of the BAM Majestic Theatre, from the unabashed juxtaposition of the BEST Products

Headquarters addition to the supple yet solid masonry of WCCO-TV in Minneapolis to the lighter-than-air resuscitation of the Rainbow Room. It's grand architecture all—serious without pretense, immensely friendly to its settings, and suffused with comfort at every level.

Ten years ago I wrote the introduction to another publication of HHPA's work, devoted to the first fifteen years of their practice. Looking back at that work and at the wonderful production since, I'm impressed by the continuing freshness of the work, by the retention of the firm's continued sense of invention. Most of all, I'm impressed by how true they've been to the course they set in the sixties, immune to fashion, ever fresh. Youthful still, and in the full stride of their project, their next ten years—and their next, and their next—will surely be filled with a thousand happy new surprises of their art.

INTRODUCTION
Mildred F. Schmertz

The founding principals of Hardy Holzman Pfeiffer Associates, Hugh Hardy, Malcolm Holzman, and Norman Pfeiffer, are of the same generation, three men who came to work together, entirely by chance, more than two decades ago. Coming from different backgrounds, each possesses strong architectural talent. The highly original work done by their firm is shaped by the special gifts, interests, architectural values, likes and dislikes, and priorities each brings to the work. How these creative forces come together so effectively to produce such unexpected, continually surprising architecture must remain a mystery. But perhaps a look at the principals' background, education, and taste will offer some clues.

As a child Hugh Hardy had a play theater in the basement. The son of a successful advertising executive, he grew up in Irvington-on-Hudson, close enough to New York City to make going to the theater a simple excursion. He soon became a passionate lover of the New York stage during the heyday of Rogers and Hammerstein's musicals, Tennessee Williams's plays, Elia Kazan's productions, and Jo Mielziner's sets. As an undergraduate at Princeton he chose to major in architecture, in response to his father's pressuring him to become an engineer. Although he had mixed feelings about Princeton, he appears to have enjoyed himself there, singing in undergraduate choral groups, acting in and directing dramatic productions, designing sets and painting scenery, broadcasting on radio, and playing the clarinet in the university marching band.

Hardy continued his architectural studies in graduate school at Princeton, where the famed Jean Labatut was nearing the end of his career as the school's leading design critic. Labatut's challenging attitude was of great benefit. "Labby played favorites, but he was good," Hardy reminisces. "He taught me to see and to understand movement through space, but did not concern himself with style." And of particular importance for Hardy, who would eventually distinguish himself by his skillful, understanding ministrations to fine old buildings,

Princeton had a brilliant architectural history department. That era's students, following a modernist curriculum, found in the teachings of the historians a validation of the great architectural works of the past.

Hardy remained stagestruck throughout his student days at Princeton, choosing as the subject for his master's thesis the design of a New York City urban renewal project that was to become, in the hands of Pietro Belluschi, Gordon Bunshaft, Eduardo Catalano, Eero Saarinen, Philip Johnson, Wallace K. Harrison, and Max Abramovitz, Lincoln Center as we know it today. He began his devoted and inspired association with Jo Mielziner by inviting the great stage designer to come to Princeton and evaluate his thesis. After graduation and a stint in the Army Corps of Engineers, Hardy went to work for Mielziner, continuing to learn how magical and poetic stage design could be. "I remember his rooftops of Paris onstage. You would gasp at their beauty, not because they were like Paris in a literal way but because he had caught the light and the forms of Paris. He was a master of light. Still, to this day, wherever I am at twilight, after the sun sets, I find myself thinking of Jo, of how he could capture all of that on the stage."

At the beginning of his apprenticeship, Hardy translated Mielziner's watercolor designs for stage sets into working drawings for use by the scenery shop. He drew the sets for *Gypsy*. Soon, however, he was invited by Mielziner to help with a project that was to turn his love of theater into avocation, putting architecture at center stage in his life. During World War II, as a camouflage specialist with the air force, Mielziner had become friends with Eero Saarinen, another such expert. The two men became co-designers of the Vivian Beaumont Theater in Lincoln Center, and Hardy found himself working for both, helping them to communicate with each other in their effort to create a building that embodied and furthered the highest potentials of stagecraft and architecture.

For Hardy, Saarinen came to incarnate what an architect could be. "He had the

steadfast conviction of a leading modernist that architecture could help make a better world, that there were new problems to solve that no one had confronted before, and that problem solving was what architecture was about. He brought a questioning attitude and an intellectual energy to architecture that was not bound by theory or historical trappings. He was inventive and original in his uses of materials. At the time I knew him, he was doing his greatest projects. In addition to the Beaumont, his work included the CBS Building, the TWA Terminal, and Dulles International Airport. I hoped to go to work for him." Saarinen's untimely death in 1961 at the age of fifty-one ended that dream, and Hardy, confident of his own powers and unwilling to work for anyone else, opened his own small office the following year in New York City, with one house and some theater remodelings on the boards. Five years later, in 1967, he made partners of his two most talented and energetic associates, Malcolm Holzman and Norman Pfeiffer.

Malcolm Holzman grew up in Newark, New Jersey. His father was a musician and a teacher of music. Although Holzman doesn't consider his early years particularly significant in his development as an architect, he did take a drafting class in high school and worked as an office boy for a local architect, making blueprints and parking cars. Having won a scholarship to Pratt Institute, he moved to Brooklyn to be near school and entered the five-year bachelor of architecture program. He enjoyed both Pratt and Brooklyn. "The nicest part of Pratt for me was that I got to meet all the other people in the art school, and in all the other Pratt departments too." It was a short subway ride to Manhattan's jazz clubs, and Holzman spent as many evenings as possible listening to musicians like Thelonius Monk, Horace Silver, and Sonny Rollins.

While he was at Pratt he apprenticed in architectural offices around the city and learned firsthand why no one likes low-level drafting jobs. Upon graduating from Pratt, he spent a year with various architectural firms that designed buildings whose quality ranged from average to poor. During this period he spent most of his evenings at Pratt's night school studying sculpture, and was considering going to graduate school to study sculpture full-time. Moving from one mediocre office to another while still hoping to do better, one day he found himself being interviewed by Hugh Hardy. "Hugh had a small office with a few rooms and one other employee. He was working on the Dobell residence in Ottawa, and on some lighting for the New York City World's Fair. When I came to the office, I didn't know anything about Hugh. I don't think there was much *to* know about him at the time." Hardy recalls that he hired Holzman because his portfolio was filled with beautiful drawings.

Seattle-born Norman Pfeiffer is the only one of the partners who knew early on that he wanted to be an architect. His grandfather, a construction superintendent for large-scale local work, often took him on site visits. By the time he was five years old, he was accompanying his grandfather to architects' offices. When he visited his grandfather's house on weekends, Pfeiffer would tape architectural drawings to the dining room table and copy them.

When Pfeiffer was eight, his father and grandfather bought some land, hired an architect, and built three houses for the family. Young Norman was encouraged to participate in building each of the houses. He laid brick, poured concrete, built cabinets, and helped install wiring, plumbing, and heating. At other times he could be found in his father's shop, crafting a variety of wood constructions ranging from birdhouses to racing carts. Like Holzman, he went directly into a five-year architecture program after high school; he graduated with honors from the University of Washington in Seattle.

Pfeiffer remembers most of his professors as quite stimulating and very committed to helping young architects learn and develop. All were practicing architects in Seattle, and while they didn't teach a particular architectural style, they approached design by concentrating on abstract issues and then moving on to the more specific ones. The school was still influenced by Beaux-Arts traditions and offered classes in freehand drawing and watercolor.

On weekends and during summers he worked for Paul Hayden Kirk, known for his unique indigenous Northwest style of architecture. Most of Kirk's work was residential, and Pfeiffer, because of his early home-construction experience, was allowed to participate in the design development of some of these houses. While he was still in college, Pfeiffer's work with Kirk led to small commissions designing apartments and houses for family friends and cabins for children's summer camps.

Eager to get to work in the real world, he nevertheless decided to do a year of graduate school at Columbia, partly as a result of peer pressure; he had won a scholarship there, having pursued it because that was what all the good students did. Coming under the influence of Columbia's Victor Christ-Janer, he found himself led for the first time into the realm of abstract theory. "He dematerialized and destylized architecture for me," Pfeiffer says. "He was existential, primordial in his thinking. He taught architecture not as style, not as buildings, not as materials, not as details, not even as design. He made me think about it as experiencing places."

Although Pfeiffer had originally intended to go back to Seattle after his year at Columbia, he decided instead to spend the summer in New York and began searching for a job. He found Hugh Hardy's name in the Yellow Pages, and walked into the Hardy office without an appointment. Holzman interviewed Pfeiffer, and the firm took him on.

By 1962, when Hugh Hardy had begun his practice, the leaders of the architectural establishment in the United States had long since won their battle against eclecticism. Such architects as Jose Luis Sert, Buckminster Fuller, Gordon Bunshaft, Louis Kahn, Eero Saarinen, Paul Rudolph, and I. M. Pei had established a rich and varied modernist legacy, essentially pluralist, derived in part from their own architectural forebears, Wright, Le Corbusier, Mies, and Gropius.

All was not well, however, in the 1960s world of architectural high culture. New players were on the scene—less talented, more expedient architects who were churning out bland, cheapened versions of modernist ideas. Eventually, of course, this is the fate of every aesthetic movement, but it was the predicament of the leading modernists that the decline had come too soon, thereby weakening their influence and making them vulnerable to opposition. Complicating matters were the formalist architects, still with us, who exalted the synthesis of style and technique as the sole aesthetic content of architecture, insisting that it be uncompromised by the real world it inhabits.

Hardy, Holzman, and Pfeiffer, whose iconoclasm, fortunately, is exceeded only by their talent, were to become among the first of their generation to challenge formalist doctrine. Their work was, and continues to be, conceived in bold, persuasive opposition to this reductive aesthetic. In their practice, these architects welcome all that is contingent in the making of architecture. In their hands, form, style, and technique are used to express commonplace, everyday experience; local traditions and culture; the value of existing buildings and landscape; the aesthetics of Main Street; ordinary building functions; and the hopes, fantasies, feelings, and dreams of clients. Today the aesthetic canon of Hardy Holzman Pfeiffer Associates is familiar, accepted, part of the particular American zeitgeist that also includes the work of Frank Gehry, Charles Moore, Robert Venturi, and Denise Scott Brown.

The earliest work of Hardy Holzman Pfeiffer Associates, done on very tight budgets, reveals their revisionist intentions, signaled by what were considered by many at the time to be peculiar shapes, startling juxtapositions, and unorthodox uses of materials. The latter quality was the first manifestation of

HHPA's unstinting attention to the materiality of their buildings, finding and perfecting handsome new applications for commonplace building products.

Houses, schools, and small experimental theaters built between 1967 and 1979 were spatially organized within systems of rotated grids and powerful diagonals, and ornamented with their guts—ducts, trusses, joists, and off-the-shelf parts. These buildings, and much of HHPA's work to follow, embody the partners' fascination with industrial forms—mills, factories, silos, refineries, Butler buildings. The style, soon to be labeled "high tech," reached its apotheosis in the late seventies and mid-eighties with such buildings as Richard Rogers' Pompidou Center and Lloyds of London and Norman Foster's skyscraper bank in Hong Kong.

Although the firm is best known for its cultural institutions—four great performing arts centers and several museums—a large proportion of HHPA's work so far has been in the fields of restoration, additions, and adaptive reuse. True pioneers in their attitude toward older buildings, the partners have a reverence for our architectural heritage that has led them to remodel and augment the structures of other eras with a judgment and a discretion that were rare at the time they began. Today they continue to do fearless additions and skillful reinventions using contemporary materials and technology in ways that are responsive to the scale, mass, and ornamentation of the buildings they join.

HHPA's quarter-century of extraordinary architectural accomplishment has never been driven by the desire to support and perfect a single canon of style; the partners have instead done their best to invent the right form and style for each project. This endeavor, painstaking yet inspired, has led them over and over again to the creation of the genuinely new, thereby extending and enriching the language of contemporary architecture.

14

INTERVIEW
Mildred F. Schmertz
with Hugh Hardy, Malcolm Holzman, and Norman Pfeiffer

Mildred F. Schmertz: **Why did you change from your earlier, more aggressive approach in buildings like Orchestra Hall in Minneapolis to the kind of historicism you show in the New Haven Free Public Library?**

Hugh Hardy: They are completely different problems and therefore require different solutions. Although I will admit to an earlier fascination with buildings that represent a confrontation between old and new, in which the juxtaposition remains unresolved, most of our work has attempted to place buildings in context, whether historic, geographic, social, or aesthetic.

2

Orchestra Hall is a new, freestanding building, the symbolic presence of traditional concert music for the city. Built in an emerging part of downtown, it was intended to be a progressive statement that linked audiences and musicians with a common architectural vocabulary, rather than separating patron and artist into different realms, as in the traditional approach. Instead of bearing the name of those who built it, Orchestra Hall is named in honor of the Minnesota Orchestra; this mix of tradition and populism is typical of Minneapolis.

The New Haven library, on the other hand, represents a completely new form of library placed, in part, in an old shell. It now has an open-stack system where there was once a separation between the books and the public. The presence of Cass Gilbert's building on the New Haven Green was too powerful to be successfully challenged by our addition to the rear, so a deferential composition that uses the same geometric organization as the original building but with different materials, proportions, and subtle variations seemed the best approach. The exterior exuberance of Orchestra Hall would be out of place on the Green except in a totally new building, and the historicist allusions of the New Haven library's addition would make no sense in downtown Minneapolis.

Norman Pfeiffer: I don't think this represents a change as much as it

4

5

demonstrates our interest and ability in doing both types of work. The same comparisons could be made about the Mt. Healthy School and the Columbus Occupational Health Center, or our additions to the Ohio Theatre and the Los Angeles Central Library. The school and the medical center are sited in open fields with little man-made context, while both additions are part of important historic buildings. In new structures we are free to pursue our own architectural interests as a part of new programs, while additions are clearly influenced by an outgrowth of the original, historic vocabulary. We do not copy, but we are inspired by existing architecture and the results show it. The joy for us is that we can be equally comfortable working on such dissimilar kinds of projects.

MFS: **But doesn't it basically come down to a matter of style?**

HH: If by that you mean surface appearance, no. The appearance of our buildings is not an appliqué but a direct result of the forces that bring them into being. The dissimilar appearance of the buildings resulted from a desire to express the essential nature of the activities they house and the communities in which they stand.

MFS: **Why did you take such a historicist approach to the Rainbow Room; why didn't you do something more contemporary?**

6

HH: There our goal was not to make a confrontation between old and new but to see them integrated into a seamless whole. This is very different from what was attempted twenty years earlier in the Exeter Assembly Hall, where old and new are clearly juxtaposed. I don't believe the results in the Rainbow Room are historicist in the sense of denying the present. The drama of arrival on the sixty-fifth floor is a totally new invention, but it feels like part of Rockefeller Center rather than a contemporary imposition. Although our new designs throughout the sixty-fourth and sixty-fifth floors use elements and materials found elsewhere in Rockefeller Center, there is, in fact, nothing exactly like them anywhere. (The

15

7. Virginia Museum of Fine Arts, West Wing service gate by Albert Paley.
8. Willamette Parking Structure, bridge with glass by Ed Carpenter.
9. BEST Products Headquarters, carpet based on Jack Beal design.

16

illuminated columns on the sixty-fifth floor, for instance, seem to belong here, but their precedent is found in our design for the lobby of Charlotte's Spirit Square.) This same game of layering old and new plays itself out in all areas of the reconstruction. Only the Rainbow Room itself is a true restoration, and even here completely new elements, such as Dan Dailey's cast-glass wall, have been introduced.

MFS: You often work with artists in your projects: Albert Paley worked on the West Wing of the Virginia Museum of Fine Arts, and many different artists contributed to the Alaska Center for the Performing Arts. Why do you choose to work with artists so often?

7

Malcolm Holzman: We work only with artists who are interested in the integration of art and architecture. Too many artists and architects see their work as separate and independent statements. But not all areas of a building need to be embellished by architects. Certain areas can become richer and more expressive when developed by an artist. Floors, doors, and fabrics can be works of art and craft. Artists we have worked with have brought their sensibilities to many aspects of a building. The gates at the Virginia Museum of Fine Arts were made by Albert Paley, the glass in the Hult Center was created by Ed Carpenter, and the pattern of the BEST Products field carpet was inspired by a folding screen by Jack Beal.

8

NP: It is evident from the spirit of our practice that we are comfortable working in collaboration. We share the belief that good ideas can come from anywhere, and artists are perfectly welcome in an inclusive architecture like ours. Not burdened by a specific architectural style, we find it easy to collaborate with and include others in the creative process.

9

Our most ambitious project in collaboration with artists is the Los Angeles Central Library. Artist-designed chandeliers, tiled and stenciled surfaces, murals, iron gates, and elevator cabs will

all be incorporated into the architecture of the new wing. In much the same way that Bertram Goodhue did in the original building in the 1920s, we are working with various artists. The precedent was clearly established by Goodhue, and it is our intention to carry the spirit of these earlier artistic works into the architecture of the new wing.

HH: This experience is also stimulating because artists have such a fearless sense of materials and they are not limited by the geometric organization of architecture. But they can also assist in enhancing walls, floors, and ceilings— building elements that are usually handled in more commonplace ways. Although difficult at times to orchestrate, the experience of working with artists is both a stimulus and an incentive for architects to get beyond the commonplace.

MFS: Your largest project to date, the rehabilitation and expansion of Goodhue's Central Library for the Los Angeles Public Library, has also been the most controversial. Why is that?

NP: Los Angeles has come to the historic preservation movement late in the game. Until recently, there was little interest in things past and, more importantly, no consensus as to the appropriate architectural response to specific historical problems. Our design for the rehabilitation and expansion of the Bertram Goodhue building has been part of the city's rediscovery of itself.

The Cultural Affairs Commission in Los Angeles has jurisdiction over all city-owned historic buildings and must approve the design of such projects. In our case they initially did not do that. The project also falls under the jurisdiction of the State Historic Preservation Office and the National Park Service, which must approve all projects that benefit from state funding or historic tax credits. Twenty-five million dollars of potential capital funding depends on certification by the state. The result is that two architectural review boards, with differing agendas, hold power over one architectural project.

10. Los Angeles Central Library, aerial view.
11. Alaska Center for the Performing Arts.
12. Hult Center for the Performing Arts.

10

From the outset it was decided that the original Goodhue building, with its three entrances and resplendent pyramidal tower, would remain as the library's front door and a dominant symbolic presence on the downtown skyline. The new addition would contain all of the subject departments and its architecture would defer to the original structure.

Our architectural inspiration for the addition came from the blocklike massing of the original building. Similar new elements formed the corners and major axis of the new wing. The new atrium was placed between these forms and the original building, which served as bookends. Just as Goodhue's tower symbolizes the heart of the original building, the atrium forms the core of the new addition, linking the various subject departments and providing what promises to be one of Los Angeles's most accessible and memorable public spaces. The architectural expression of all this was originally far more modern and contrasted in form and material to the more traditional elements of Goodhue's building. We thought the design, composed of waving terra-cotta walls that supported a stainless-steel-and-glass atrium skylight punctured by clerestory windows accented in alabaster, represented an appropriate response to the problem of relating old and new. We also felt strongly that the new wing should not confuse the public by appearing to be part of the original. We believed that such dissimilar vocabularies were compatible and could coexist to form a composition that acknowledges the past and the future. Unfortunately, the two architectural review boards agreed with each other to not agree with us.

Modifications to the initial design, which took a year to complete, consisted of removing the atrium's peak, lowering the mass of the skylight, and modifying the design with more familiar massing and fenestration patterns. Terra cotta, now flat, still forms the primary infill material between the new stucco masses. The new wing is different in spirit from the first design and is done with far less contrast to the Goodhue building. When the new

wing is completed there will be no doubt that it was inspired by the original.

MFS: Which of your projects give you the most pleasure?

HH: Those built for the public. I feel a particular joy seeing places we have imagined for people actually being animated by their movement and presence. It is exhilarating to see architecture come alive this way.

NP: Those that were made to enhance an art form, i.e., museums, theaters, concert halls. The pleasure comes as much from the process, which involves close collaboration with artist-users, as it does from the finished product, which results from the resolution of the conflicting needs of clients and our own needs as architects.

MFS: What is your favorite HHPA project?

NP: I would say the Hult Center in Eugene and the Alaska Center for the Performing Arts, because both exhibit a variety of dissimilar architectural vocabularies within a single project. Each theater's interior has its own distinct architectural treatment, while the performance spaces themselves form a marked contrast to the public lobbies that connect them. They present the greatest amount of artistic flexibility for the user and the greatest amount of visual variety for the audience.

On the outside of the Alaska Center, seemingly disparate architectural forms are united into a single architectural composition by common materials that are woven continuously through. In Eugene, the large, naturally textured concrete forms of the theaters are juxtaposed to the multipeaked modern glass vocabulary of the lobby.

MFS: Malcolm says your firm enjoys making things that are incomplete. But how do you feel about additions to your work by others?

HH: Changes are inevitable, especially in a dynamic society like ours. Beginning

17

11

12

18

with the premise that buildings can result from juxtapositions—between old and new, between volumes and materials, between the symbolic identities of the parts—we must accept additions and changes as part of architecture. The question is how they relate to the original, whether they obscure or reinforce the original intent. Our Children's Museum in Brooklyn has been changed many times, by new exhibitions and administrative needs, but the integrity of the building is still intact. Our concert hall in Denver is receiving a new exterior context in a way that now appears to be unsympathetic, but the place where music is made will not change.

NP: At the Los Angeles County Museum of Art, we developed a long-range master plan for the renovation and future expansion of the museum. At the heart of the plan is a large central court that provides access to all of the buildings as well as a dozen other future building sites.

Our new building there, the Robert O. Anderson Building, for contemporary and modern art, established a new architectural vocabulary for the museum, setting the tone for future new construction as well as the renovation of the three original buildings. New materials as well as a new scale were introduced into the composition, and these also influence future work.

Before the Anderson Building was complete, the museum received a generous gift of Edo prints and along with it a building design by Bruce Goff. The Pavilion for Japanese Art could be easily placed because there was an overall planning concept for expansion. While it bears little resemblance to the Anderson Building, to the other existing structures, or to those planned for the future, it sits comfortably, like a piece of sculpture, next to them in appealing contrast. It is a delightful exception to a more unified complex and adds a welcome surprise to the museum experience. It reinforces the idea that this museum is too vital to be complete.

MFS: I've heard you speak of the importance of landscape. How is that

13

represented in your work?

HH: First of all, the siting of each building must be a response to the natural environment, even in urban areas. I suppose our opera house in Cooperstown is the most obvious example of building in a landscape because the movable walls of the auditorium permit audiences to see the surrounding gardens and trees before and after performances. The separation of cars onto an adjacent hillside permits the public to approach on foot around a small pond (actually part of the fire-protection system) and arrive at the opera house with a completely different experience than the suburban shopping center, where the sequence is car, parking lot, front door. Finally there is the siting of the opera house, which is placed as part of a complex of farm buildings so that they fit together into a complementary whole.

MFS: You often speak of the distinctions between architecture and scenery. Having made both, how do you see them as different?

HH: Scenery is ephemeral. It is intended to be a surrogate for reality. Architecture attempts to reconcile different realities—outside versus inside, form versus use—and present them in concrete terms. It speaks directly, with the force of corporeal truth. Scenery and architecture are often combined, as in baroque churches, Disney hotels, and some developer buildings. As the inflationary forces of the 1980s caused many buildings to be built to increase land value without regard for their long-term survival, a new form of disposable architecture appeared that *is* scenery.

MFS: How often does your firm use scenery?

HH: We often use it to temporarily solve problems. Take our installation at the New York Botanical Garden. Our temporary kiosks, pylons, and platforms conveyed the illusion that this vast 250-acre garden had somehow been changed and made more friendly, less remote and confusing. In fact, the garden

14

is physically the same, but the presence of these lattice structures, which change with the seasons, provides orientation and shelter in a lighthearted and ephemeral way that more permanent-seeming architecture could not achieve.

MFS: Why is so much of your work done for cultural institutions?

NP: Our own curiosity and constant search for new architectural expression is often well matched to their institutional goals and objectives. Out of this interaction come individual solutions crafted to the specific goals and objectives of a particular organization rather than the repetitive stylistic expressions of commercial work.

Also, many institutions have existing buildings of great distinction. Adapting them to new program requirements, developing an appropriate relationship between old and new, has always been of great interest to us.

MFS: In most of your work, the new complements the old, rather than contrasting with it. Why have you chosen this approach?

NP: We believe that in most instances a new building designed to contrast with its historic neighbor is an appropriate and valid approach, but it is a difficult response for most clients and users to understand and accept. A more literal borrowing from or abstraction of the original is more commonly accepted. The consensus of landmark commissions, landmark conservancies, and other such groups around the country seems to indicate a more sympathetic relationship between old and new. While the guidelines developed by the National Park Service to control the certification of historic buildings discourage literal copying, they still lean toward a sympathetic response to the old.

Our new forty-three-story hotel in downtown Los Angeles is sited next to one of the city's finest historic buildings, the former Barker Brothers Building. It is our first major project to take a strongly contrasting approach. Here a very

modern glass building will be joined to a rusticated limestone-and-masonry building. The curtain-wall system and the color of the glass will be manipulated to relate parts of the new hotel to key features of the historic building. While the new hotel will be clearly modern, it bears an appropriate allusion to its neighbor.

MFS: As young architects emerge who enjoy the freedom of design ideas that you three helped make possible, how do you keep your work relevant?

HH: There's never enough good architecture, and while it's true that architecture enjoys a freedom of expression unknown when the three of us went to school, the results are not necessarily better buildings. In fact, there's an excess and indulgence in much of today's architecture that saddens me. In trying to be up-to-the-minute, much of today's work is in fact a caricature of what we worked for in our earlier assault on the status quo. Gratuitous angles, disorienting plans, and an overwrought selection of materials obscure rather than enliven many contemporary buildings. At the same time, a new awareness of the environment and a less self-conscious use of history is beginning to emerge, developments that speak well for the future of this most public of the arts.

NP: I must admit it's quite amazing to see the proliferation of projects being built—particularly in Southern California—that incorporate many of the architectural ideas we began exploring when we started working together in the 1960s. Many of these concepts found form in our early work and continue to emerge today where appropriate. Ironically, the major projects we are doing in California now involve significant historic buildings in which our inclusionist approach takes on a different kind of relevance. The range of possibilities in restoration is far more finite than in designing new, freestanding buildings. We have become more involved in the re-presentation of architectural ideas generated by others, in the appropriate interpretation of their work for the future, than in making a contemporary statement.

19

16. Cooper-Hewitt Museum.
17. Stanford University, detail of Richardson quadrangle.
18. B. Altman's Midtown Centre.
19. Cleveland Public Library.

20

MFS: What concerns do you have for today's architecture?

HH: I worry about the current dalliance with theory as the generator of architectural form, about buildings that can be understood only in terms of literary values rather than through direct experience. Architecture should not need to be decoded to be understood. Although it represents a series of conscious choices that take place in an intellectual framework, this should not obscure public enjoyment of the results.

More troublesome still is the idea that architecture is somehow restricted and hampered by tradition. If one accepts the idea that the profession represents a two-thousand-year-old language of enclosure enriched by past associations, the thought of creating the new without benefit of this resource becomes absurd. Whether in the anthropomorphic forms of Michael Graves, the abstract historicisms of Robert Venturi, the vernacular manipulations of Charles Moore, or the challenging sculptures of Frank Gehry, architecture is enriched through its connections to what has gone before. The modernists were misled not by their embrace of the machine but by their rejection of the past. It seems odd to go through all that again in the name of borrowed literary theory.

MFS: Malcolm says your firm never does restorations. Hugh says you do. Whom do I believe?

16

HH: Both of us. He means restoration in the scientific sense, the attempt to re-create the past. I mean it in the symbolic sense, the attempt to evoke memories. Ada Louise Huxtable called our work at the Cooper-Hewitt Museum "interpretive" restoration. That's the key difference between an effort to preserve the past—which is impossible—and the possibility of evoking it, as in the Rainbow Room.

NP: We sometimes do both. At Stanford University we're working on part of the original quad designed by H. H. Richardson. Due to the recent earthquake, which was unforgiving to these buildings, the entire interior

17

structural system—walls, floors, columns, roof—will be removed and replaced. The outside of the sandstone buildings will be restored to their original condition, while the inside will be a new interpretation of the character of the past.

MFS: Wasn't your proposed addition to B. Altman's department store presented as the completion of Trowbridge and Livingston's design? How does that fit in with your statement that you can't re-create the past?

18

HH: The Altman's design represents the adjustment of an ill-proportioned composition, a change that the New York City Landmarks Preservation Commission accepted as legitimate. Whether Trowbridge and Livingston would have added six floors to their design in this way is not the point. Here is the opportunity to see a commercial structure enlarged and changed to accommodate a mixed-use occupancy in a sympathetic manner. We thought that choice was more legitimate in the urban context than creating confrontation, using the store as a pedestal for a totally different architectural form.

MFS: Would you have done this if there were no landmarks commission?

HH: Perhaps. But the client would probably not have paid for such a complete realization.

MFS: You have entered only a few competitions and, with the exception of the Willard Hotel, have built nothing as a result of competitions. Why is this?

HH: The collaborative and explorative nature of our practice works better when there are clients, a program, and a dialogue. We use clients' input as a stepping stone to establish a design direction. Too often competitions are rigged, or they're beauty contests, or they're judged by unknown rules. Nonetheless, we recently won competitions for the expansion of the Cleveland Public Library and for a new

19

20. Rainbow Bridge U.S. Toll Plaza.
21. BEST Products Headquarters, Phase 1 site plan.

gateway for the U.S.-Canadian border at Niagara Falls.

MFS: Today collaboration in architecture is the rule rather than the exception. How has your collaborative partnership evolved and how will it change?

MH: Twenty-five years ago, Hugh, Norman, and I worked on all of our projects. In essence, good ideas were pursued and developed and lesser ones were discarded. The authorship of ideas was not as paramount as the execution of good architecture. As the firm grew in size, more individuals participated in the process and the circle was expanded. Today the three founding partners still collaborate on the most complex projects. Since the majority of the firm's projects are still modest in size, the collaborative role is frequently shared by a partner, an associate, and a project architect. The circle has been expanded again and also divided so it can work together or in parts.

NP: Now that we have two offices, the circle has expanded even farther. But even as recently as the Los Angeles Central Library the three of us spent over three years in close collaboration right down to the custom furnishings and paint colors. I'm sure we'll continue to do this on major new commissions in the east and the west.

MFS: Does your work have some affinity with that of other architects, painters, sculptors, or photographers working today? Are you part of a zeitgeist?

MH: Unlike when we started out, there are a lot of people working now with whom we have something in common. But we are not aligned with a particular movement or style. Happily, there are many choices now, and no single style is correct for a particular type of building.

MFS: Are there architects with whom you feel a commonality?

MH: There is a commonality of interest with some, including Frank Gehry and

Richard Rogers, with all their emphasis on industrialization. We also share Bruce Goff's exploration of new uses of materials, the idea that you can use common materials in uncommon ways. His buildings are marvelous. In Wright's later years, even he was borrowing from Goff.

MFS: I think you receive some of your inspiration from contemporary art.

MH: Yes and no. There is some relationship between the kind of art I enjoy and the architecture I have an interest in. One aspect of painting is the creation of a two-dimensional surface, and what to do with this surface. A common choice is to distort the surface to give it a sense of depth or perspective. When we make buildings with large, public rooms, we frequently distort the volumes to make these rooms intimate. We attempt to make them seem smaller than they are. When we plan a concert hall with 2,500 seats, we want the audience to feel as though they are in a place with 150 seats. We find ways to focus their attention, somewhat in the way painters do.

Another concern in art is the correct cropping of an image. Painters have learned a lot from photography in this regard. And architects have learned a great lesson from both arts. One frequently sees cropping in architecture today. One of the most deadly aspects about postmodern architecture, with its pediments, end towers, and symmetrical windows, is that it is all complete. The contemporary mind wants more challenge than that. Marcel Duchamp suggested earlier in this century that the spectator can complete the work of art. I think people today would rather complete our buildings in their mind's eye than have everything spelled out for them.

MFS: How do you use cropping devices in your buildings?

MH: The question is, how much of a fragment does there have to be to allow one to imagine the whole? Take the plan for the BEST Products Company Headquarters. We built a segment of a

22

22

23

24

curving building facade in such a way that one can imagine the form completed. We imply that this great wall could become a circle. In our Arts Center at Middlebury College we have a large circle in the center of the plan. It doesn't form a complete cylinder, but people will nevertheless have a sense of being in something whole. Cropping also occurs when we pattern surfaces. The manner in which the diaper pattern on the facade of BEST Products is cropped at the ends of the wall implies continuation.

Painters find ways to subvert the flatness of the picture, and I like that. Good paintings, like good architecture, are interesting both from a distance and up close. Some buildings look terrific from a distance, but when you get up close there are no details to look at. Some architects get all the screw bolts lined up perfectly for close inspection, but there is no bigger image to see. In our work we strive for both.

MFS: To quote Kenneth Frampton: "When much of modern building is experienced in its actuality, its photogenic quality is denied by the poverty and brutality of its detailing." This is not true of your work. How do you manage to be an exception?

MH: Our building exteriors are almost never made of a single material. At the Los Angeles County Museum of Art, for example, we use terra cotta and glass block in new ways, getting the manufacturers to modify these products to accomplish our design. Such combinations of materials respond to natural light and give the building its scale.

MFS: Your firm is well known for getting fine results in spite of tight budgets. Most of your buildings appear to be more expensive than they are. How do you do this?

MH: One way is to find bargains in regional materials. For a project we are working on in Omaha, Nebraska, we found someone in the community who still fires bricks in century-old beehive

25

26

kilns, the last two operating in the city. The nature of these kilns is that they are uncontrollable; as a result, you get different shapes, colors, and sizes of bricks. Another regional supplier, who is in the tombstone business, sells granite remnants for $80 a ton, cut eight inches thick, and polished on both sides.

At Middlebury College the most appreciated buildings are constructed of dimensional stone, thick blocks that support themselves. But in 1990 we can't afford the same stone laid up in the original method. Instead, we are using sidewalk curbing blocks erected with concrete-block backup. These types of materials provide economy with quality and give regional character to our buildings.

MFS: The design of each of your buildings focuses on symbolism and meaning relating to the nature of the institution to be housed. How do you communicate these symbolic aspects through formal devices?

HH: When we designed the Mt. Healthy School in Columbus, Indiana, it was difficult to make the building look like a typical school because it had an open plan, organized around the functions of team teaching. Indeed, when I presented our design to the school board and explained the logic of all the diagonals, the layering, and the clustering, the leader of the conservative faction on the board said, "Mr. Hardy, it doesn't look like a school." The images carried in the public mind are very powerful and you must understand them. You can manipulate them, you can perhaps transform them, you can adjust them, but you have to know they are there. Often, however, questions of symbolism can be resolved with a few deft moves. Mt. Healthy started to look like a school after we put a flagpole and flag out front.

MH: We sometimes express the nature of a theater by making the building a marquee. For WCCO-TV in Minneapolis, finding appropriate symbolic content for the viewer on the street turned out to be difficult. We made a portion of the building a base to display the TV-

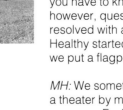

27

26. Middlebury College, McCullough Student Center, curbing blocks.
27. Mt. Healthy School, main facade with flagpole.
28. WCCO-TV Headquarters, broadcasting equipment.

28

broadcasting equipment above. Unfortunately, some people noticed only the masonry base and others were offended by the equipment on the roof. Often our symbolism is misread. In our Nebraska project we proposed a large window in the shape of the state, which is almost a rectangle. The university's Facilities Planning and Space Management office was offended. Direct symbolism is not for everyone.

MFS: HHPA's work is strongly driven by programmatic concerns. How do you develop a program?

NP: We try to begin without preconceived notions. We develop the program and try to discover the forms that are inherent in it. We have labyrinthine discussions with our clients. To a school board that has always built ten classrooms by putting five on each side of a corridor we propose other options. In designing the Columbus Occupational Health Center in Indiana, we studied the entire experience of going to a hospital or a doctor's office and tried to make it more humane.

MFS: You bring to all your work an open mind and a willingness to begin at the beginning.

NP: I think we do that consistently, although fresh programmatic starts are harder to accomplish when we are working in noninstitutional development ventures in which the limits of economy and efficiency drive the show. Tight budgets do not allow for a lot of exploration. But we try to leave no stone unturned. We are designing a new hotel in L.A. with the Macklowe Organization. The resources we have are finite, and the challenge is to figure out how to work with them to create more than just grids of mullions and glass or patterns of marble in the lobby.

MFS: All of HHPA's work is enhanced by wit and playfulness. Could this be one of the reasons you receive so little attention from the academic critics?

NP: Perhaps early in our careers we fought the rules so hard that we offended people. On the other hand, our work is

not categorically pure; we do not attempt to be stylistically uniform. We have not spent a lifetime perfecting a single aesthetic idea. We have not been a part of some mainstream. We have not come from a definable past, and we are not headed toward a predictable future. To get critical attention in academia, architects must make stylistic commitments, hone the perfect thing, be constant to a frequently articulated philosophy. When critics write about something, they must compare it to other things.

Another reason could be that our buildings are usually far richer on the inside than the outside. Most architects elaborate their exteriors and treat a building as an object, a piece of sculpture. Academic critics seem to be better able to handle this.

MH: I think academic critics have not come to grips with the way we work with old buildings. We are concerned about our built heritage. Our firm does not undertake pure historic preservation or restoration work. The old buildings we most frequently come in contact with need to be altered or added to in some way. This automatically generates a dialogue between new and old construction. There are two easy ways to add to an old structure: one is to clone it; the other is to build something in stark contrast to it. Either approach lends itself to easy criticism. This is the type of discourse most frequently read. If cloned, is it sympathetic, or has it bloated and obscured the original? If conceived in contrast, is the original overpowered? We have completed projects in both modes, but the work that interests us most lies somewhere in between. We attempt to change old buildings in ways that are compatible and reasonable, not to undermine them. We endeavor to extend the thinking that is already there in a contemporary way. Critical appraisal of this design approach is not prevalent.

HH: We didn't begin by writing a manifesto, by saying we are the origin of a new architecture, and it is going to be this. Academic critics are more comfortable with architects who do that

23

24

because it makes evaluation easier. They are also more comfortable with questions of style.

MH: I view what we are doing as a lifetime's worth of work. It won't be done until we get to the end. Whereas academic critics most frequently view each building as its own completed piece of life, I view all our work as being connected. We are struggling to make architecture that we think is authentic. We are not cribbing other people's stuff, even though there are similarities between our work and other people's work. We are trying to do something that is of interest to us and meaningful to the people with whom we are making our buildings, something that represents a reflection of our time. We may never make buildings that are perfect, complete, and totally resolved, but I think the fact that there is an incomplete quality about them is in some way the best expression of how they were conceived. Perhaps this is what makes them as good as they are. We have learned that it takes a long time to master how to design a good building. The first twenty-five years of our professional lives have been spent gaining that mastery.

MFS: What is the future of HHPA?

HH: It is obvious that the profession is becoming increasingly specialized. The key to recognition and survival in a field of greater and greater competition is to develop a distinctive product through style, building type, or rhetorical strategy. The idea of architecture as a profession that provides services is fading in favor of the notion of a profession that shapes products. This makes the future of generalist firms hard to predict. Our range of project types, our explorations into many different architectural vocabularies, and the apparent dissimilarity of our projects prevent a neat packaging of our work for those looking for ways to categorize.

Nonetheless, we believe there is a place for our approach to architecture, and we remain dedicated to an architecture that results from connections between discovery and need, aesthetics and use.

NP: We've recently opened an office in Los Angeles, primarily to be closer to our West Coast work. But, more importantly, we want to expand our practice in the commercial world, and Los Angeles is a city where considerable commercial development is expected. Working within a developer's limited economic means is a challenge we welcome; we believe that our inquiring approach to design can find an expression in the commercial market as well.

MFS: How will your future projects be different from your past work?

MH: They won't be. Aside from the obvious functional requirements, the issues addressed in our designs will be much the same, although the results may appear different. We are working out certain basic issues in our projects: how to add to an existing structure without cloning or undermining the original; how to make large public spaces intimate; how to make inexpensive structures with quality materials; how to integrate a structure with its surroundings.

MFS: How will an architectural historian fifty years from now sort out HHPA from its contemporaries?

HH: Who cares? But I will try to answer your question. I have always thought that history has its own agenda. History is like a giant trunk that you loot to serve your purposes on a given day. History is for the living, not for the dead, but the more you can offer history, the better. The more games and revels and costumes you give future generations, the more they can play in the trunk. I think it is wrong to even try to imagine what historians will think of what we do. I see how carefully other professionals have attempted to position themselves, but I don't believe the results will justify the effort.

MFS: What would you most like to be remembered as?

HH: Architects whose inquiring attitude encouraged a fresh examination of architecture.

29

1. Saint Louis Art Museum, master plan.
2. Salisbury School, plan.
3. Orchestra Hall, lobby detail.
4. North Carolina School of the Arts, master plan.

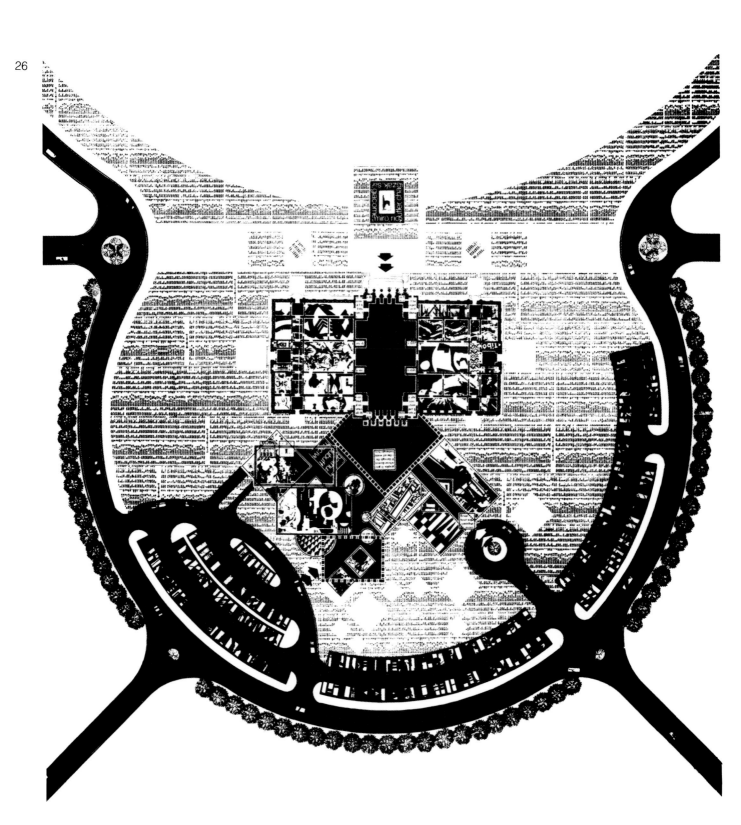

A PROCESS OF CONSCIOUS CHOICE
Hugh Hardy, Malcolm Holzman, and Norman Pfeiffer

Architecture is now the most public of arts. Once the sole province of royalty and entitlement, architecture can now belong to everyone. It can connect the world of ideas with life in the street, making buildings that are accessible to all without the constrictions of arcane theory or complex rhetoric. Buildings can be made for public enjoyment; they can be places of celebration and shared pleasures.

The creation of architecture is distinguished by a process of conscious choice. It is not the expense of a structure but the intelligence with which its elements are selected and put together that separates architecture from mere building. Lavish materials, costly construction methods, and unusual techniques may be used, but to succeed they must clarify, not obscure, the original intent.

Every architect who practices today is forced to come to terms with modernism, a movement that attempted to erase architecture's past in the name of a new social order. This new architecture of the people emerged as a socially minded response to the appalling living conditions that resulted from industrialization and as an aesthetic reaction to Victorian excess. It was based, in part, on the desire to create housing and public spaces that were stripped of pretense. It advocated buildings that were hygienic and suffused with light and air to promote good health and a sense of well-being. New methods of construction were pursued, presaging a new order, a new way of seeing the elements of architecture. Purged of all ornamentation, this environment was to be one of simple essentials: pure structure, abstract planar enclosures, basic materials, and sleek furniture; all in buildings designed ideally for flat sites.

But by limiting the legitimate elements of architectural enclosure, removing all historical associations, and relying more on theory than experience to justify the results, modernism led to a monotony that alienated those for whom it was intended. Instead of remaining a populist

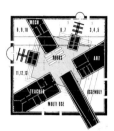

2

3

4

movement, modernism was taken up by the wealthy to convey status, eventually becoming a form of corporate chic. Shorn of its populist underpinnings, it became a style for a select few.

In reaction to modernism's collapse, architects now struggle to find new ways to organize the elements of architecture. Some embrace history with wide-eyed enthusiasm; others temper it with a heavy dose of irony. Some reject all that has gone before in yet another attempt to invent forms that are free of past associations. Against this cultural background HHPA has pursued two different goals. One has been to explore new ways to define and employ the elements of architecture: plans based on rotated grids; enclosures whose sections are not congruent with their plans; industrial products used as materials for finished surfaces; the imagery of incomplete buildings and fragmented interiors. The other goal has been to integrate new buildings into a continuity of architectural expression: rather than create buildings, *de nouveau*, in opposition to their context, HHPA often creates buildings that complement existing structures while still communicating an awareness of the present.

These various devices may appear contradictory; indeed, combining all of them in a single building would lead to chaos. But HHPA's intention is not to follow a single unified theory of design. It is, rather, to find the right architectural expression for each project, whether it is located in a dense urban setting, in a rural landscape, or beside a highway. Our hope is to expand the boundaries of architecture, to create buildings that are appreciated for their rich imagery, their ability to seem familiar on many different levels of understanding.

As each generation of architects has confronted modernism, it has also had to come to terms with history. The problem of what to do with old buildings—how to serve them as well as ourselves—springs from the conflict between aesthetics and practicality. All Greek Revival buildings, for instance, may come from common

5. Demolition of Pennsylvania Station, 1962.
6. BAM Majestic Theatre.
7. New Haven Free Public Library and courthouse.

design principles, but their organization and purpose can differ wildly. Some are meant to show off, some to represent the ideals of government, some simply to be good neighbors. The approaches to the restoration and reuse of old buildings must be as varied as the forces that brought them into being.

Ironically, Pennsylvania Station, whose demolition led to the formation of the New York City Landmarks Preservation Commission, has become the great icon of preservationists, more important in memory than it was in fact. It was destroyed in 1962, all the Roman grandeur and ceremonial pomp giving way to blatant function and uninspired commerce. Was this confrontation between preservation and development necessary? Did it have to be an either/or situation? Was it essential to demolish the entire complex in order to achieve the present uses? If a less doctrinaire, less confrontational approach had been taken in the planning and development of this block-long site, could a less brutal architecture have resulted?

As this type of urban development proves, dismissing the past can lead to a landscape of confused anonymity, a present without meaning. But although preservation and restoration of old buildings fulfills our need for cultural continuity, they require care and sensitivity. Even if true restoration—a complete turning back of the clock— were possible (or legal), it would be of questionable value to contemporary use. Perhaps paint finishes and original detailing can be duplicated, but today's safety requirements, lighting levels, and standards of comfort are so drastically different from those of earlier eras that present-day occupants would find the results of true restoration uninhabitable.

The attempt to recapture the past through restoration can re-create only an approximation of what once was. Not only are restored buildings too bright and clean to be physically accurate, but when they appear 100 percent new, their place in time is falsified. The most realistic restorations are those that can accept the passage of time as part of

their essential nature. Buildings from other periods are important to us not only because of their aesthetics but also because they document the survival of values so different from our own. Efforts to remove the psychic distance that separates us from them only renders the original false.

In our restoration work we have sought to heighten the basic character of each building, whatever its stylistic vocabulary, but not to possess it so tightly that the intervening years are squeezed away, leaving only a gaudy copy. The results of our explorations are therefore as diverse as the communities they serve.

While the return of activity to an abandoned structure can make its preservation possible, does the architectural restoration that accompanies it have to involve a wholesale re-invention of the original? In our restoration of the BAM Majestic Theatre (1987), the original fabric of the interior remains clearly visible, but the components of contemporary theater technology have been placed in full view and the audience-performer relationship has been greatly altered. Instead of the 2,400 people accommodated by the original auditorium, this restoration includes seating for only 900. Contemporary audiences, who are now used to the intimacy of television, would find the original two-balcony theater vast and impersonal; hence a reduced and reconfigured reconstruction. But the character and organization of the original room are no less clear for having been altered for contemporary needs.

When adding on to old buildings, purists may demand a juxtaposition of old and new so that the two are revealed by opposition. However, we feel that there is no need to avoid the gentler forms of continuity offered by a less aggressive view. For instance, HHPA's 1990 addition to a neo-Georgian library on the New Haven Green would no better serve its purpose by being an assertive juxtaposition. Such impudence might have momentary appeal if seen isolated as a single, new structure; but in the historical context of Cass Gilbert's

6

7

8

9

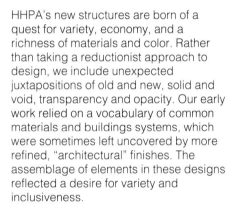
10

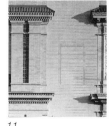
11

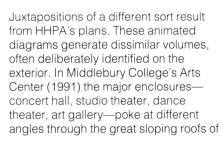
12

original building and the Green itself, the results would be more an irritant than an insight.

We believe that an interpretive restoration can form part of a new composition without compromising either old or new. In our invention of new public spaces to complement a restored Rainbow Room, or our design for a 330,000-square-foot addition that doubles the size of the Central Library in Los Angeles, we do not deny the validity of the original designs. A purist philosophy, one that narrows the aesthetic limits of architecture, seems too limiting for our pluralist society. In a country characterized by diversity, why should there be only one way to make architecture?

HHPA's new structures are born of a quest for variety, economy, and a richness of materials and color. Rather than taking a reductionist approach to design, we include unexpected juxtapositions of old and new, solid and void, transparency and opacity. Our early work relied on a vocabulary of common materials and buildings systems, which were sometimes left uncovered by more refined, "architectural" finishes. The assemblage of elements in these designs reflected a desire for variety and inclusiveness.

Such eclecticism has shaped the design of several recent HHPA compositions. Projects such as the expansion of the Currier Gallery of Art in Manchester, New Hampshire (1982), the Galbreath Pavilion at the Ohio Theatre in Columbus, Ohio (1984), and the McCullough Student Center at Middlebury College (1991) demonstrate an intermingling of modern and traditional elements that provides both cultural continuity and visual contrast.

Juxtapositions of a different sort result from HHPA's plans. These animated diagrams generate dissimilar volumes, often deliberately identified on the exterior. In Middlebury College's Arts Center (1991) the major enclosures—concert hall, studio theater, dance theater, art gallery—poke at different angles through the great sloping roofs of

13

14

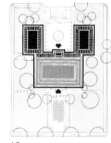
15

the structure. These contrasts in form are heightened by the use of different materials to distinguish each volume.

29

We have spent considerable effort investigating the use of materials. Contemporary buildings are increasingly conceived as veneer over a structural frame, and the resulting thinness of the exterior wall tends to make all materials appear the same. In opposition to this trend, we are seeking to make brick look like brick, stone look like stone, glass look like glass. Our effort is to give these surface veneers the richness of detail and the stable appearance that architecture deserves.

HHPA's work, whether with new buildings or old, covers an exceptionally wide range of project types. Each design is a deliberate attempt to avoid conforming to a preconceived stylistic approach. Rather than pursue new projects as the confirmation of a unified abstract theory, we see architecture as a way to enhance, sustain, and celebrate the distinctive characteristics of each site and program. We delight in the full range of possibilities that architecture represents. Diversity is our goal. Our pursuit of its limits continues unabated.

BUILDINGS AND INTERIORS

HADLEY HOUSE
Martha's Vineyard, Massachusetts, 1967

32 For a client who requested "a house that nourishes without tiring, that changes from day to day," HHPA produced one of its most exuberant early compositions. This structure, built for author-playwright-journalist Arthur Hadley and his three children, was designed to serve his year-round living and working requirements. It is an idiosyncratic house for a client of strong opinions, combining the traditional techniques of stick construction with images of collision, fragmentation, and incompletion. It juxtaposes two orthogonal grids, one at a 45-degree angle to the other, resulting in a series of spaces, linked both horizontally and vertically, whose variety yields ever-changing perspectives. Though the house is a play on the saltbox form, no single living area is totally defined by this volume. Instead, the space flows continuously, from the living areas around the chimney (with a fireplace that, at the client's request, is big enough for cooking), through the kitchen and dining areas, spiraling up the staircase, and doubling back across a bridge above the living room. Apart from utility spaces, the bedroom and a small office are the only enclosed spaces in the house.

This residence contains intimate, cavelike spaces for warmth and winter shelter, in contrast to open areas that are bathed with light. Natural light is introduced overhead in several ways, creating a variety of elusive, shifting patterns on the interior surfaces. Exposed structural framing and mechanical ducts contrast with finished wood and slate. Ladders, bridges, flagpoles, and other appurtenances provide unexpected experiences within this variegated spatial environment.

Isolated on a 320-acre plot on Martha's Vineyard, the house is designed to gracefully complement its setting: the

1. South facade.
2. Second floor plan.
3. North facade.

1

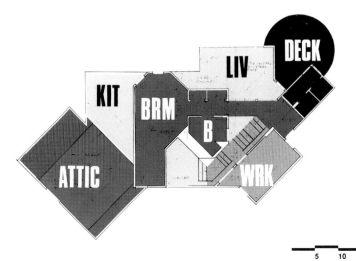

2

5   10   20

fresh-water environs of Homer's Pond, with a panoramic view of the Atlantic Ocean. Despite its implicit saltbox form, the shingle-clad exterior of the house features truncated eaves and dormers, balconies, and a crow's nest. Small fragments adjacent to the main house (a result, metaphorically, of the collision of forms) were built as cabins for the children; these were subsequently replaced by a guest house, which offers more private quarters. In 1984 the owner commissioned a new volume to be grafted onto the original—a major addition of a sunlit, plant-filled living space.

4. View from living room toward kitchen.
5. Bedroom.
6. Stair.

5

6

ROBERT S. MARX THEATER, PLAYHOUSE IN THE PARK
Cincinnati, Ohio, 1968

36   When completed in 1968, Cincinnati's 672-seat Robert S. Marx Theater at Playhouse in the Park was regarded as a radical, innovative structure. An extremely tight budget of less than $1 million (or $1,443 per seat, considerably less than the cost of conventional theaters) compelled the architects to make both functional and aesthetic virtues of necessity.

For economy the walls are built of concrete block, only one layer thick, applied to a steel frame. In the auditorium functional elements such as catwalks, theatrical lighting, ladders, and mechanical and structural systems are all frankly exposed and arranged in contrasting grids to give the space an impression of richness, despite minimal means. The complete openness of these systems is also highly practical, providing easy access for hanging scenery, positioning lighting, and making other adjustments for stage productions. The only contrasting "soft" elements are upholstered seats and carpeting on the stairs.

The budget permitted only a minimal lobby, initially designed as a grand concrete firestair with extra-large platforms. Here, too, ornamentation is provided through utility: ventilation ducts and air diffusers are left exposed to become works of sculpture in stainless steel. The colorful carpeting on the floors and ceilings absorbs sound and animates the space, which is further enlivened by exposed vertical fluorescent lights; forty-foot-tall mirrors both unify and amplify this active place.

The building's asymmetrical plan is as aggressive as its aesthetic. The Marx Theater was built with a thrust stage, one of the first in American theaters. Designed to accommodate theatrical productions of a strong artistic director, the configuration of stage and seating provides the flexibility of twenty-four different entrance possibilities for performers. Because seating wraps around the stage, the actors and the audience are brought into close proximity, and no one sits more than seventeen rows away from the stage.

1

2

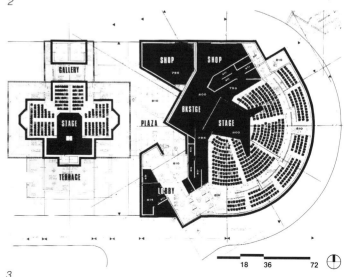

3

4

5

6

1. Hillside view.
2. Plaza level entrance.
3. Plaza level plan.
4. Thrust theater.
5. View of lobby looking toward entry.
6. Lobby.

ASSEMBLY HALL, PHILLIPS EXETER ACADEMY
Exeter, New Hampshire, 1969

38 The idea of unity through contrast, which the architects explored in the late 1960s, guided this renovation at Phillips Exeter Academy. A chapel built to seat 700 was made into an assembly hall for 1,100 by inserting a new, curved steel balcony with 400 seats into the existing space. The use of contemporary materials (such as round, chrome-covered columns, exposed beams under the balcony, and a corrugated-steel deck—not visible in the photographs) contrasts vividly with the original 1914 Cram, Goodhue, and Ferguson design. This juxtaposition of new and old elements both animates the room and creates a far tighter, more functional gathering place.

Intimacy and focus are provided by a small, curved presentation platform that projects in front of the original proscenium, permitting recitals and small group performances. A curved, wooden acoustical soundboard discourages theatrical performances, for which the auditorium is not well suited. An improved rake in the orchestra seating accommodates upholstered benches whose form is a response to that of the stage projection. The steps of the U-shaped balcony above oppose the configuration of the bench seating below, further invigorating the design.

To make the contrast between new and old components more pronounced, portions of the ceiling were removed to accommodate the new balcony and to provide for easier lighting. The original plasterwork was painted and glazed to accentuate its architectural detail. Portraits of founders and dignitaries that had lined the walls were restored, rehung, and illuminated. In the process of this transformation, original design features were strengthened so that they can contribute to a lively dialogue between existing and new elements.

---

1. Existing chapel, circa 1967.
2. Main level plan.
3. View from balcony.
4. View from entry.
5. Entry detail of balcony.

1

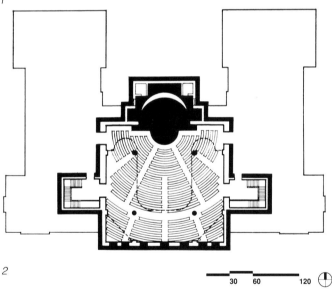

2

30 60 120

3

4

5

MT. HEALTHY SCHOOL
Columbus, Indiana, 1972

40 The Mt. Healthy School is located in farmland outside Columbus, Indiana. Its philosophy of team teaching and individual student development is supported not by the large, barnlike interiors of typical late sixties and early seventies open-plan schools, but by a series of highly variegated spaces that allow for different types of activities.

Key to the plan are the three classroom clusters that correspond to the standard academic divisions of kindergarten through second grade, third and fourth grade, and fifth and sixth grade. Each cluster accommodates upwards of 180 students and is designed to function almost like a one-room schoolhouse, with six loosely defined class areas per cluster. This permits large-group, small-group, and individual instruction to go on simultaneously. Different areas of the clusters are architecturally delineated in a variety of ways: changes in floor level, natural and artificial light, fixed furniture arrangements, movable teaching devices, and a wide range of juxtaposed materials, finishes, and colors.

At the heart of each cluster is a small instructional materials center, which is operated in conjunction with the central facility and shares its programs. This arrangement enables students to take part in the learning process that best suits their level of achievement.

Partial-height partitions are used throughout the interior, except around mechanical-equipment areas, the kitchen, and the gymnasium. An open, central path connects the three clusters with other major interior spaces, including the gym, the art room, and administration and service areas. Because the volumes of enclosure are not congruent with the plan, movement through the building offers

1. View from upper cluster level.
2. Main level plan.
3. View toward clusters.
4. West entrance facade.

1

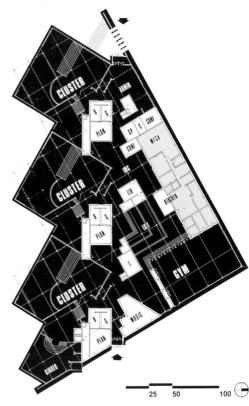

2

3

4

spatial variety and an ongoing sense of discovery.

The interior spaces are illuminated by 1,000 feet of four-foot-tall clerestory windows that pass diagonally across all activity areas. Large sections of industrial glazing were also originally provided in the exterior walls of the clusters to afford fine vistas of the countryside, but they were eventually removed to reduce energy consumption. In addition, the building is illuminated by both incandescent and fluorescent light in various patterns and intensities.

---

5. Common assembly space.
6. Circulation path.
7. Cluster.
8. View of various cluster levels.

43

6

7

8

CLOISTERS CONDOMINIUMS
Cincinnati, Ohio, 1973

44   Named for the secluded nature of the site, the Cloisters Condominiums occupy a steeply sloping piece of land atop the east bank of the Ohio River. This townhouse development, designed to fit the character of the surrounding Mt. Adams community, looks more like a group of individual buildings than a large multifamily dwelling. Seen from a distance, it has the vernacular scale and feel of neighboring nineteenth-century housing. A major design objective was to give each unit unobstructed views of the Ohio River and the Kentucky countryside beyond.

This development contains seventeen spacious two-bedroom units. Typical "A" units, set on the upper, flat area of the site, have window projections angled to take full advantage of the view while lending variety to the basic rectangular plan. Spatial diversity and individuality have been provided by reversing the plan of every other unit, so that windows occur in different places. Typical "B" units, which step down the site, have no window projections, but the alternating location of the balconies above gives variety to the living areas below. The repetitive unit plans developed to accommodate the flat and sloping characteristics of the site also permitted a lower budget and greater expediency in construction.

The wood-frame structure is supported on wood posts, eliminating the need for massive foundation walls or the destruction of vegetation. The exterior of the Cloisters is sheathed with vertical cypress siding, and the roofs are covered with terra-cotta tiles. Masonry party walls, which provide fire separation between every two units, are left exposed; these, along with oak boards and painted plaster, define the major interior wall surfaces. Now that the wood has weathered, the units fit gracefully into their context.

1. Mt. Adams facade.
2. Unit plans.
3. View of south corner.

1

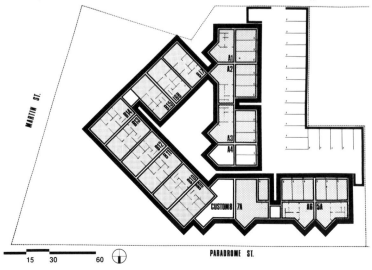

2

COLUMBUS OCCUPATIONAL HEALTH CENTER
Columbus, Indiana, 1974

46 Instead of concealing routine working functions behind opaque walls, as hospitals do, this design brings as many functions as possible out into the open. Access to the activities within both educates and reassures users while minimizing the boredom that usually accompanies visits to a health facility. Spaces that require only aural privacy, such as laboratories, are enclosed by glass and are visible to passing patients and staff. Spaces that require visual privacy, such as changing rooms and certain testing areas, are surrounded by eight-foot-high partitions. Spaces requiring both aural and visual privacy, such as examination rooms, are completely enclosed from floor to ceiling.

The Columbus Occupational Health Center is a small structure of only 21,000 square feet. It primarily provides physical examinations and testing for employees of Cummins Engine Company and treatment for occupational illnesses and ailments. A large central waiting space, which leads to all medical functions, is bisected by two gently sloping circulation ramps that connect the three half-levels of the building. Circular seating pods are placed throughout this open space. A direct, private circulation system of staircases can be used by patients and staff during examinations and treatment. A strong color palette is liberally used throughout.

The health center uses standard elements in novel ways. The exterior, sheathed in black glass, is diagonally intersected by a continuous skylight in mirrored glass, constructed of standard greenhouse parts. This skylight, which illuminates the central circulation area and fills the interior with a constantly changing play of light and shadow, extends beyond the building's perimeter to form a porte cochere.

1. View from west.
2. Entrance view.
3. Site plan.
4. Lobby waiting area.

1

2

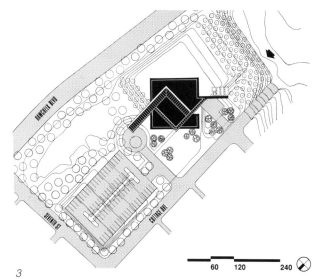

60 120 240

ORCHESTRA HALL
Minneapolis, Minnesota, 1974

Orchestra Hall was conceived as a study in contrasts. The outer form of the auditorium is a simple brick box, but it is juxtaposed with multiglazed, offset public spaces enclosed in stripes of glass and metal. Inside, the auditorium is a straightforward space, designed with acoustical excellence as the overriding objective. Working with consultant Dr. Cyril Harris, the architects took the traditional, shoebox-shaped concert hall form and made it appear more intimate than its 2,600-seat size might suggest, through the use of a geometric progression of balcony fascias, a warm color scheme, and the absence of a proscenium. Stage and audience seating are integrated into one space by patterning the ceiling with a random arrangement of plaster cubes that wraps down the back stage wall. On the periphery of the auditorium three balconies are stepped and staggered in an innovative sequence designed to improve sight lines from the side seats.

The second major programmatic requirement was that the building enhance concertgoing for audience and orchestra members alike. The building was named Orchestra Hall in honor of the renowned Minneapolis Symphony Orchestra—not a conductor or donor. Backstage areas use the same design vocabulary, materials, and exposed building systems as the lobby areas, and both enjoy views of Peavey Plaza. HHPA also created the site plan for Peavey Plaza by locating the building back from Nicollet Mall. This not only creates a major urban space, but also optimizes public accessibility, views, and the relationship of the building to its context. M. Paul Friedberg subsequently developed the landscape design.

Orchestra Hall was conceived and built in the astonishingly short space of sixteen months, two months ahead of the eighteen-month schedule called for in the building program. It was also realized within tight budget constraints. Both feats were made possible by working with a well-established form for the auditorium and by a close collaboration among client, construction manager, and architect.

1

2

1. North facade.
2. View of lobby looking toward entry.
3. Orchestra level plan.
4. Concert hall from second balcony.

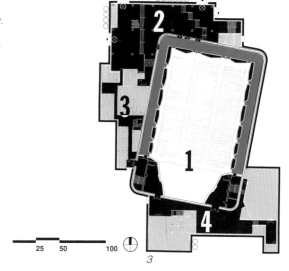

25   50   100

3

FIREMEN'S TRAINING CENTER
Ward's Island, New York, 1975

50 The Firemen's Training Center is not only one of the first modern campuses in the nation for firefighting but also the largest. It was built on twenty-six acres of newly created landfill in the upper reaches of New York's East River. This gave the architects an opportunity to plan and landscape a dramatic site with spectacular views of river bridges and the Manhattan skyline. HHPA also designed the center's nine buildings.

A diagonal access road defines the site's east-west axis and separates noisy training and service activities from the education and administration building. The training buildings include mockups of typical New York City building types— a tenement, a loft structure, a storefront— all designed to be used repeatedly so that trainees can practice their skills under simulated fire conditions. These basic concrete structures, faced with brick and patterned with horizontal stripes, are contrasted with the metal-clad education building set across the main axis. The simplicity of the education building's form is belied by a few details that hint that this is not an ordinary building. Two contrasting fenestration patterns animate its north facade. Corrugated-steel culverts are diagonally inserted into the earth berm to provide building access. A water storage tank, painted bright red, is adapted for a formal, vestibule-like space that provides entry to a richly varied spatial sequence.

Contrasts between the building's simple exterior and the intricately designed public spaces inside are surprisingly dramatic. The lower floor's main corridor is an array of brightly colored materials and shapes. The classrooms are rectilinear boxes without windows—a response to the client's desire to limit distraction and ensure concentration— organized along diagonal corridors. The placement of rotated volumes within the roof's sloped enclosure creates a great variety of residual open spaces along the full 365-foot length of the building. A mezzanine floor housing administration areas opens into these spaces and encloses the classroom areas below.

1

2

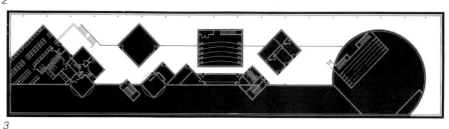

3

20   40   80

1. Training buildings: loft, tenement, and single-family structures.
2. Administration and education building.
3. Administration and education building, balcony level plan.
4. Aerial view of site looking toward Manhattan.
5. Entry of administration and education building.

COOPER-HEWITT MUSEUM/ NATIONAL MUSEUM OF DESIGN
New York, New York, 1976

The 1901 Andrew Carnegie mansion on Fifth Avenue may not be the most outstanding example of the architecture of its era, but the building's handsome materials and innovative systems—along with the fact of its survival—give it distinction. Converted into a museum for the Cooper-Hewitt collection seventy-five years after its completion, the building was an early example of adaptive reuse in New York, one of the first of what are now called "interpretive restorations." Some of its spaces have been restored to their original state, some have been only slightly altered to make them suitable for museum purposes, and still others have been transformed.

The building is one of the last remaining freestanding houses on Fifth Avenue overlooking Central Park. It features a use of materials and craftsmanship typical of its period, from the teak parquet flooring and richly carved paneling and balustrades on the interior to the big, pink granite sidewalk slabs that surround the house on three sides.

In altering the house to become the Smithsonian Institution's National Museum of Design, HHPA left intact nearly everything of serious consequence about the original structure. The basic axial arrangement of the house was respected. The wildly eclectic public rooms on the first floor, each designed in a different period style (as was fashionable at the time of construction), were left largely untouched to serve as novel settings for exhibitions, despite the fact that the "white box" was considered the only proper museum environment for the display of decorative art objects in the mid-seventies. Only contemporary lighting and display surfaces were added. Rather than restricting the galleries to a set form of presentation, the presence of period

1. Restored north facade.
2. Restored south facade.
3. Main level plan.
4. Great Hall.
5. Great Hall, 1938.

1

2

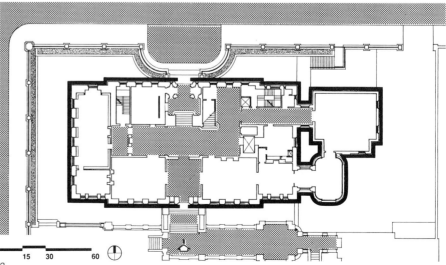

15   30   60

3

4

5

styles permits collections to be exhibited in a variety of ways.

Original elements such as chandeliers, lights, balustrades, and columns were cleaned and reinstalled, and environmental control systems were integrated with the existing architectural details. Minor alterations were made in the main entrance hall, where new recessed, adjustable spotlights and pairs of period wall sconces now provide the illumination once furnished by a miscellany of floor lamps. Although none of these lighting elements is in fact original, the result appears correct.

On the second floor several small bedrooms were converted to one long exhibition gallery by removing the original walls and ceiling. This simply detailed gallery forms a deliberate contrast to the main stair hall, which is embellished with a wood-paneled wainscot, carved columns, pedimented door frames, and a plasterwork ceiling.

One of the most significant architectural alterations derived from the need to improve vertical circulation for public use. This involved removing the organ loft of the main entrance hall and installing a public elevator in its place. As in other parts of the house where alterations were intended to be unobtrusive, the architects reworked surrounding woodwork so that this addition appears to be part of the original.

6. Restored entrance foyer.
7. Carnegie dining room after restoration.
8. Restored drawing room.
9. Restored conservatory.
10. Detail of restored chandelier in Great Hall.

7

8

9

10

BROOKLYN CHILDREN'S MUSEUM
Brooklyn, New York, 1977

56 The Brooklyn Children's Museum, the oldest such institution in the nation, is also consistently one of the most forward-looking. Founded in 1899, the museum spent most of its early years in two houses in the Crown Heights section of Brooklyn. In 1968, while its permanent home in Brower Park was being planned, the institution moved to MUSE, a temporary facility designed by HHPA in a converted pool hall and automobile showroom. There the museum's director experimented with various kinds of hands-on presentations, appealing to children's natural curiosity and their instinct for play while providing education about the physical world. Many of these concepts were incorporated into the environment of the new museum.

To preserve the openness of Brower Park the architects proposed an underground facility whose exterior could be used for both structured and unstructured activities. The result was a rooftop playground and open-air theater that combines an assemblage of pre-engineered elements borrowed from industry, transportation, and agriculture. A 1907 Queensboro Bridge kiosk, for instance, became the museum's street-corner entry pavilion.

The public interior of this reinforced-concrete box is essentially a one-room, 19,600-square-foot exhibition space whose four levels are buried up to forty feet below grade, with one corner exposed to daylight. The space is intersected by a 180-foot-long series of corrugated-steel culverts that descend from the entry kiosk to an enclosed courtyard on the lowest level. This People Tube, which glows with a spiral neon rainbow and has a stream flowing down one side, is broken into sloping sections, with each segment opening onto one of the four exhibition levels.

---

1. Rooftop bridge.
2. Courtyard.
3. Upper level plan.
4. Rooftop playground and adjacent park.

1

2

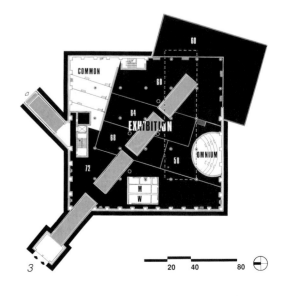
3

20 40   80

5

Throughout the museum a participatory learning process is emphasized. Changing exhibits are designed so that children can take part in a variety of activities. Workshops, a library, a dance studio, and photography and darkroom areas are combined with a marketplace to provide additional learning opportunities. On the lowest level a large steel industrial storage tank encloses a small auditorium. The entire building is designed to encourage and accept change, ensuring that future needs can be accommodated.

5. Lower exhibition level.
6. Middle exhibition level.
7. Circulation path through exhibition area.

6

SCULPTURE HALL AND EAST WING, SAINT LOUIS ART MUSEUM
St. Louis, Missouri, 1977

60 This great neoclassical monument, loosely modeled after a Roman bath, has not had an easy life. Built for exhibition use in the 1904 St. Louis World's Fair, it was poorly understood and badly marred in later years, especially during the heyday of modernism, which held America's Beaux-Arts legacy in scorn. Many of the building's surfaces were encrusted with layers of pseudo-settings built for the display of art objects. Its axial plan was obscured, its circulation patterns blocked, its noble proportions and symmetries violated. Skylights leaked and lighting was inadequate or nonexistent. Its once prominent architect, Cass Gilbert, had been all but forgotten.

Before undertaking this restoration HHPA investigated Cass Gilbert's career, turning for inspiration to such masterworks as the U.S. Custom House (1907, New York), the Woolworth Building (1913, New York), the St. Louis Public Library (1933), and the U. S. Supreme Court Building (1935, Washington, D.C.). Two major objectives were formulated: the reclamation of Gilbert's axial plan and the celebration of his use of natural light.

The main axes were redefined by clearing the interior of all extraneous additions and reestablishing the basic circulation routes. The sculpture hall, where these principal axes cross, was stripped of an improvised bookstore and a miscellany of exhibits to reveal its soaring architectural vaults. The original proportions were restored in the gallery spaces. New doorways were framed by moldings copied from Gilbert's own, and windows and a blind arch were opened to natural light. A soft, warm color scheme, varying subtly with changes in natural light, was introduced throughout. A skylit attic, formerly used for storage,

1

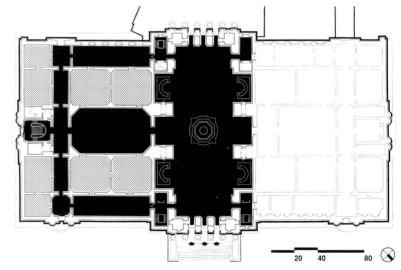

2

1. New window in existing East Wing facade.
2. Upper level plan.
3. Main entrance facade.

was rescued and transformed into a gallery for prints, drawings, and photographs.

Lighting and mechanical systems were reevaluated and modernized. Gilbert's liberal use of daylight was wonderful (the building was also one of the first to use electric lighting), but, if unfiltered, light can damage artworks. His system of skylights, laylights, and clerestories was reconstructed and reglazed, using a sophisticated filter system to block ultraviolet light and direct natural light. Lighting studies were undertaken to determine how best to combine electric light (used to focus attention on the viewing portions of the gallery walls) with changing, natural ambient light from above. Advanced environmental control and security systems were installed, all concealed within the structure.

As in many other projects, HHPA's work in St. Louis comes under the rubric of interpretive restoration. Some details left unfinished in the original were completed by HHPA. Others, such as a new curving grand staircase leading down to extensive pre-Columbian galleries, were executed with traditional materials, but in a frankly contemporary manner. In spirit the east wing of the museum has been fully restored to the splendor envisioned by Gilbert. The pristine clarity of the building's axial plan and the light-filled ambience of its spaces can once more be seen as the orderly, masterful creation of a great architectural intelligence.

4. Restored Sculpture Hall.
5. Original Cass Gilbert moldings and casework; murals by Elmer Garnsey.
6. Restored exhibition galleries.

5

6

BOETTCHER CONCERT HALL
Denver Center for the Performing Arts, Denver, Colorado, 1978

64 The first concert hall in the United States in which the audience fully surrounds the stage, this auditorium reflects the cultural aspirations of a community that wanted a unique symphonic performance room. Boettcher's unusual form was determined by Brian Priestman, the conductor of the Denver Symphony Orchestra, who found it an intimate and entirely natural way of gathering the audience around music-making. This nontraditional plan for the permanent home of Denver's symphony also suited the city's sense of itself as an open-minded, progressive community. Using Hans Scharoun's brilliant surround hall for the Berlin Philharmonic as precedent, the architects designed a concert hall of great warmth and drama.

Intimacy and acoustics are principal issues in the design of any concert hall, but here they posed an even greater problem than usual, given the challenge of placing 2,750 seats in this unusual configuration. One major advantage of the surround concept is that it brings seats closer to the stage; at Boettcher 80 percent of the seats are within sixty-five feet of the stage platform. To enhance the feeling of intimacy and to prevent the interior from looking like the inside of a bowl with monotonously rising tiers of symmetrical rows, the seating was divided into terraced, staggered segments. This design gives the audience a sense of sitting in individual

1. Site plan.
2. Orchestra level plan.
3. Concert hall seating tiers.
4. Overleaf: View of concert hall.

1

2

sections and yields a large number of desirable "front mezzanine"-type seats. Arranged asymmetrically, these segments give each seat a different perspective of the stage.

Working in close collaboration with acoustician Christopher Jaffe, HHPA designed a canopy of 106 sound-reflecting translucent acrylic disks, many of which can be raised or lowered to tune the hall for specific events. These disks in part replace the reflective surfaces provided by the traditional "megaphone" enclosures of shoebox-shaped auditoriums. As in Orchestra Hall in Minneapolis, the architects chose to spend most of the limited $13 million budget on the auditorium's interior, to create a memorable room for music. The opulence of the interior is heightened by the contrast with the relatively spartan lobbies, which employ a subdued color palette.

Although designed primarily as a single-purpose hall, Boettcher is also used for modern dance and chamber opera. The hall is part of the four-square-block downtown Denver Center for the Performing Arts, which consists of several cultural facilities, joined by a glass-roofed galleria designed by Kevin Roche.

---

5. Ceiling with acoustical diffusers.
6. Detail of balcony.
7. Lobby stair.

69

6

7

LANGWORTHY RESIDENCE
New York, New York, 1979

70 The design of this residence, which replaces a Greenwich Village town house that was accidentally blown up by the Weathermen in 1970, was almost as explosive as the detonation that made replacement necessary. At issue was the "appropriateness" of the new facade. Because the original had been part of a row of historic (but greatly altered) 1840 town houses officially designated as New York City landmarks, no new structure could be built on the site without the approval of the Landmarks Preservation Commission. Gaining that approval entailed several controversial public hearings, and in the process the plan became a cause célèbre.

Although only the exterior needed the commission's approval, the architects wanted the exterior to reflect the interior. The original long, narrow rectangular volume of the house is opened up through the creation of half-levels set between front and back at an angle, generating long, diagonal views. On the exterior the rotated plan is expressed on the middle two floors by a projecting bay and a recessed door. At the same time, to relate this facade to the other buildings on the street, the cornice line is retained, along with the attic windows and stoop.

The "wrinkle in the wall," as Village residents called it, proved to be the most controversial element in the design. Although bay windows are commonplace in the Village, no such historical precedent existed on this street. The opponents of the plan protested that it was "out of harmony" with the rest of the block, and suggested that reproduction would be a better solution. The architects argued—on architectural and historical grounds—that for over a hundred years additions and subtractions had been made on the block and that these were now part of its basic character. Furthermore, they said, an exact reproduction would be based on conjecture.

The facade was built as proposed. Rather than seeking literal duplication, the design blends old and new to achieve an appropriate mixture of materials, scale, and texture, as well as a compatibility of architectural elements.

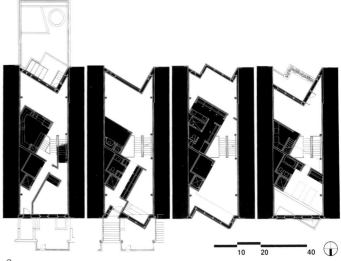

1

2

3

1. Site after blast, March 6, 1970.
2. Site after town-house demolition.
3. Plans of four new levels.
4. New street facade.
5. Living area.

4

5

BEST PRODUCTS COMPANY, INC. HEADQUARTERS, PHASE I
Richmond, Virginia, 1980

72 The owners of BEST Products had very definite notions of what they needed in their new corporate headquarters: a building that had a distinctive image, with the liveliness and the noncorporate look of the ad hoc offices they had been occupying in a company warehouse. It also had to be expandable and functional.

The resulting building occupies one quadrant of a cloverleaf interchange in suburban Richmond. The curve of its access road influenced both the master plan for the site and the commanding, organizing curve of the building. The main facade, designed to expand along the plan's semicircular perimeter, has a diaper pattern of translucent and reflective glass block and a terra-cotta cornice and base, terminating in a watercourse animated by fountains. This facade established a strong image for the company without resorting to the kind of corporate bombast often seen in suburban headquarters buildings. Its historicist allusions to sixteenth-century Venetian patterning and Renaissance water spouts contrast with a pair of Art Moderne carved stone eagles and glass lanterns (originally created by René Chambellan for the now-demolished East Side Airlines Terminal Building in New York), which flank the entrance bridge.

At the rear, rectangular private offices jut out into the landscape, forming a series of small courtyards and gardens that are shielded from the road. In contrast to the glass-block front, the building's notched back is clad in white fiberboard panels horizontally patterned with windows of dark insulating glass.

Inside, the glass-block facade wall appears to stand free while a second floor level zigzags along it, creating a changing series of twenty-eight-foot-high

1. René Chambellan's eagle and lantern, with entry facade beyond.
2. Main level plan.
3. Watercourse at front entry.

1

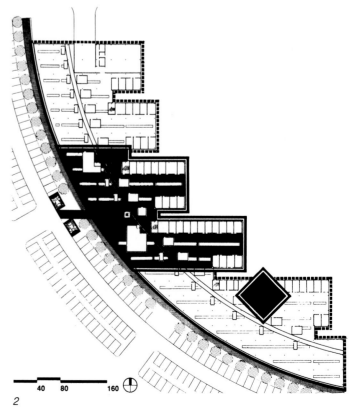

40   80   160

2

4

5

4. View of main facade from upper level.
5. Cafeteria.
6. View of lobby from upper level.

open spaces the length of the plan. The glass block admits a soft, even light that is unusual in a working environment and provides an ideal setting for displaying the company's contemporary art collection. Artworks are placed throughout the offices and illuminated by a special, independent lighting system. An elevator, complete with a restored Art Deco cab salvaged from renovations at Rockefeller Center, provides secondary access to both floors.

The main circulation route through the 68,000-square-foot space is a mosaic-tiled walkway that follows the arc of the facade. Freestanding cedar-clad rooms house mechanical and sanitary services, acting as dividers between the open offices, which are located on both sides of the walkway. Clerical spaces are further defined and enclosed by movable acoustical panels and by a grand architectural device specially designed by HHPA—an eight-foot-high cabinetry wall containing storage and electrical and computer systems for each work station. It is painted a Colonial blue-green and embellished with a traditional architectural cornice.

7. Circulation path.
8. Boardroom with table by Ed Zucca.
9. Typical open work station.
10, 11. Private offices.
12. Overleaf: Main entrance at night.

8   9

10

11

MADISON CIVIC CENTER
Madison, Wisconsin, 1980

80 In early 1970 Paul Soglin, the mayor of Madison, decided to undertake the recycling of two major State Street commercial buildings into an arts center in hopes of bringing people back to a dying downtown. To many observers this seemed like a high-risk act: neither building was particularly distinguished, the private sector demonstrated scant interest, and there was little precedent for using a cultural center to hold a city together. Besides, an ambitious design for a civic center on one of Madison's two magnificent lakes had already been commissioned twenty years earlier from Frank Lloyd Wright, a daunting presence in his native state even years after his death. Wright's design continued to dominate public interest, and although bids for the ambitious project had repeatedly come in over budget, many citizens still hoped to see it built.

But among the advantages of Soglin's plan was the fact that the expected cost of recycling abandoned structures was at least $2 million less than that of new construction. Equally important, the buildings were located in Madison's commercial core on the major axis that links its two foremost institutions, the University of Wisconsin and John Russell Pope's State Capitol. The prospect that these two State Street structures in close proximity to a substantial, older residential community could become a catalyst for downtown redevelopment seemed promising.

HHPA made the former Capitol Theater, designed in 1928 by Chicago movie palace architects Rapp and Rapp, into the Civic Center's performance hub. This refurbished movie house is now the 2,100-seat multipurpose Oscar Mayer Theater. Its stage was extended and its original ceiling coves newly illuminated in three colors of incandescent light. Plaster

1. *Capitol Theater, circa 1928.*
2. *Site plan.*
3. *Main entrance to Civic Center.*

1

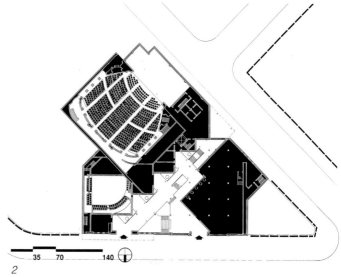

2

walls, ceilings, and balcony surfaces were painted and stenciled in 1928 style; new aisle carpeting was rewoven from the original designs; and decorative accessories of the period were added to heighten the ambience.

The new 370-seat Isthmus Playhouse was tucked into former retail space built as part of the Capitol Theater. Carpet-covered benches below and a balcony with a few rows of loose chairs above provide the seating. The thrust stage and demountable rear stage wall of the playhouse give it the flexibility to accommodate children's theater, dance, lectures, chamber music, civic meetings, and many other uses.

The principal gallery of the Madison Art Center occupies the main selling floor of the former Montgomery Ward department store. Additional galleries, support space, and workshops are located on other levels.

The Hispano-Moorish facade of the theater is flanked by new infill brick-and-glass facades where smaller buildings once stood. Doorways in the original building openings lead into a four-level public thoroughfare called the Crossroads, which runs diagonally through the building to join three exterior entrances with ten points of interior access to major activities. The Crossroads holds the center together, serving as lobby, informal performance space, background for displays, and shortcut through the block, and giving access to both theaters, the Madison Art Center, and other community spaces on the upper floors.

The Civic Center, undertaken in conjunction with a rebuilding of State Street to designs by M. Paul Friedberg, has largely succeeded in the revitalization of Madison's main downtown street, demonstrating that older structures, even if less than first-rate architecture, can be worth recycling. Such buildings form part of the urban fabric and can again become useful, giving the streetscape a sense of continuity and coherence that new buildings often do not provide.

---

4. View from balcony of Oscar Mayer Theater.
5. Orchestra level below balcony.
6. Stage of Oscar Mayer Theater.
7. Restored plaster surface with new stencils.
8. New chandelier created from old components.

83

5

6

7

8

9

10

9. *Isthmus Playhouse, from entry.*
10. *Isthmus Playhouse, from balcony.*
11. *View from Crossroads to Madison Art Center.*
12–15. *Details of Crossroads.*

11

12

14

13

15

MUSIC AND DANCE BUILDING, ST. PAUL'S SCHOOL
Concord, New Hampshire, 1980

86 The campus plan of St. Paul's School, founded in 1856, was originally developed by Frederick Law Olmsted. When St. Paul's decided to build a performing arts center, the architectural challenge was to determine the massing and general shape of the building, as well as to locate it so as not to overwhelm the existing modestly scaled structures. The solution was to separate program functions—a music room, dance room, and small room for drama—to diminish the building's apparent size. The small theater was attached to the existing Memorial Hall, and the music and dance rooms were divided into two seemingly separate volumes, connected by a common underground floor that contains locker rooms and rehearsal spaces.

The building is sited on a hillside at the center of the campus. Its two volumes are set at a right angle on opposite sides of a major campus circulation route. The building's presence has been further reduced by inserting both volumes into the hillside. The sloping-roof forms are borrowed from nineteenth-century New England mill structures. Materials used on the building's exterior are similar to those of adjacent buildings: brick facing for most walls and copper seam cladding on the roofs. For contrast, one exterior wall of each volume is surfaced with corrugated mineral fiber panels and horizontal bands of glazing.

The two main interior spaces are the music room and the dance studio. In the music room industrial elements (exposed steel framing and ducts, metal stairs and railings) are contrasted with traditional ones (incandescent wall sconces, wood moldings, and Shaker-style wood chairs). Warmth is achieved by using oak and cedar boards on floors, ceiling, and balcony surfaces.

1. Exterior of music room.
2. Site plan.
3. Music room.

1

2

15   30   60

HULT CENTER FOR
THE PERFORMING ARTS
Eugene, Oregon, 1982

88 The Hult Center for the Performing Arts is intimately connected with Eugene, Oregon, once "The Lumber Capital of the World" and today home of the state university. The steeply sloping roofs of its lobby recall the towering mountains of the Pacific Northwest setting. The lobby's spectacular four-story-high wood columns and ceiling are made of specially selected trees found in the region. The involvement of thirty regional painters, sculptors, and craftsmen resulted in the creation of fifteen works designed for the building's interior.

Flat-roofed, poured-in-place concrete volumes enclose and soundproof the two multipurpose auditoriums of the Hult Center: the 2,500-seat Silva Concert Hall and the 500-seat Soreng Theater. In addition there are public spaces, a rehearsal hall, and support spaces—all linked by an enclosed bridge to a 500-car garage. HHPA prepared the master plan for the performing arts center and adjacent convention center and hotel, which together form Eugene's two-block civic center complex.

In developing the program the clients and the architects concluded that in order to provide the widest possible range of choices, the two theaters should be entirely different from each other. The large Silva Concert Hall is a grand, formal space, both romantic and baroque in feeling. The sinuously curved balconies and large ceiling arches unify the room in a series of embracing arcs. The segmented curve of the proscenium arch is repeated throughout the theater. (The house curtain is the work of regional artists.) The ceiling is a unique basket-weave pattern, made of plaster, expanded metal, and fiberglass; it has both the absorptive and reflective qualities to fulfill acoustical criteria.

---

1. Lobby roof.
2. Mezzanine level plan.
3. Exterior view of four-level lobby.

1

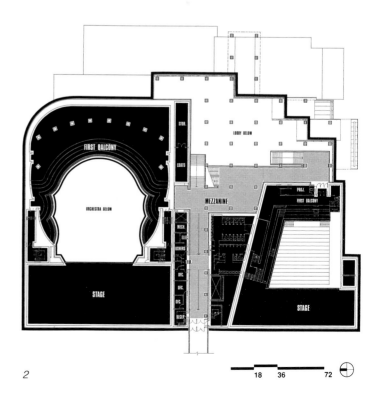

2

4

5

As in all of their performing arts spaces, the architects have gone to great lengths to reduce the hall's apparent size and to foster intimacy through a skillful shaping of seating levels. The configuration of the Silva balconies is unusual. Each has its own curve, and the upper balcony extends beyond the mezzanine to bring seats closer to the stage. If the hall is traditional in feeling, it is modern in its integration of technology. It has a well-equipped stage and a sophisticated electronics-assisted resonance system, which allows the hall to be adapted to a full range of musical and dramatic productions.

The Soreng Theater is a trapezoidal room designed for a variety of production types. It features exposed catwalks and ladders and no permanent proscenium, an openness that increases flexibility.

At night, the center's glass-walled lobby serves as its own marquee, lighting up the streets and giving the city of Eugene a vigorous urban identity.

4. "Marble glass" by Ed Carpenter in pedestrian bridge to lobby.
5. Soreng Theater.
6. Clay tiles by Catpaw Pottery in lobby.
7. Porcelain mask by Mary Ann Fariello.
8. Lobby.
9. Overleaf: Silva Concert Hall.

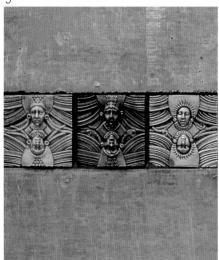

6

7

THE JOYCE THEATER
New York, New York, 1982

94   The Joyce Theater was built to fill a gap in available performance spaces. With dance in the early 1980s bursting out all over, new or experimental companies had to make do with performances either in church basements and gyms or in halls that were too large and too expensive to rent. An affordable 500-seat theater was clearly needed to serve New York City's dance community.

Converted from a 1941 movie house built on the foundations of three brownstones, the Joyce Theater is a near-total reconstruction. The interior was completely gutted. All that remains of the original is the black-and-white brick patterning of the facade, the tenement walls of the interior, and the exposed steel trusses and precast-concrete roof planks. All the rest—the lower facade (modeled after the original above), the Art Deco marquee, the glass bricks and neon, the two-level lobby, the terrazzo floors, the indirect cove lighting—is the architects' invention. A single steeply raked seating "dish," replacing the previous orchestra and loge of the old movie house, offers excellent sight lines. New side balconies step down along both of the bare brick side walls, furthering the intimacy between audience and performers.

By continuing the original movie house's black-and-white patterning across the adjacent storefronts in a straightforward manner, the Joyce Theater illustrates a different approach from that normally taken by HHPA when working with existing structures. This design is neither a contrast of new with old nor a confrontation that pointedly comments on the character of what was there before. Instead, everything fits together as one piece, making new and old a seamless whole.

---

1. Main entrance, from street.
2. Main entrance, from lobby.
3. Lobby plan.
4. Theater plan.
5. Main facade.
6. Existing Elgin Theater, 1980.

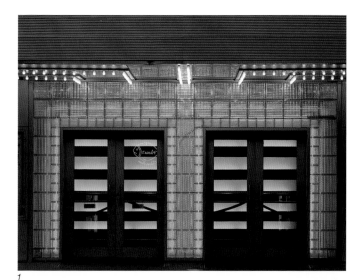

1

2

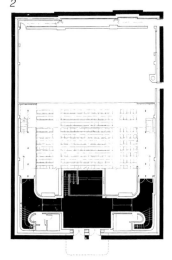

3

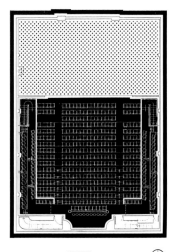

4

12 24   48

5

6

7. View of theater.
8. Detail of lobby paneling.
9. Stair to lower-level lounge.
10. Detail of stair handrail.
11. Elgin Theater interior, 1980.

97

8

9

10

11

WILLARD HOTEL
Washington, D.C., 1982

The story of the Willard, the historic "Hotel of Presidents," considered by many to be Washington's greatest hotel building, is a strange and complex architectural saga that seems hard to reconcile with the building's current success. By the early 1960s the Willard had fallen into disuse and was slated for demolition under a development scheme to upgrade Pennsylvania Avenue east of the White House. Only a last-minute public outcry succeeded in saving it from the wrecker's ball.

In 1978 the newly established Pennsylvania Avenue Development Corporation held a limited competition to select an architect/developer team to restore and expand the hotel. This was a serious challenge: how to make a sympathetic addition to a prominent architectural monument.

Without actually copying Henry Hardenbergh's 1901 Beaux-Arts structure, HHPA's scheme is still sympathetic to it. The architects were able to study Hardenbergh's other great buildings (most notably the Plaza Hotel and the Dakota Apartments) at first hand in New York. The new extension borrows the imagery of the old Willard, which is based on a French Second Empire chateau, and treats it in a fragmented, contemporary way.

The addition is composed of four corner facade elements that echo the scale and details of the earlier building's 14th Street corner, together with its cornices, dormers, porticoes, and bull's-eye windows. Their massing, however, is different, for they are set back and at an angle to Pennsylvania Avenue before they step back and up from the street. As they approach the original building they also step back to form an open-air plaza, linking Pennsylvania Avenue with F Street through a pedestrian arcade. A freestanding classical gateway continues the building line of Pennsylvania Avenue while framing the entrance to the public plaza. The plan was conceived with the urban context in mind, to prevent the large addition from overwhelming the scale of Pennsylvania Avenue.

1

2

1. Drawing of Pennsylvania Avenue facade
(left to right): Washington Hotel, new addition,
and original Willard Hotel.
2. Restored and expanded Willard Hotel.

PINGRY SCHOOL
Bernards Township, New Jersey, 1983

100 The most unusual aspect of this commission for the design of new quarters for the 750-student Pingry School was the program itself. It called for accommodating the day school's facilities in a single structure (thirty-six classrooms and laboratories, a library, an auditorium, administrative spaces, and extensive indoor athletic facilities, including two gymnasiums and a swimming pool). Another remarkable aspect was the budget: even by 1983 standards, $78 a square foot was restrictive.

Combining many dissimilar volumetric spaces into a single building was the design's point of departure. HHPA created a V-shaped structure of two wings that meet in a central clocktower. Large-scale spaces (including auditorium, gyms, and pool) are placed toward the front. In the rear, two levels of classrooms, laboratories, and dining rooms are rotated at a 45-degree angle to the corridor, resulting in a sawtoothed rear facade. This produces not only a split-level building, but front and rear facades with radically divergent configurations. Since the two facades have completely different functions and orientations, it made sense to distinguish them even further by using contrasting materials and fenestration patterns.

Pingry's front, which requires minimal fenestration, is clad in two colors of concrete block with a stripe of polished black granite. This facade's detailing refers indirectly to the traditional structures occupied by the school over its 125-year history. The two-story terra-cotta entry portico is also an allusion to the clocktower of Pingry's last home and a response to an adjacent clapboard church tower that forms the other end of the entrance axis. With its patterned expanse, the masonry facade serves as

1. Front facade.
2. Site plan.
3. Main level plan.
4. Main entrance.
5. Overleaf: Rear facade facing woods.

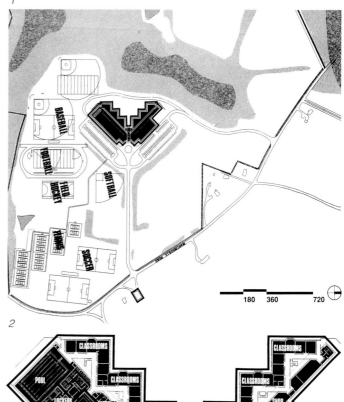

1

2

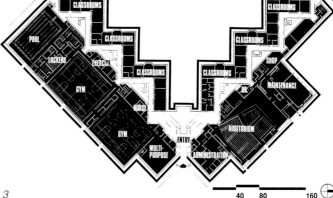

3

6

an appropriate backdrop for the school's playing fields. The rear facade has continuous industrial, ribbon-sash windows, which allow natural light into the classrooms and admit views of the lush rural landscape. It is clad in sand-colored corrugated metal, peeled back over the windows to form protective awnings. The straightforward materials—concrete block and industrial metal, used here in nonstandard ways—were chosen for reasons of economy.

Behind the portal is the interior's most dynamic space, a three-story, dramatically skylit interior, in and around which are clustered the central stair, the student lounge, and the library—the symbolic heart of the building. Beyond are skylit corridors, "exploded" as a result of the classrooms' rotation to yield multistory triangular spaces that serve as meeting and lounge areas, and sometimes as open classrooms as well.

The Pingry School gave HHPA its best architectural opportunity to address a question that it had long been asking: why should the front and back of a building be the same? It demonstrates that each orientation of a building can respond to its site on its own terms.

6. Residual space at stair.
7. Common area at lowest level of lobby.
8. View of lobby from library level.

7

SCHOLASTIC, INC. OFFICES
New York, New York, 1983

106 Scholastic, Inc., the publisher of classroom journals familiar to generations of children, sought to consolidate its entire staff, which had been housed on eight unconnected floors of a 1950s building, into a single facility. The company took three floors of newly constructed space atop the old John Wanamaker warehouse in New York, giving HHPA the opportunity to execute a tightly structured scheme that manages to provide both diversity and informality.

With only 90,000 square feet to house 500 people, space had to be carefully organized. But because the client wanted the employees to have some latitude in arranging their individual work spaces, the design also had to be flexible. To create diversity within order and to avoid the labyrinthine spaces characteristic of densely inhabited offices, HHPA developed a plan with a varied geometric organization. Each of the three floors has a distinctive layout, circulation scheme, and color palette; each level is experienced differently as one moves along the varied routes of the black-and-white tile pathways. A central stairwell, illuminated by a skylight, joins the three floors, revealing the orientation and geometry of each.

In planning the work spaces, the architects carefully considered the interaction between light and spatial organization. The client agreed that editorial work, which accounts for most positions in the organization, does not require windowed offices. Perimeter spaces could therefore be used for circulation, giving everyone the pleasure of views and light and helping avoid mazelike corridors. Three different heights of partitions define open offices and editorial cubicles. These are graduated from low (near the perimeter

---

1-3. Plans of tenth, ninth, and eighth floors.
4. Stair at ninth floor.

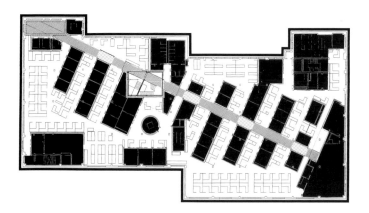

1

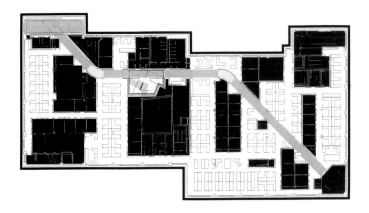

2

3

18   36   72

wall) to high (toward the floor's center). This scheme allows the maximum dispersal of natural light to the interior. Electric illumination is provided throughout by inverted industrial fixtures arranged in linear patterns.

The partitions surrounding the clerical spaces are standard off-the-shelf components, flexible enough to meet the changing requirements of new office equipment and work assignments. Other types of enclosures are created by found elements (such as an existing wooden water tank, transformed into a conference room) and by fixed drywall partitions (used to separate executive spaces from staff areas).

The project was completed on a tight schedule in only twelve months from planning to occupancy. Construction took just ninety days, including installation of all support services such as plumbing, wiring, and mechanical equipment.

5. Building's original water tank, now reused as a conference room.
6. View of stairs, looking from the eighth to the tenth floor.
7. Circulation path.
8. Executive office.

109

6

7

8

WCCO-TV COMMUNICATION CENTER AND HEADQUARTERS
Minneapolis, Minnesota, 1983

Small in size but forceful in demeanor, WCCO-TV's headquarters building has had a major impact on downtown Minneapolis. The clients, when it came time to expand, decided to stay put and make a contribution to downtown instead of relocating to the suburbs, like most TV-station owners. Mindful of the station's reputation as the voice of the Upper Midwest, the clients sought a contemporary building that fit into its urban context and frankly acknowledged its function as a broadcast center without being overwhelmed by a high-tech appearance. The building also had to equal the design quality of HHPA's Orchestra Hall (1974), located directly across the street.

In a downtown increasingly transformed by tall buildings, HHPA created a blocklike, stepped masonry structure that rises to four stories at the corner of Nicollet and Eleventh in response to the stone mass of nearby Westminster Church. Though not large, the building has great presence, even a sense of monumentality. It serves as a pedestal for the constantly changing panoply of communication technology that announces the building's function: a 100-foot-high broadcast tower, satellite dishes, electronic interference shields, weather equipment, and so on. This contrast between the solid base and the high-tech equipment above is one of the structure's most distinctive features.

The predominant building material is Minnesota stone cut against the grain. If cut with the grain, as in many contemporary Minneapolis buildings, the material is rather colorless and uniform in appearance. But cut against the grain, as in the 1930s Farmer's and Mechanic's Bank, a beloved downtown Art Deco landmark, it becomes an elegant building material, yellowish but shot through with

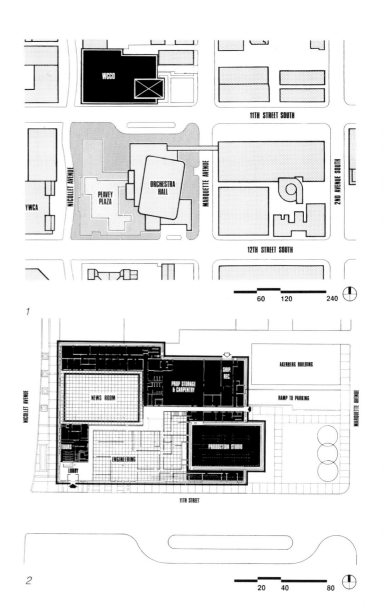

1. Site plan, showing relationship to Orchestra Hall and Peavey Plaza.
2. Main level plan.
3. Nicollet Mall facade.

4

red and purple. With its variegated hues and range of finishes, the stone takes on different colorations in the changing light. The WCCO building's other major material, copper, is also Minnesota-crafted and is used on sloping roofs, skylights, and walls in an original application of self-sealing ribbed shingles.

On the Nicollet Mall facade there are large windows that allow passersby to look directly into the newsroom, furthering the public's knowledge of the building's function. A circulation corridor zigzags through the interior and permits visitors to tour the newsroom, the control rooms, and the station's 50-by-100-foot freestanding studio.

The handcrafted qualities of WCCO's headquarters building have won a place in the hearts of Minneapolitans and appear to have spurred a revival in the elegant use of Minnesota stone. For HHPA, the commission came as a welcome opportunity to complete another side of Peavey Plaza, planned and initiated with their Orchestra Hall ten years earlier.

4. Production studio.
5, 6. Interior details.
7. Newsroom.

5

6

114

8

9

8. View from Nicollet Mall.
9. View with Peavey Plaza and Orchestra Hall in foreground.
10. Tower and office elements.
11–14. Exterior details: copper facade windows, copper roofs, Minnesota stone, and stone and copper juncture.

10

11

12

13

14

GALBREATH PAVILION
AT THE OHIO THEATRE
Columbus, Ohio, 1984

116　Designing an addition to a theater rather than the auditorium itself is not a typical assignment for HHPA. But then almost nothing about the Ohio Theatre *is* typical. This 1928 movie palace was one of the first to be designated a National Historic Landmark. It has perhaps the most splendidly ornate interior ever created by the movie palace architect Thomas W. Lamb. It also has a prominent setting, adjacent to the Ohio State Capitol, a landmark structure begun in 1860 after designs by landscape painter Thomas Cole.

When a group of Columbus citizens began to slowly and lovingly restore the Ohio Theatre, they realized that even though the building's life as a first-run movie theater was over, it could still be used as a performing arts center. However, new support facilities—expanded lobby spaces, an enlarged stage, additional dressing rooms, rehearsal rooms, and administration offices—were needed to make the conversion possible. Because little space was available on the constricted site, the architects were challenged to design a modest, twenty-one-foot side extension and a thirty-foot rear extension that could accommodate all these needs and still be of such quality that it would not compromise the landmark theater.

The auditorium and existing lobby were restored. The public spaces were greatly expanded by the width of the new Galbreath Pavilion, which runs nearly the full length of the building. It provides concessions, rehearsal rooms, banquet facilities, and other amenities required in a contemporary performance facility. The major design device is a grand staircase that allows patrons to circulate upward to the various levels of seating and downward through the levels of the lobby, giving ample opportunity for people-watching during intermissions.

---

1. Ohio Theatre, 1981.
2. Site plan.
3. Expansion plan, main level.
4. View of theater complex (left to right): Esplanade, Galbreath Pavilion, original theater.
5. Galbreath Pavilion and Ohio Theatre.

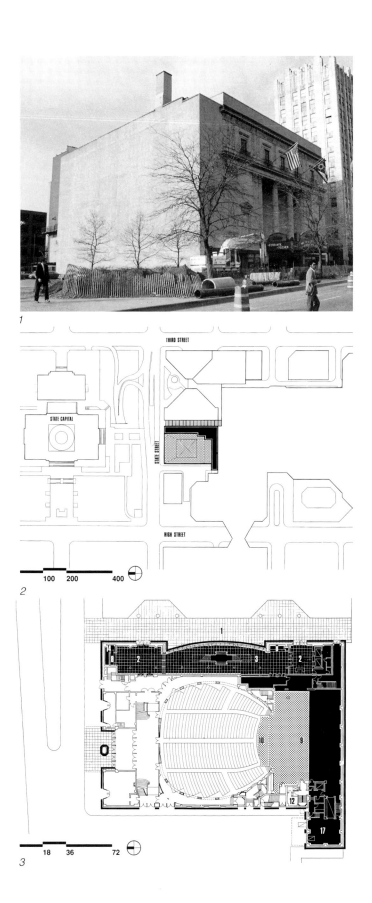

1

THIRD STREET
STATE CAPITAL
STATE STREET
HIGH STREET

100　200　400
2

18　36　72
3

4

5

6

An illuminated bronze and crystal handrail, carpeting with a pattern and colors taken from Lamb's resplendent interior, and an undulating wall of glazed, plum-colored terra cotta add sparkle to the space. Lamb's original marquee entrance is augmented by new entrances from a glass-roofed galleria. This walkway connects the state capitol with a new shopping mall and office buildings adjacent to the performing arts center. In warm weather it becomes an outdoor extension of the lobby.

Lamb's exterior is far more restrained than his exuberant interior. HHPA was able to approximate Lamb's shades and shadows by using brick instead of terra cotta for pilasters and cornices on the facade facing the capitol. An entirely new grand gesture was added in the galleria with a great curved-glass window wall that rolls in and out of the pavilion's structural grid.

This restored and improved structure is now recognized as the official state theater of Ohio. Though it has won several design awards, its success lies as much in its effective operation as in its architectural design. The Ohio Theatre has been a financial success, inspiring other efforts to convert historic theater structures in downtown Columbus for contemporary use.

6. *Interior of Ohio Theatre.*
7. *Pavilion stair.*

RIZZOLI INTERNATIONAL 57TH STREET BOOKSTORE
New York, New York, 1985

120   For twenty years Rizzoli's flagship bookstore was a landmark presence on Fifth Avenue, an exemplar of Old World elegance and luxury. When the store was forced to move, the design challenge was to relocate this beloved institution to a new address without essentially altering its character. Complicating the problem was the fact that the new location (the former Sohmer Piano Showroom, on West 57th Street) was larger than the old, with 6,000 square feet of space, and of an altogether different configuration, with three floors instead of two. A further complication was the requirement that the move be accomplished in less than five months.

To preserve the store's associations and character, HHPA moved several key pieces of carved casework and four chandeliers from the Fifth Avenue store to 57th Street. These elements are integrated with new cherrywood cabinetry, a new marble floor similar to the old one on Fifth Avenue, and a custom-designed carpet with a Renaissance-inspired pattern. The old Adamesque plasterwork ceiling has been retained and glazed to give it a traditional appearance.

These elements provide sufficient connection with the Fifth Avenue store to make the new store's design "an essay in continuity," a thought that pleases both client and architect. But many improvements were also made. The lighting, for instance, was greatly improved. Each bookshelf is now individually illuminated. This not only makes browsing easier and more pleasurable but increases the drama and theatricality of the interior. Completely new mechanical and electrical systems were also installed.

1-3. Third, second, and first floor plans.
4. 57th Street facade.

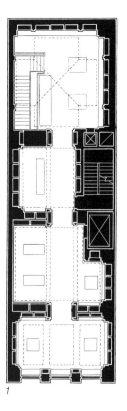

1

5   10   20

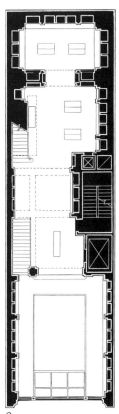

2

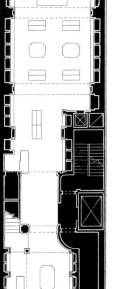

3

6

5. Second-floor interior.
6. Detail of glazed ceiling with Hermès
chandelier.

WEST WING,
VIRGINIA MUSEUM OF FINE ARTS
Richmond, Virginia, 1985

124 Among contemporary architectural
commissions few are more problematic
than adding new gallery space to an
existing museum. The addition has to
relate to the original, but it has to be
architecturally engaging as well, despite
demanding program requirements that
call for what is essentially a featureless,
environmentally sealed box.

These challenges were implicit in
designing the new 90,000-square-foot
West Wing of the Virginia Museum of Fine
Arts in Richmond. The museum was
housed in a 1936 limestone and brick
neo-Georgian building and three later
additions, none of which followed the
stylistic details or proportions of the
original.

By devising a relatively inexpensive
method of masonry construction that
uses large stone blocks, HHPA turned
the West Wing's facades into an essay in
limestone. The play of textures created
by a rusticated base and bullnose
together with alternating bands of smooth
and ribbed limestone enliven the West
Wing's facade and reduce its apparent
size. The wall surfaces appear to change
colors under varying light conditions, to
advance or recede, to take on shadow
and depth. Without copying the
architectural vocabulary of the original
structures, the walls speak of tradition
with a subtle and richly inflected voice.

The interior presented the architects with
an equally formal challenge. Built to
house two special but very different
collections of art, the West Wing had to
display each to advantage yet maintain
their separate characters. For the
installation of a collection of eighteenth-,
nineteenth-, and twentieth-century small-
scale objects, donated by Mr. and Mrs.
Paul Mellon, HHPA designed a series of
intimate galleries specifically scaled to

---

1. Existing museum complex, circa 1980.
2. Partial plan of Robert E. Lee Memorial Park.
3. Virginia Museum of Fine Arts, main level plan.
4. West Wing, south facade.
5. West Wing, from Robert E. Lee Memorial Park.

1

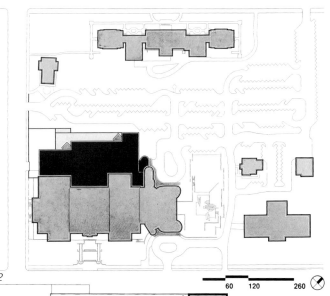

2

60   120   260

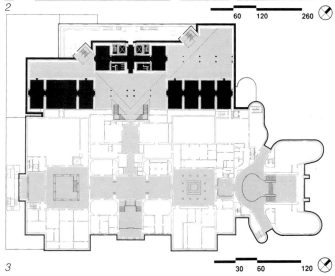

3

30   60   120

4

5

6

the pieces. To accommodate the changing installation of large-scale artworks and decorative art objects from the collections of Sydney and Frances Lewis (only 10 percent of which can be exhibited at any time), the architects created airy, loftlike spaces.

The West Wing galleries are entered through the existing buildings from a double-height entrance hall whose walls and floors are finished in Italian marble. The stone is arranged with the darkest pieces at the bottom and the lightest at the top, so that light appears to be entering from above even when the rooftop skylights are dark. With its sensual and elegant use of materials, the West Wing emerges as a tactile piece of architecture, inviting people to experience its surfaces and the art objects it holds.

---

6. *Mellon Galleries.*
7, 8. *Changing exhibition areas, Lewis Galleries.*

7

128

9

10

9. Service-yard gate by Albert Paley.
10. Detail of stair.
11. Marble hall.

WELLESLEY COLLEGE
SPORTS CENTER
Wellesley, Massachusetts, 1985

130 Wellesley's handsome campus is distinguished by the Olmsted Brothers' landscape plan and many fine Gothic Revival buildings. When called upon to design a vast new sports center (140,000 square feet) for the college, the architects could have chosen a site far from the central campus in order not to overwhelm the existing structures. Instead, to maximize the sports center's accessibility and practicality, they placed it near residence halls, an auditorium, and a major campus entrance, a decision that necessitated skilled site placement.

An existing gymnasium was demolished and a 1939 recreational building was renovated to house dance studios, squash courts, locker rooms, and a multipurpose gymnasium. The new field house, which holds courts for tennis, basketball, and volleyball, is carefully concealed from the main part of the campus and integrated with the 1939 structure and a separate new swimming pool structure. The new L-shaped configuration of the whole is sited so as to reduce its apparent mass from the main campus.

Access from the central campus is through a small courtyard, past a crenellated, diaper-patterned stair tower. Beyond the sports center are the open playing fields. The visitor moving through the complex is thus treated to a series of slowly receding perspectives. Only across the sweep of the playing fields can the full extent of the new structures' volume be seen. From this perspective their gabled roofs and taut-skinned forms (clad in steel panels and brick) appear as both an abstraction of and a complement to the campus's collegiate Gothic architecture.

---

1. *Existing gymnasium, 1983.*
2. *Second floor plan.*
3. *First floor plan.*
4. *View from playing field.*
5. *View from beyond field house.*

1

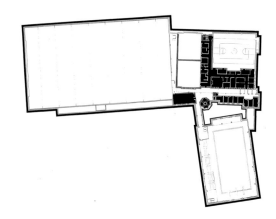

2

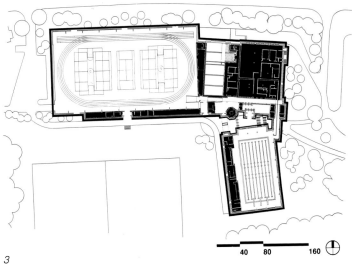

40   80   160

3

4

5

132

6

7

6. Detail of railing.
7. Entry stair.
8. Field house.
9. Overleaf: Natatorium.

BEST PRODUCTS COMPANY, INC. HEADQUARTERS, PHASE II
Richmond, Virginia, 1986

136　In the six-year interval between the first and second phases of its corporate headquarters building program, BEST Products acquired another catalogue-showroom retail business and nearly doubled its sales. As a result, twice as much space as originally anticipated was needed in the Phase II extension, but it had to be constructed with the same cost per square foot as Phase I.

To accommodate the program's volumetric requirements, the architects had to break the original two-story cornice height envisioned by the master plan and construct a three-story expansion using less expensive materials. HHPA was nonetheless able to make a transition between the two parts by submerging part of the expansion below grade and allowing only half of the third floor to rise above the curved glass-block and terra-cotta wall that extends along much of the new facade, thus preserving the height of the original facade. The remainder of the addition's exterior is clad in three shades of eighteen-inch-square mineral fiber panels.

An entirely new element is the blue entry portico that divides the extension in two. The portico roof leads into a great linear atrium, nearly seventy feet at its highest, which opens out into green spaces beyond. Its stepped walls, marble-clad circulation core, and partially translucent roof create a dynamic space in the otherwise straightforward interiors.

---

1. Rear facade.
2. Site plan.
3. Main entrance.
4. Detail of glass-block and terra-cotta base.
5. Detail of shingle wall.

1

120　240　480

2

3

4

5

138

6

7

8

6. *View of atrium looking toward entry.*
7. *Entry vestibule.*
8. *Atrium stair.*
9. *Atrium lounge.*

ROBERT O. ANDERSON BUILDING AND TIMES MIRROR CENTRAL COURT, LOS ANGELES COUNTY MUSEUM OF ART
Los Angeles, California, 1986

140 Few works of contemporary architecture resolve as many competing program requirements as the Robert O. Anderson Building at the Los Angeles County Museum of Art. Three classicized buildings from the 1960s by William L. Pereira were already in place around an empty plaza. Besides providing 115,000 square feet of exhibit, support, and administrative office space, the new building also redefines the museum's presence on Wilshire Boulevard and establishes a clearly identifiable entrance to the complex.

A master plan was developed by HHPA for the entire museum complex in 1981. The Anderson Building has been built as part of a program of phased construction. It was planned as the fourth side of a 55,000-square-foot covered central court. All public services are centralized around the Times Mirror Central Court, including a new restaurant, a museum shop, and membership and art-rental areas. The partially roofed Central Court unifies the entire museum at plaza level and is crossed by bridges that connect the buildings at upper levels. This eliminates the psychological deterrent of having to pass between galleries without weather protection.

From the street the building presents a new public image of the museum. Its facade of buff-colored Minnesota stone, glass block, and green terra-cotta stripes—shimmering and sensual— relates directly to Wilshire Boulevard's Art Deco and Art Moderne heritage.

The interior galleries are arranged enfilade, with windows at the end of axes to provide orientation. The top floor, which contains the pre-1945 permanent collection, is the most traditional in its detailing, with moldings, a heavy base, and cornices. It also has the smallest

1. Existing museum complex, circa 1965.
2. Site plan.
3. Axonometric.
4. Wilshire Boulevard facade of Robert O. Anderson Building.

1

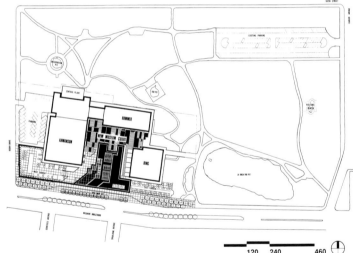

2

120   240   460

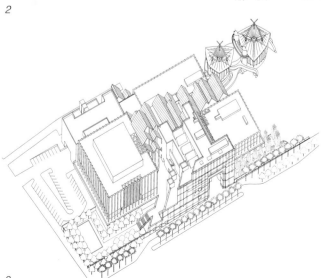

3

galleries. The middle floor, for post-1945 art, has somewhat larger galleries and simpler details. The bottom floor, a neutral box for changing exhibitions, is almost without detail, and its large open galleries can accommodate a variety of artworks.

The upper floors have natural light, provided on the top floor by overhead skylights and on the second floor by a traditional skylight turned on its side. Glass blocks and louvers also let in California's abundant natural light while screening out ultraviolet radiation.

5. Detail of glass-block, terra-cotta, and porcelain panels.
6. Detail of west facade.
7. Detail of Wilshire Boulevard facade.
8. Sculpture courtyard.

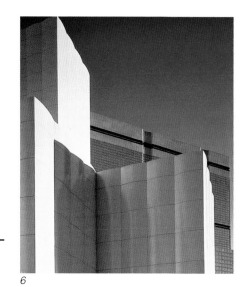

6

7

8

9. Second-floor gallery, Robert O. Anderson Building.
10, 11. Third-floor galleries, Robert O. Anderson Building.

10

11

12

The Robert O. Anderson Building

13

The Robert O. Anderson Building

ALICE BUSCH OPERA THEATER
Cooperstown, New York, 1987

148 Nineteenth- and twentieth-century architectural themes come together in this opera house used during the summer months on Lake Otsego in upstate New York. Built on a turkey farm, the opera house takes its design cues from the adjacent vernacular buildings. Wood is liberally used on the principal facade of traditional, shedlike forms and throughout the interior, but the theater has a steel frame, clad for the most part in corrugated metal to satisfy the building code.

The building is carefully sited to take full advantage of its Arcadian setting. Patrons arrive on terraced parking levels to the west of Route 80 and reach the opera theater by walking across a meadow and around a small pond with swans and cattails. From the outdoor lobby the parking area disappears into the landscape, preserving the bucolic tranquillity of the scene.

To take further advantage of the setting, this home for the Glimmerglass Opera Company is designed as an open-air pavilion with screened walls covered by eight sixteen-by-twenty-four-foot rolling doors that can be closed for matinee performances or during inclement weather. The interior is reminiscent of the nineteenth-century European opera houses whose intimacy and fine acoustics were often the precedent for successful performance halls in America. Its decorative latticework ceiling has an overlay design based on nineteenth-century American quilting patterns.

The intimate interior has 600 seats on the orchestra floor and 300 on the balcony. The large stage (ninety-six by forty-five feet) and the sixty-nine-foot-high fly loft provide ample resources for handling scenery. The orchestra pit can accommodate up to eighty musicians.

---

1. View toward entry.
2. Balcony level plan.
3. Ground level plan.
4. Aerial view of site, looking toward Lake Otsego.

1

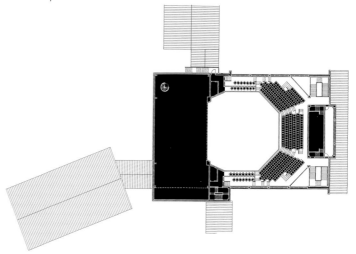

2

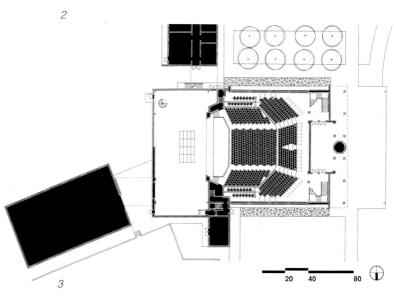

3

20 40 80

Several farm buildings on a small knoll adjacent to the theater are now used for support functions. Rehearsal rooms and additional support buildings are planned to be constructed nearby and will be integrated into the landscape plan. Terraces surrounded by ornamental flower borders are being gradually added each season.

5. Open-air orchestra and balcony seating.
6. Detail of balcony stair.
7. Theater ceiling.

150

5

6

BAM MAJESTIC THEATRE
Brooklyn, New York, 1987

152   Built in 1903, the Majestic was a lively performance venue during its heyday, even serving as a tryout house for George Gershwin. Its transformation reflects changing demographics in the surrounding community and current ideas about the performing arts. Its rehabilitation seems particularly appropriate for an adventuresome organization like the Brooklyn Academy of Music, sponsor of the annual Next Wave Festival.

"Reparation" rather than "restoration" may best describe this project. The theater has not been restored to an imagined earlier state, but rather repaired to appear at the point of disintegration where it was found after a decade of abandonment. But the theater has also been transformed: extensive changes in its stage and seating have altered the traditional performer/audience relationship, making it more intimate than a conventional proscenium theater.

To create a dramatic arena that suggests a Greek amphitheater, HHPA reduced the original interior's three seating tiers to two, sloping seats down from the mezzanine level to a new stage that projects twenty-one feet in front of the proscenium. To improve sight lines, the upper balcony was reduced from twelve rows to seven. Upholstered benches on the main floor and high stools with backs and small armrests in the balcony have replaced conventional seating. For standard productions the projecting part of the stage can be removed and replaced with additional seating or an orchestra pit.

Inspired by Peter Brook's Bouffes du Nord in Paris—a similarly "ruined" theater that serves as both laboratory and stage for the innovative director—the new BAM Majestic opened in 1987 with his

1. Original theater section.
2. New theater section.
3. Orchestra level plan.
4. Renovated street facade.
5. Street facade, circa 1904.

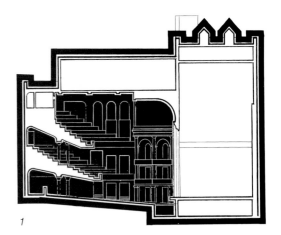

1

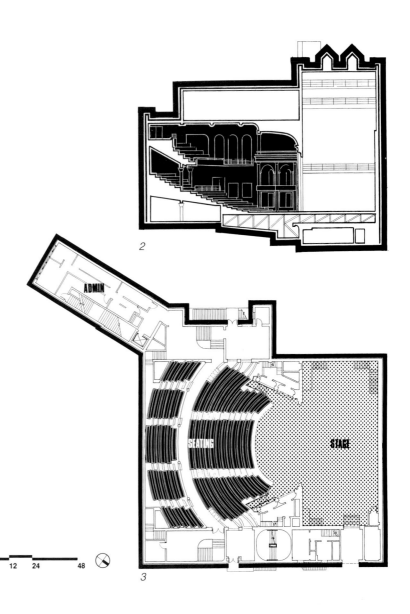

2

3

4

5

production of the epic, nine-hour *Mahabharata.* The peeling layers of paint and crumbled plaster attest to the passage of time, allowing audiences to imagine the building's earlier lives: first as a Brooklyn neighborhood theater, then as a movie palace, and finally as a home to religious services. Water from a leaking roof damaged many of the interior surfaces, creating a rich tapestry of peeling paint and spalled plaster. The theater's current state appears to be the result of this natural process. Some surfaces are new, however, but even these have been distressed and hand-painted to complement existing textures and colors. The exposed steelwork has been spray-fireproofed; the lighting equipment is directly visible and undisguised.

6. *Reconstructed theater interior.*
7. *Detail of stage.*
8. *View of orchestra level, with balcony above.*
9. *Detail of scenery.*
10. *Stabilized theater boxes for the production of Peter Brook's* Mahabharata.

6

7

8

9

RIVERBANK WEST
New York, New York, 1987

Riverbank West, in a once neglected area at the west end of 42nd Street, was developed to provide affordable, middle-income housing. Despite the development's height, its patterned facade, stepped profile, and landscaped entry courtyard recall buildings of an earlier era.

Although originally conceived as a black-and-white tower to complement two celebrated skyscrapers on 42nd Street—the Chrysler and McGraw Hill buildings—and to convey a distinctive architectural image, the design was subsequently modified to beige and brown in response to the developer's preferences. By manipulating and patterning balconies, fenestration, and brickwork, the architects convey a memorable image with an economical building.

The facade is made entirely of standard products in standard colors: beige and terra-cotta colored giant bricks, cantilevered concrete balconies with glass handrails, and off-the-shelf aluminum windows. Except for cabinetry in the lobby, no custom work was involved.

The building boasts splendid views of the Hudson River, the Palisades, Upper New York Bay, and Manhattan. A health club containing a lap pool, an exercise room, and squash courts offers services not found in comparable rental buildings. A vine-clad redwood pergola leads through a landscaped entrance courtyard to the lobby, providing privacy and a welcoming sense of entry from the street.

---

1. Ground level plan.
2. View across the Hudson.

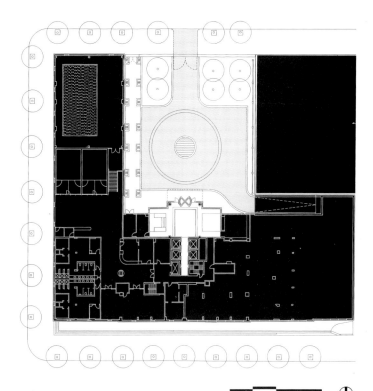

1
18 36 72

3. Detail of south elevation.
4. Detail of masonry.
5. 42nd Street elevation.

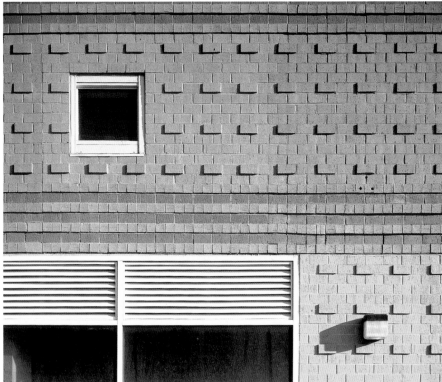

3

4

RAINBOW ROOM AND ROCKEFELLER CENTER CLUB
New York, New York, 1987

160   Half the challenge of revitalizing the interiors of the Rainbow Room and its associated spaces on the sixty-fourth and sixty-fifth floors of the RCA Building at Rockefeller Center was to make certain that the experience of arriving at this rooftop perch would fulfill the visitor's expectations. Unlike the original, where visitors stepping off the sixty-fifth-floor elevator were faced with a dull corridor and no view, they are now greeted by a spectacular reception lobby that leads to the ultimate twentieth-century urban vista. By creating a series of richly banded and illuminated piers that march in jazzy enfilade across the floor to end in a smart salute to the Empire State Building and the World Trade Center beyond, HHPA achieved a dramatic effect in a very limited space. But how to ensure that the rest of the 50,000-square-foot Rainbow complex would live up to such an introduction?

The architects rejected the idea of designing high-style contemporary interiors. A premise that ignored the Rainbow Room's fabled status as a romantic thirties icon or disregarded the strong design vernacular that characterizes Rockefeller Center would run the risk of soon appearing dated. Instead they chose to reinterpret a classic style that would last well into the next century.

Working in close collaboration with restaurant impresario Joseph Baum and graphic designer Milton Glaser, HHPA restored the Rainbow Room and reconstructed 18,000 square feet of other public spaces on the sixty-fifth floor. They rebuilt the entire sixty-fourth floor for the Rockefeller Center Club, providing private dining and banquet facilities. These spaces had never been fully unified by any design premise, and the many accretions over the years only

1

1. *Rainbow Room, 1934.*
2. *Restored Rainbow Room.*
3. *Plan of 65th floor.*

2

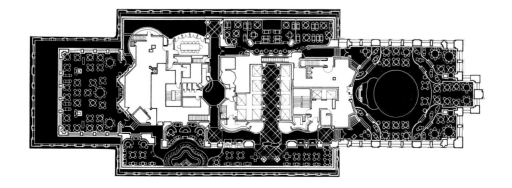

3

15   30   60

made matters worse. Some views were even lost when window walls were given over to service functions and traffic corridors. The public now has access to the complete perimeter of the sixty-fifth floor, parts of which were raised to give diners panoramic views over the limestone parapets.

New rooms such as the Radio City Suite (an Art Deco homage to Donald Deskey, the interior designer of Radio City Music Hall), the Pegasus Suites, the Rainbow Pavilion, and Rainbow and Stars were designed to accommodate contemporary business and entertainment needs, both day and night. Materials found throughout Rockefeller Center are used on both floors. Deep and lustrous mahogany contrasts sharply with the flash of milled aluminum and polished bronze. Cast glass, with its tactile glow, abuts sleek, lacquered wood. Adventurous geometric patterns enliven the thick carpeting, and ceilings abound with layers of frosted, patterned glass, illuminated from within. Each of these elements reinterprets the unique design vernacular of American Modernism.

4. Rainbow Grille, with Dale Chihuly's "Macchia" glass sculptures.
5. Rainbow Room.
6. Bar at the Rainbow Promenade.
7. Detail of Radio City Suite.
8. Center Suite C, "Hommage à Deskey" cabinetry.

5

6

7

8

164

9

10

And for the grande dame herself, the Rainbow Room, HHPA executed a loving rather than a literal restoration. Original details were painstakingly researched in remaining office records and in libraries in New York, Philadelphia, and Washington. Elena Schmidt's brilliant interior design was faithfully re-created, with aubergine silk fabrics for the walls, crystal balustrades, and a domed ceiling edged in gold leaf, which glows with the changing multicolored lights that give the room its name. The newly rebuilt dance floor, thirty-two feet in diameter, once again revolves and is surrounded by three tiers of seating. The technology throughout has been updated, with sophisticated lighting, sound, and mechanical equipment systems, all carefully concealed and integrated with original details. Some obvious improvements have been made. The Rainbow Room entrance has been shifted to the south in order to heighten the drama of arrival, and a nondescript wall above the bandstand has been replaced by an illuminated bas-relief of cast glass by Dan Dailey.

9. Detail of Rainbow Grille.
10. Ladies' lounge.
11. Rainbow Promenade seating.
12. Overleaf: Arrival area on 65th floor, on axis with the World Trade Center.

ALASKA CENTER FOR
THE PERFORMING ARTS
Anchorage, Alaska, 1988

168 The Alaska Center for the Performing Arts has a festive air that goes a long way toward dispelling the darkness of the long winter nights in subarctic Anchorage. The large building (175,000 square feet) was carefully designed to prevent it from becoming a hulking presence in the relatively modest scale of the city's downtown. Each of the three auditoriums is identified by separate entrances, lobbies, and roof shapes. Beneath the entrance porches are gabled vestibules that recall Anchorage's small cottages and allude to some of the improbable juxtapositions still found in the center of this frontierlike city: a small, yellow clapboard house sitting next to a reflective-glass office mid-rise, or a small log building neighboring a high-rise condominium.

Many of the lessons learned by HHPA in their earlier theaters and auditoriums were put to use here. The center's three halls are deliberately differentiated in size, geometry, and imagery in order to increase variety and maximize performance possibilities. An ambitious program integrating works by regional artists directly into the architecture helps to relate the massive building to its community. The lobbies are warmly illuminated and sheathed with patterned-glass curtain walls. Views of the multilevel spaces animate the surrounding streets and beckon the public inside.

The largest of the three performance spaces, the 2,100-seat Evangeline Atwood Concert Hall, is a multipurpose auditorium with electronically assisted acoustics developed by Christopher Jaffe. Parterre sections at the back and the sides of the orchestra, as well as mezzanine and balcony seating, are angled along the faceted sides of the hall, while the main orchestra seating is

---

1. Entrance porch.
2. Orchestra level plan.
3. Main entrance, marked by "Visual Music" light sculpture by Eric Staller.

1

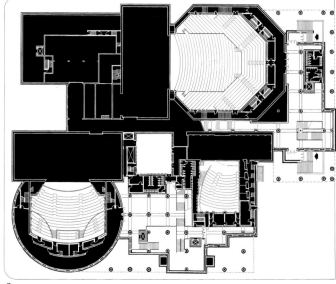

2

40   80   160

parallel to the stage. This fragmentation helps bring audience and performers into a more intimate relationship. The room's most distinguishing feature is the geometric shaping of the ceiling, which was inspired by the aurora borealis, one of the Arctic's most spectacular natural features.

The 800-seat Discovery Theater is dominated by opposing curves in the ceiling and floor, which create a gentle slope toward the stage and focus audience attention. The asymmetrical 350-seat Small Theater can accommodate speeches, films, or full musical and theatrical productions. The catwalks and rigging are left exposed to offer multiple points of access and express the room's function.

The art program for the Alaska Center differs from the program for the Hult Center in an important respect. In the Hult Center individual works of art were applied to the architecture, whereas in the Alaska Center designs representing the region's landscape, vegetation, and atmosphere were converted into designs for fabrics, carpets, and glass, and adapted as an integral part of the architecture. The color palette for the two small theaters, for instance, was inspired by artists' renderings of leaves and berries in different seasons. The custom carpeting in the center's main lobby, which connects all three theaters, was based on Nancy Taylor Stonington's renderings of the Alaskan poppy, enlarged to giant size. An electronic frieze designed by Eric Staller runs across the outside cornices. This computerized light sculpture, which flashes, brightens, and fades in a variety of colors and patterns, lends considerable drama to the surrounding streetscape, even when the theaters are dark.

5

171

6

7

4. View of lobby from upper level.
5. Small Theatre.
6. Native Alaskan mask in lobby.
7. Colored-glass "Labyrinth" lobby windows by Ed Carpenter.
8. Detail of lobby stair.
9. Detail of lobby carpet, designed by Nancy Taylor Stonington.
10. Overleaf: Discovery Theater ceiling.

8

9

174

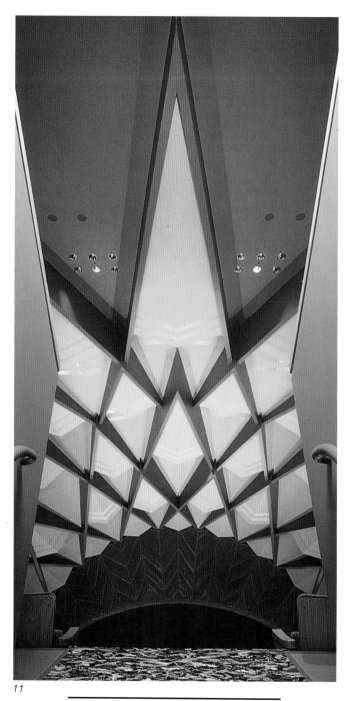

11

11. View of "Aurora" ceiling from third balcony of Evangeline Atwood Concert Hall.
12. Proscenium of Evangeline Atwood Concert Hall.

MAIN LIBRARY,
NEW HAVEN FREE PUBLIC LIBRARY
New Haven, Connecticut, 1990

176 Cass Gilbert's stately neo-Georgian library is a model of architectural decorum. Although it is an imposing, important public building on the New Haven Green, it is sensitively scaled and styled to harmonize with its Colonial Revival neighbors. The 65,000-square-foot addition is similarly restrained, respecting Gilbert's original and its neighbors while nearly tripling the building's size.

The bulk of the new, four-story addition is sited to the rear of the existing building and replaces an outmoded, closed-stack structure. To the east this addition is scaled down to two stories, in deference to Gilbert's facade and the classical portico of the neighboring courthouse.

The addition architecturally complements rather than copies the original. It uses the same vocabulary of elements and proportions, but different materials and patterns. Whereas Gilbert's facade consists of red brick walls set within a framework of white marble, the addition is composed of square masonry units within a frame of darker red brick. The proportions of the fenestration on the two buildings are identical, but the window patterns found in the original are not repeated in the addition. Gilbert's cornices and belt courses are of Vermont marble, whereas the new ones are of brick. This addition ties old and new together without undue sentiment or presumption.

Though the interior has been radically altered to improve its functions, the original public entry has been retained, along with Gilbert's axial plan. The building is still entered through the grand oval stair hall, beyond which lies the triple-height Main Hall—which remains the focus of the interior—flanked by double-height reading rooms. All of these spaces have been interpretively restored.

1. Site plan.
2. Main level plan.
3. West elevation.
4. View of library from New Haven Green.

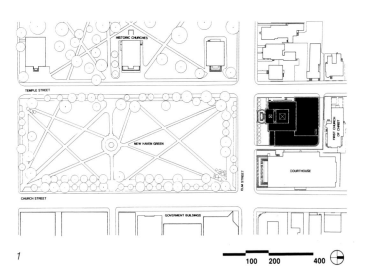

1

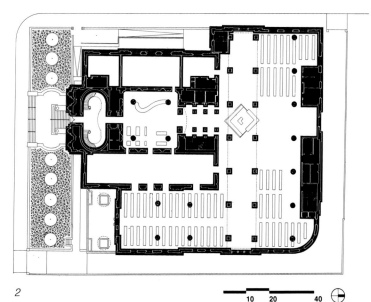

2

3

4

5

Besides the greatly expanded physical space, the principal interior change is the replacement of closed stacks by an open-stack system that gives the public direct access to collections. Other key elements include the addition of large flexible spaces that allow for changes in departmental priorities; sophisticated computer systems; and new administrative office space for the Free Public Library system.

The original building's symmetrical plan extends into the addition, continuing existing circulation patterns. New seating areas throughout the open stacks encourage browsing and reading and diminish the institutional quality of row upon row of bookshelves. In major public areas the building's poured-in-place concrete construction is left exposed to form a decorative ceiling surface and maximize ceiling clear heights.

5. *Reading area in new addition.*
6. *New stack wing.*
7. *Informal seating on main level, with stained glass by David Wilson.*
8. *Children's library.*
9. *Main Hall.*

6

7

8

LILLIAN VERNON RESIDENCE
New York, New York, 1991

180   This Fifth Avenue duplex is in marked contrast to other HHPA interiors. Charged with transforming a nondescript series of spaces into an environment for setting off a collection of antique and contemporary furnishings, decorative art objects, and sculpture, the architects dispensed with many of their usual strategies—exposed ducts, bold juxtapositions, layerings of pattern upon pattern—and opted instead for minimalist restraint.

Employing a restricted palette of colors and materials, along with subtle modulations between elements and meticulous detailing throughout, HHPA simplified the space while at the same time heightening the drama provided by an occasional deliberate contrast: a dark marble fireplace against a white plaster wall, lustrous wood paneling enlivening a prevailingly monochromatic scheme.

The furniture is limited to a few select items to maintain openness and an even flow of space. Illuminated niches and recessed shelves in the living room contain artworks, eliminating the need for vitrines and giving depth to the planar surfaces of walls. A cantilevered bench serves as both window seat and shelf. Lowered ceilings set at an angle throughout the public spaces conceal ducts and delineate specific areas. Changes in floor height signal transitions between formal and less formal areas.

These pared-down spaces appear spartan and serene, exhibiting an unusual combination of the dynamic and the sensual. The angled lines of the partially lowered ceiling, the recessed niches, and the long, asymmetrical built-in cabinets interact with one another against the rectilinear envelope to create subtle tensions. The curvilinear forms of the stairwell further counter the rectilinear enclosure and, along with the luxurious materials—terrazzo, veneer wood, pigmented plaster, thin metal wall coverings—impart drama to the space. Stainless-steel detailing in doorhandles, pulls, and light fixtures contrasts decisively with the natural materials.

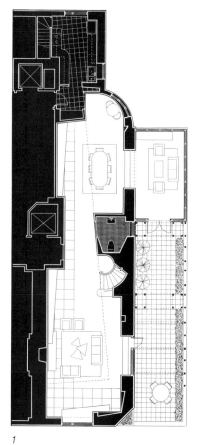

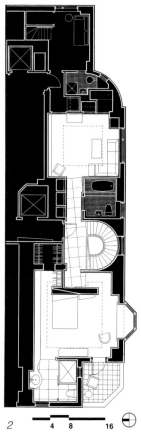

1

2   4   8   16

3

4

1. Lower level plan.
2. Upper level plan.
3. Entertaining area.
4. Dining room.

McCULLOUGH STUDENT CENTER AND ARTS CENTER, MIDDLEBURY COLLEGE
Middlebury, Vermont, 1991

182 Both of these projects, situated on Middlebury's beautiful campus near the Green Mountains of Vermont, steer a difficult design course between a respect for tradition and strong individuality. Like many of Middlebury's older stone buildings, which are modeled after early New England mill structures, they have spare, geometric forms and steeply pitched roofs, and they are set in the open landscape.

In designing the addition to the historic 1912 McCullough Gymnasium to create the new student center, the architects studied various programmatic volumes—from a single large structure to simple individual masses on each side of the gymnasium—before deciding to divide the program into a series of pavilion-like structures. These are set back from the gymnasium's main facade, leaving three of its sides largely unobstructed while concealing two sides of the architecturally unsympathetic, boxlike Brown Pool addition, which was erected behind it in 1963.

By designing the two largest elements as octagonal stone pavilions and subordinating them in height to the main building, the architects reduced their apparent bulk and allowed the earlier building to dominate. Two smaller octagons of white clapboard—another traditional building material at Middlebury—supplement these forms. The additions, which hug the complex to preserve the openness around it, house meeting rooms, a mail room, and various other spaces. The former gymnasium is used for social activities that require a large open space.

1. Site plan, with McCullough Student Center (top) and Arts Center (bottom).
2. Student Center, main level plan.
3. Student Center, east entrance.
4. Student Center, view of stage from balcony.
5. Student Center, view of balcony from stage.

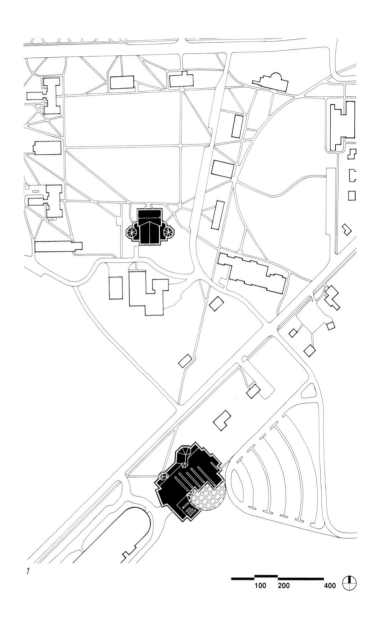

1

100 200 400

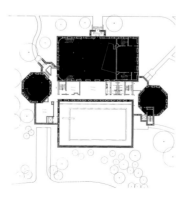

2

30 60 120

3

4

5

184 The arts center was built to strengthen the school's programs in both the performing and the visual arts. It houses a 400-seat concert hall, a 300-seat theater, a 200-seat dance space, and five art galleries, as well as teaching and rehearsal spaces and a music library. The trustees opted for one large building rather than several small buildings to create opportunities for cross-pollenation among the arts and to provide a single focal point accessible to both the Middlebury community and the general public.

The architects exercised special care in designing this 100,000-square-foot facility. Its exterior is designed as a long and relatively low profile, a rectangle overlaid and re-formed with squares, circles, and octagons held together by a common skin. The component parts are designed to be clearly readable once one has become acquainted with the building. The large octagon is the concert hall; the rotated, projecting form is the studio theater; other identifiable shapes are the dance theater, the art gallery, and building entrances. Each department retains its own unique character, and the arts center's exterior expresses the building's various interior functions. The exterior's low profile, peaking at fifty feet above the music hall, echoes the gentle, verdant mountain landscape.

Though constructed primarily of pink and gray granite with a copper roof, the arts center is not an extravagant building. Stone is used in its roughest form, cut into large blocks, to emphasize its solidity. Inside, the large, multilevel circulation corridor also serves as a lobby.

6. Arts Center, north elevation under construction, October 1991.
7. Arts Center, main level plan.
8. Arts Center, detail of stone and clapboard juncture.

6

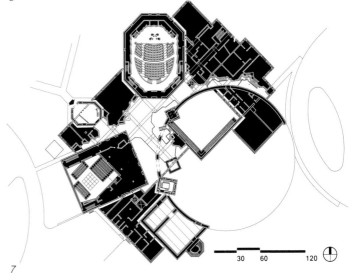

7

30 60 120

8

9

10

9, 10. *Arts Center, lobby under construction, October 1991.*
11. *Arts Center, concert hall under construction, October 1991.*

COMPETITIONS, PROJECTS, WORKS IN PROGRESS

BUNKER HILL: LOS ANGELES MUSEUM OF MODERN ART AND MUSEUM PLAZA
Los Angeles, California, 1980
Competition

The Museum of Modern Art is a key element in the four-block development in downtown Los Angeles known as Bunker Hill. The goal of this plan is to enhance the area's quality of life by providing unique architecture with a human scale while also strengthening its identity as the region's cultural and commercial hub.

The plan is deliberately public in posture, locating the museum's cantilevered cubistic form on the primary corner of the new Grand Avenue. This tree-lined promenade is a string of public plazas, courts, fountains, sheltered arcades, and sidewalk cafés, adorned with ornate street furniture and textured pavement, which integrate the five million square feet of Bunker Hill's new development with existing public and private development. Museum Plaza extends the promenade to the steps of the new museum. It is planned as a terraced garden, shared by an adjacent luxury hotel, that holds an outdoor café and displays of visual and media arts. It also serves as an access point to a new public-transit network.

The museum itself is designed as a deeply notched glass volume, six stories high, that cantilevers at an angle over the plaza. It is finished with transparent, translucent, and opaque glass to vary the quality of light throughout the museum's one-, two-, and three-story-high gallery spaces. Consisting of four major parts— formal galleries, informal artist/public spaces, a landscaped urban park, and support areas—the new museum offers a kaleidoscope of design possibilities that celebrate the unresolved contradictions inherent in the idea of a museum of modern art.

The museum, at skewed angles to the promenade, breaks with the more formal order of the surrounding development, a distinction that is heightened at night, when the museum is illuminated.

1

1. Ground-level view of museum model.
2. Rendering of Maguire Thomas proposal for Bunker Hill.

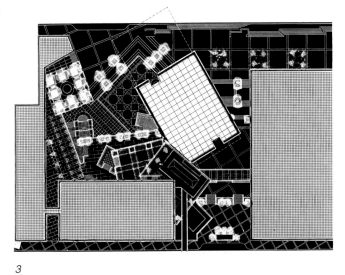

3

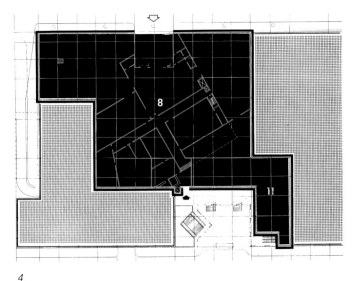

4

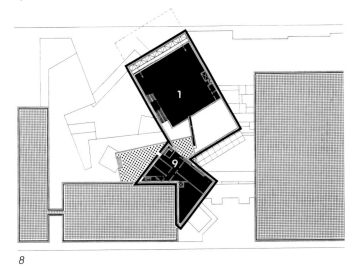

7

8

3. Landscape and roof plan.
4. Lower level plan.
5. Plaza level plan.
6. Main level plan.
7. Level two plan.
8. Level three plan.
9. Level four plan.
10. Level five plan.
11. Longitudinal section of Museum Plaza.

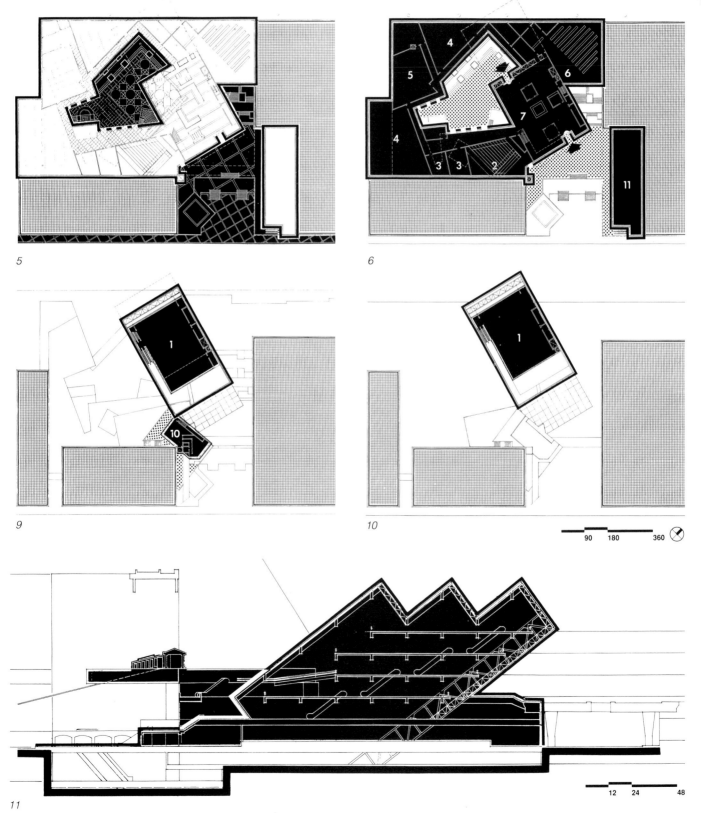

5

6

9

10

90 180 360

12 24 48

11

NEW-YORK HISTORICAL SOCIETY
New York, New York, 1984
Project

194   The 1908 building that houses the New-York Historical Society was designated a New York City landmark in 1966. Located on the west side of Central Park between 76th and 77th Streets and surrounded by other landmarks, this neoclassical building is also part of the 76th Street historic district.

In response to the society's program to expand its facilities and develop its property and air rights, this project was designed to take full advantage of an unusual real estate market. The main components of the project are the restoration of the society's existing building; a vertical addition to expand the society's bookstacks; the renovation of an existing town house and the construction of two new town houses; and the construction of a twenty-three-story apartment structure located above and adjacent to the existing building.

The restoration plan for the society's present building includes replacing the facade's glass blocks with the original glazing system, restoring the roof to the original standing seam copper profiles, cleaning and repointing the stone, and painting the steel metalwork. The proposed enlargement provides three floors for the expansion of the society's archives and a total of 28,000 square feet of new space for the bookstacks.

The existing town house on the society's western property line (used originally by the society for storage) is renovated and restored for residential use. Two new town houses, placed adjacent to the entrance of the new apartment complex, are designed as residential structures similar in size and height to the existing low-scale turn-of-the-century row houses on West 76th Street.

---

1. View looking north along Central Park West, 1984.
2. Site plan.
3. Central Park West elevation.

1

90   180   360

2

3

4

10 20   40

A 163,000-square-foot apartment structure is added to the top of the existing building. Located along Central Park West, this addition carries the base's tripartite organization upward through a series of setbacks. Each facade is composed differently. The north facade forms a transition between the historical society's present building and the truncated form of 7 West 77th Street, an adjacent fifteen-story apartment house. On 76th Street, the new building adopts an informal and asymmetrical configuration as it steps away from the midblock town houses. The massing on the 76th Street side restores the street walls and cornice heights of the historic district and establishes a transition between the low-rise midblock houses and the taller portion of the new structure, which is typical of buildings on Central Park West.

---

4. North elevation, along 77th Street.
5. New view looking north along Central Park West.
6. New view looking south along Central Park West.

5

6

INTERNATIONAL CULTURAL AND TRADE CENTER/ FEDERAL OFFICE BUILDING COMPLEX
Federal Triangle, Washington, D.C., 1989
Competition

198 The International Cultural and Trade Center and Federal Office Building project is the culmination of the development of the Federal Triangle, an area on Pennsylvania Avenue that, although originally designed sixty years ago, remains unfinished. The new design addresses a variety of contextual and symbolic issues and satisfies the requirements of a complex program.

The challenges presented by this development included the configuration of 3.1 million square feet of mixed-use space on an odd-shaped eleven-acre lot; the accommodation of over 2,300 cars; the restriction of the building height to under 134 feet; and the use of neoclassical design elements to relate to the Pennsylvania Avenue site between the Capitol and the White House. The proposal breaks down the large volume into formal geometric masses whose forms are associated with the design of the city. The new ICTC-FOB is composed of two major building blocks, punctuated by five pavilions, three rotundas, and circular exterior and interior spaces.

A rectangular pavilion at Pennsylvania Avenue and 13th Street is the largest of the new buildings and the only one to include a major pedestrian entry. It houses activities relating to the performing arts and the ICTC. Four smaller pavilions are located at the corners of the primary structure to surround a central rotunda. Their symmetrical, recessed facades make reference to the pilasters that line the exteriors of adjacent federal buildings. They are divided into base, shaft, and cornice, and are punched with sets of windows articulated to different degrees. All the elements have balustrades and gable tile roofs to complement adjacent structures.

---

1. 1901 McMillan Plan of Washington, D.C.
2. Aerial photo of site.
3. Massing study.
4. Model of pavilions and rotundas along 13th Street.

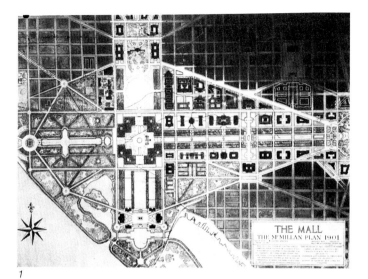

1

2

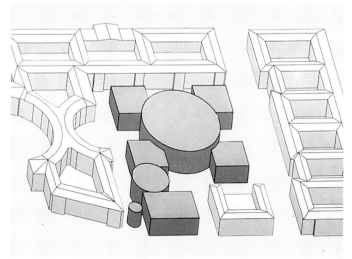

3

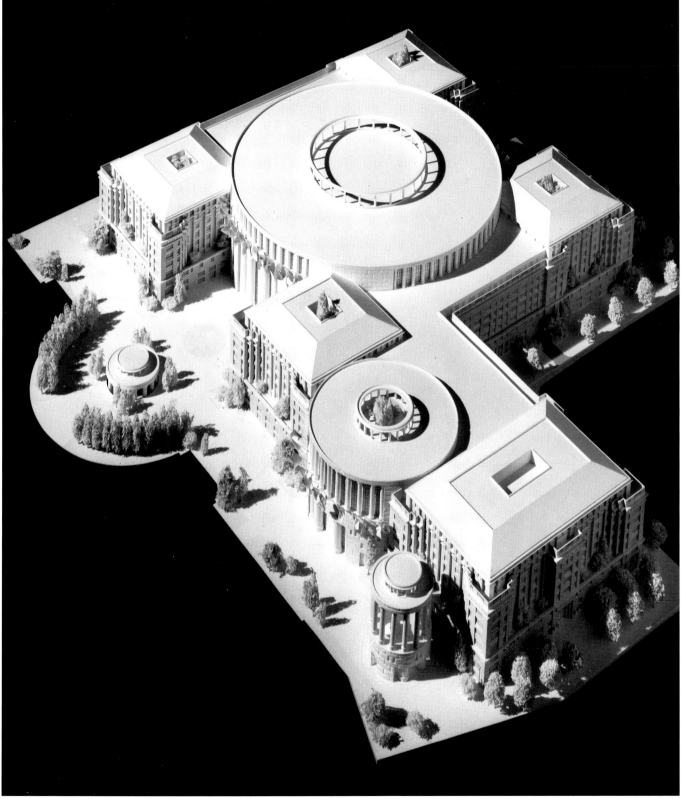

200 In addition to the pavilions, three rotundas are used to reduce the apparent mass of the scheme. They display basic, neoclassical elements and use cyclopean columns and stone blocks topped with circular colonnades. The freestanding Woodrow Wilson Memorial, which acts as the Pennsylvania Avenue gateway to the project, is sixty-six feet in diameter and open to the exterior. Its facade contains fourteen columns to represent the fourteen points Wilson enumerated in the Treaty of Versailles. The second rotunda, near the former junction of 13th and D Streets, is partially assimilated into the building and measures 160 feet in diameter. The third, 344-foot-wide rotunda is embedded within the four surrounding pavilions. Its strongly curvilinear form emerges at the exterior of the building to the west and east, on axis with the adjacent Commerce Building.

At the center of the large rotunda is the 150-foot-wide Geosphere, a ten-story spherical atrium that links a variety of spaces for governmental and international trade activities. Its grand colonnade maintains the same tripartite division and dimensions as the exterior of the main building. Natural light is filtered down into the space through a glass skylight above. The geosphere features plaster coffers, a scagliola colonnade, and a marble base and columns. The flooring, made of polished terrazzo surrounded by granite banking with bluestone inserts, extends the exterior paving materials into the building's interior.

The ICTC-FOB is designed to maximize the use of natural light: the faceted exterior generates as many surfaces as possible from which to reflect light; the curtain wall used at the rotunda entries admits light and provides views of the surrounding structures; and the outdoor courtyards behind the building's cornices and atop its pavilions admit light into interior areas.

5

6

5. 13th Street facade.
6. View along 13th Street to Pennsylvania Avenue.
7. Space in central rotunda of Geosphere.

7

8–19. Model of levels and study of internal functions.

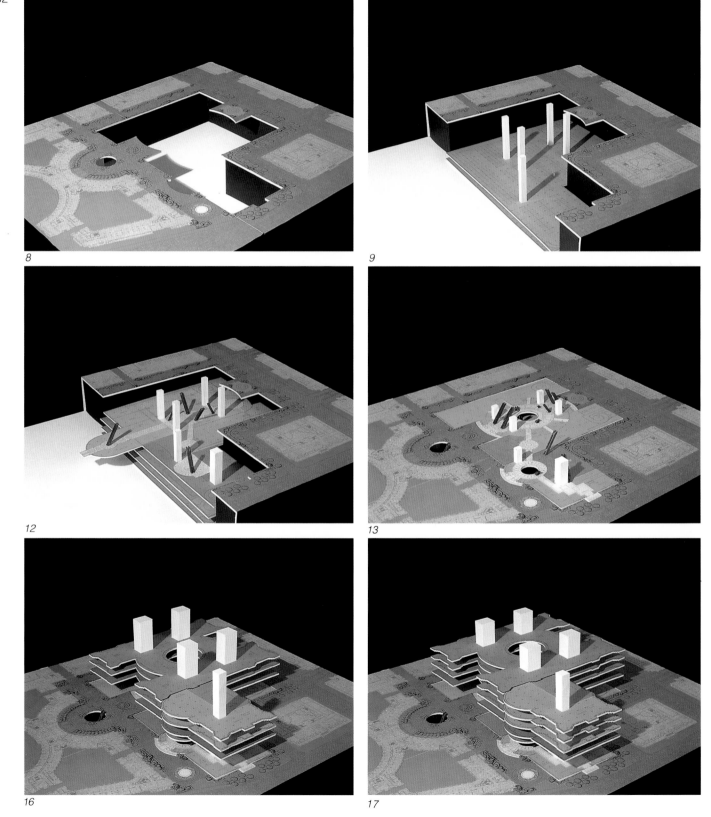

8

9

12

13

16

17

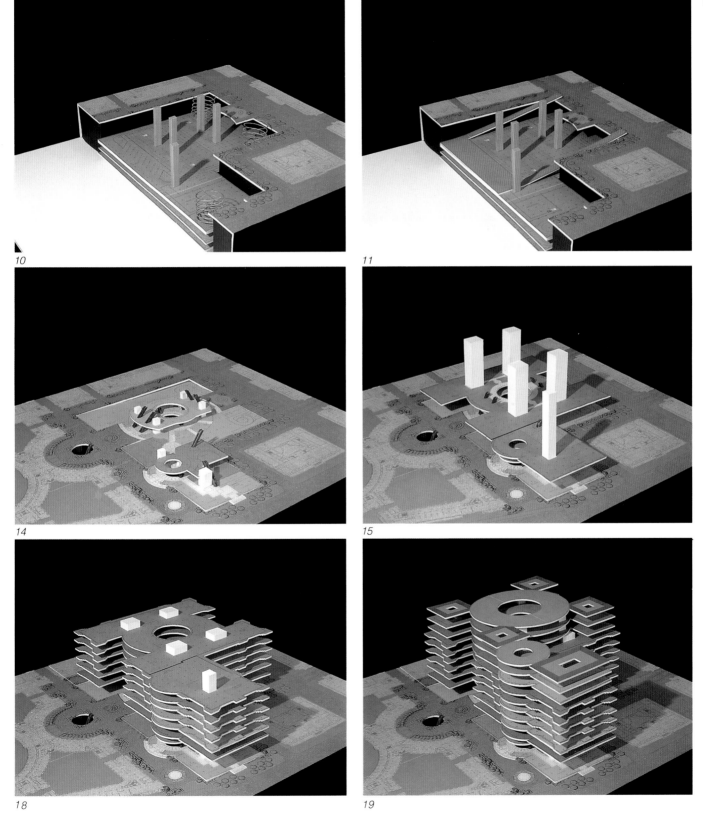

10

11

14

15

18

19

RAINBOW BRIDGE U.S. TOLL PLAZA
Niagara Falls, New York, 1990
Competition

204   The fifty-year-old Rainbow Bridge at Niagara Falls, New York, which connects Canada and the United States, is the most heavily traveled northern point of entry to the U.S. The expansion and reconstruction of the U.S. toll plaza and customs inspection building is the first phase of a $30 million program to modernize and beautify the approaches to the bridge and double its vehicle capacity. The design facilitates the processing of people and vehicles while respecting the site's grandeur. It is based on a marriage of function, setting, and symbol and speaks of the interwoven history and shared ambitions of the two countries.

The major components of the design are the expansion of the plaza; new customs booths and integrated lighting and signage; the addition of administrative and public facilities in a building that spans the roadway; new duty-free shops; and a new bus inspection facility.

This expansion broadens the existing plaza to a width of more than 400 feet, with twenty-two inspection lanes and five toll lanes. The faceted-glass customs booths are positioned in a curving row. Above them, an open network of trusses supports the main building, a crescent-shaped glass structure that houses immigration and customs offices, toll facilities, and support spaces. The building's concave facade is made of dichroic glass, which fragments natural light into shifting patterns of color and shadow by day; the facade is floodlit by night. This "bridge" is supported by piers made of stone from the surrounding area.

Two light towers illuminate the bridge apron and the north elevation of the building. A secondary inspection line is protected by a translucent glass shelter that provides a soft glow at night. Extensive landscaping at grade and bermed to the roof levels of the duty-free shop and bus/pedestrian inspection building is designed to integrate the new plaza with the natural environment.

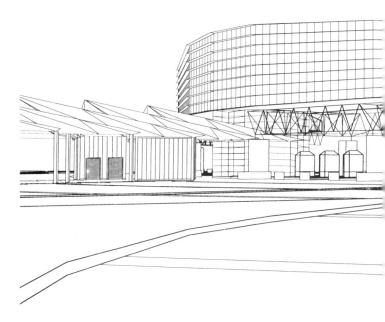

1.

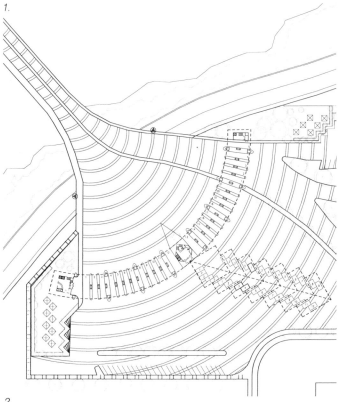

50   100   200

2

1. View from United States approach.
2. Site plan.

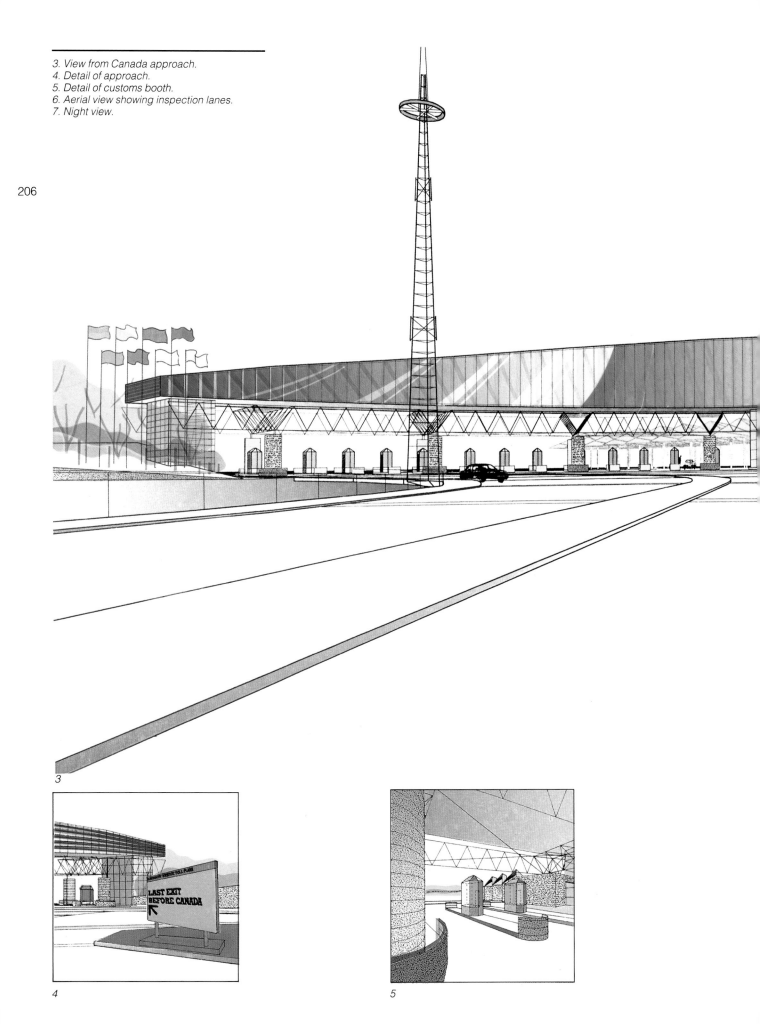

3. View from Canada approach.
4. Detail of approach.
5. Detail of customs booth.
6. Aerial view showing inspection lanes.
7. Night view.

206

3

4

5

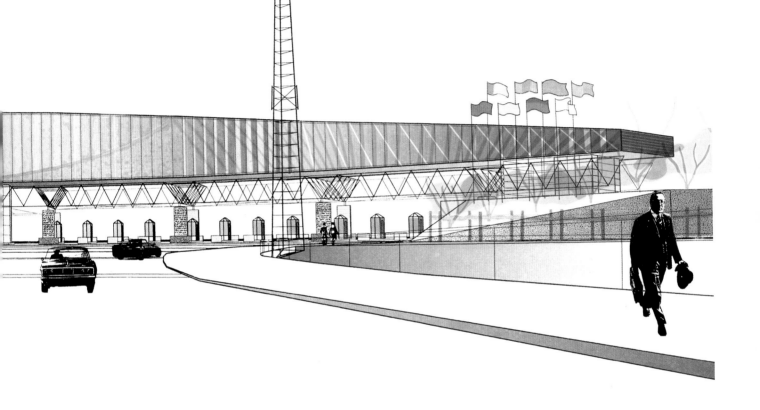

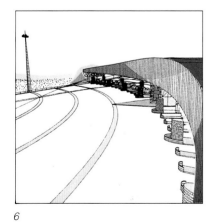

6

7

NORMAN ROCKWELL MUSEUM
Stockbridge, Massachusetts, 1988
Competition

208 The new home for the Norman Rockwell Collection is the Linwood Estate, which also includes a carriage barn, a shed, outbuildings, and the relocated Rockwell studio. The program calls for a museum building and the enhancement of the surrounding landscape. The new, 30,000-square-foot museum, made of wood and masonry, completes the fourth wall of an enclosure formed by pine and spruce trees at the rear of the Linwood house. It stands parallel to the studio and diagonal to the main house.

The interior public spaces are organized around a ten-foot-wide continuous circulation path, which accommodates large audiences and allows for the arrangement of the galleries in a controlled sequence, with entrance and exit through the same door. The galleries follow the slope of the hill, and visitors descend and ascend by means of a ramp that runs the length of the building and creates a connection with the outdoors through the judicious placement of windows. Details in the galleries include wood floors, baseboards, wainscoting, beamed ceilings, and inset carpets.

Four interior galleries of equal size are provided for the display of objects that require no natural light and need special environmental control for conservation. Most of the museum support spaces are located below the galleries in an area that also serves as a connecting link to the Linwood house. Within the roof volume of the galleries is an upper level that contains administration areas. Here dormers provide vistas of the surrounding countryside.

Visitors approach the museum through a small opening in the western row of tall pine and spruce trees adjacent to the parking lot, which is located in an open area a short distance from the estate gates. A vista from this point to the opening between the museum and the house guides visitors up a gentle slope. The landscape is terraced into three distinct areas, each of which features planting, paving, sculpture, and seating. From the upper terrace, visitors can see the museum and the rolling landscape.

1

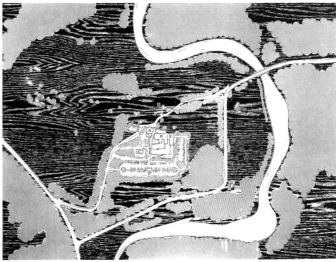

500 1000 2000

2

1. View of model from east, showing museum
and Linwood house.
2. Site plan.
3. View of model from west.

3

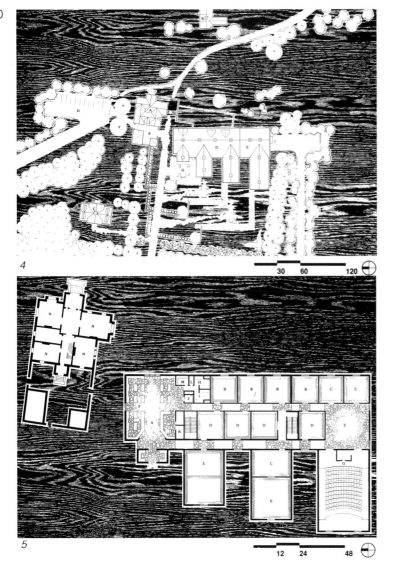

4

5

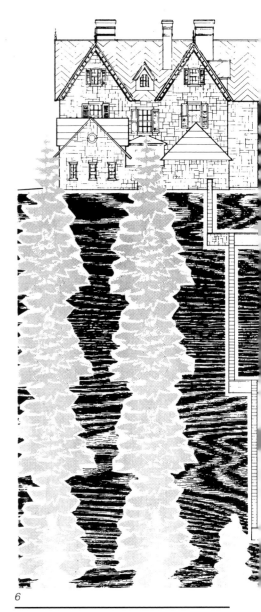

6

4. Roof and garden plan.
5. Main level plan.
6. West elevation, showing museum approach via terraces.

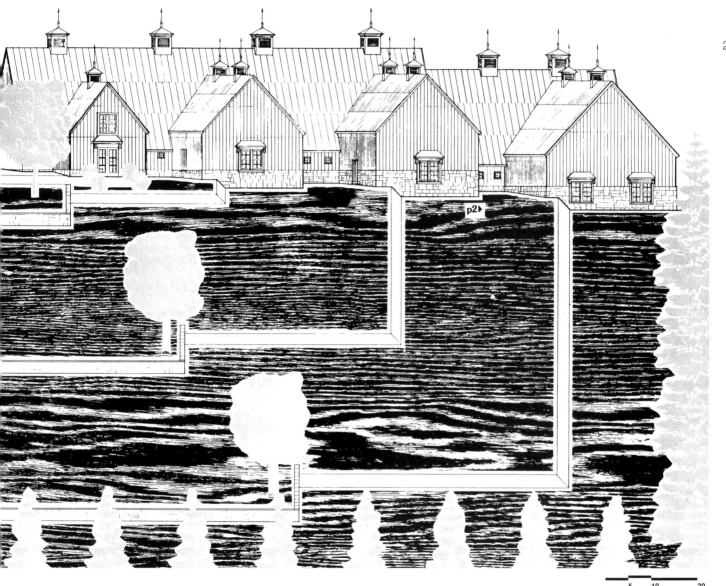

5   10   20

FINE ARTS EDUCATION BUILDING, UNIVERSITY OF NEBRASKA AT OMAHA
Omaha, Nebraska, 1992

The program for the initial phase of this project includes three major building elements: a gallery; a main component for classrooms, laboratories, and support spaces; and a flexible theater. The design takes advantage of the site's sloping terrain by including outdoor courtyards, providing a vertical organization of common program elements, and relating major building entrances to existing parking lots and important pedestrian paths.

The one-story gallery wing is oriented east-west to allow for optimum natural light and to create a protected entrance courtyard with the adjacent science center. The second, largest building element accommodates all studio, laboratory, and office spaces. It is placed diagonally on the site, maximizing southern views and exposure, and follows the current pedestrian path that leads from the parking lots, acting as a thoroughfare between the parking and the main pedestrian mall. At the southwest corner of this central structure, a hexagonal elevator/stair tower functions as the main public entrance and lobby. It provides a circulation hinge between the building and the future addition of a radio and television facility together with a proscenium theater.

The undulating, textured brick facades of the exterior foreshorten and articulate the building's longest component. The double-loaded interior corridor has a series of windows that open onto areas for art- and drama-teaching activities. Offices on the mezzanine level receive natural light through clerestory windows extending the full length of the structure. The gallery and theater are distinguished by their asymmetrical forms, the granite finish of their exterior walls, and their gable roofs. The various masonry materials used for the building were selected to harmonize with the existing architectural character of the campus.

1

2

---

1. Aerial view of site, 1988.
2. Site model, Phases I and II.
3. Site model.
4. Site plan.

3

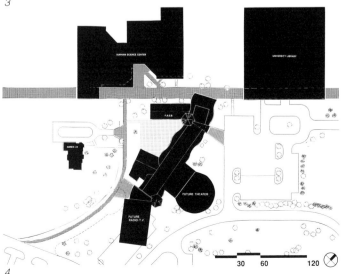

4

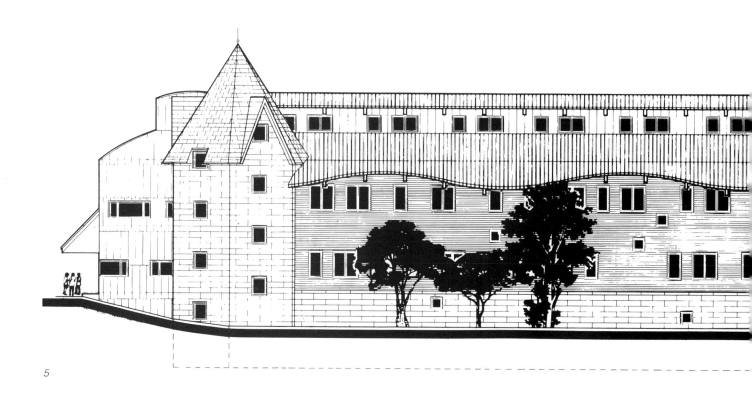

5

5. East elevation, Phase I.
6. Main level plan, Phase I.
7. Construction photo, July 1991.

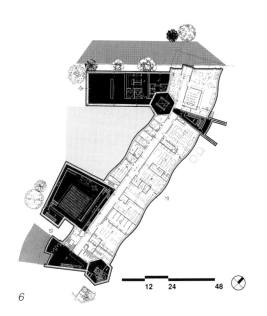

12 24   48

6

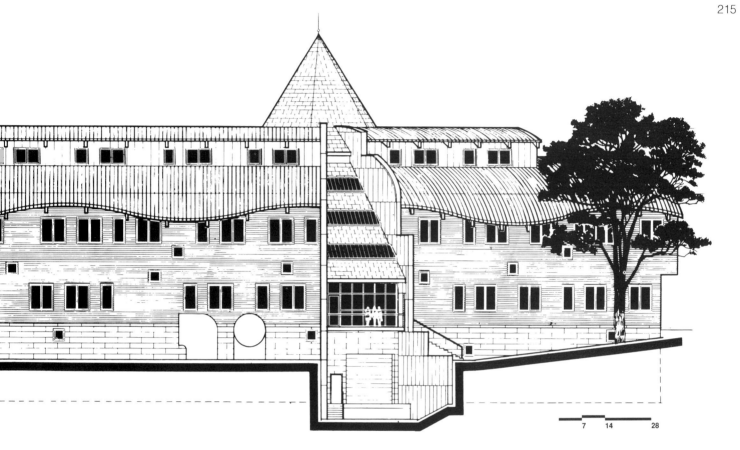

7

CLEVELAND PUBLIC LIBRARY
Cleveland, Ohio
Work in progress

216 This competition-winning design for the expansion of the Cleveland Public Library, the nation's third-largest municipal lending library, retains the classical stature of the landmark building originally envisioned in the city's 1903 Group Plan. It also provides a new functional organization that integrates the existing 1925 structure, designed by Walker and Weeks; a new addition, which doubles the facility's present size; and an enhanced Eastman Garden.

The addition is designed to meet the library's future functional and technological needs; to respond to the formal arrangement and aesthetics of adjacent civic buildings; to express both the library's neoclassical origins and today's technology; and to improve upon the public garden it encompasses.

The development of a larger and more efficient library was based on the decisions to demolish an adjacent building and to re-create the garden, which allows for the linking of the addition to the historic main building. The resulting design affects less than 5 percent of the landmark's exterior fabric and sets the library's east facade as a dramatic internal focus of both the garden and the addition. The library now embraces the garden, dramatically enclosing the space, using it as a point of orientation and a source of light throughout the addition.

The two-part addition is connected to the existing building with a stepped glass-and-metal structure that preserves the landmark's architectural integrity and its relationship to the Group Plan. The addition is anchored on the opposite end of the link by a masonry pavilion, a classically organized design that relates to the area's architecture and provides the library with a new main entrance on a significant street. Inside, the addition is integrated with the original building. Each subject department is found on a single floor, and most materials continue to be shelved in the library's progressive, open-stack tradition.

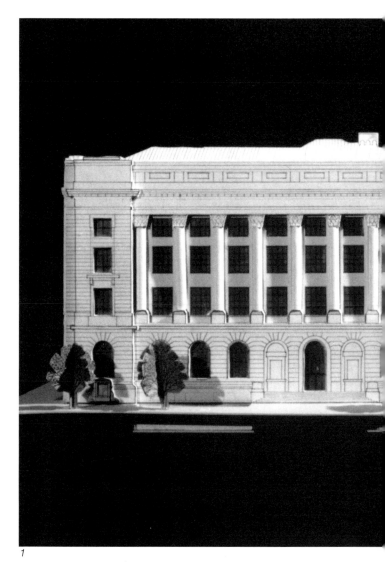

1

2

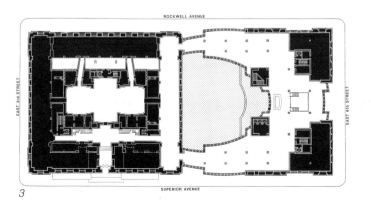

1. Model, showing main facade.
2. Existing library, circa 1930.
3. Main level plan.

3

ROCKWELL AVENUE

EAST 3rd STREET

EAST 6th STREET

SUPERIOR AVENUE

25   50   100

4

4. *View looking east.*
5. *Context elevation.*
6. *Left to right: north-south section, east-west section, side elevation.*

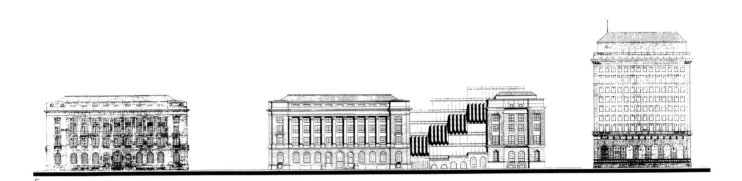

5

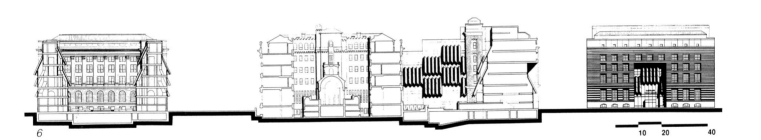

6

10 20   40

HOTEL MACKLOWE
Los Angeles, California
Work in progress

220 This $80 million luxury hotel and conference center in downtown Los Angeles, developed by the Macklowe Organization, sits on a 38,000-square-foot site. It is linked to the landmark Barker Brothers Building, at 818 West Seventh Street, and is located not far from the expanding Los Angeles Convention Center.

Part of a development plan for the entire block, the Macklowe project presents the challenge of visually tying a new structure to an existing, adjacent landmark and two other proposed high-rise structures. The major unifying element is an internal cross axis of open space that cuts through the project at midblock.

The design program, which responds to economic and space constraints, includes five major stacked components: five levels of parking, with underground loading and service facilities and a forty-foot-high motor court to avoid street congestion; a seven-story base with public spaces; a three-story public conference center; a 700-room, forty-three story hotel; and a rooftop pool and health club.

The design calls for a curtain-wall system of aluminum and glass, whose coloration and patterning are used to distinguish the hotel from its conference center base. The latter is visually linked to the dense base of the Barker Brothers Building at street level and tops off at the cornice line of the older building. The hotel's granite and marble horizontal bands complement the landmark's historical elements.

The interior features of the building include a skylit lobby and grand staircase that lead to seven levels of bars, restaurants, and a private club, as well as an 8,000-square-foot ballroom. High-tech teleconferencing and computer equipment are basic amenities.

---

1. Site plan.
2. Seventh Street elevation.

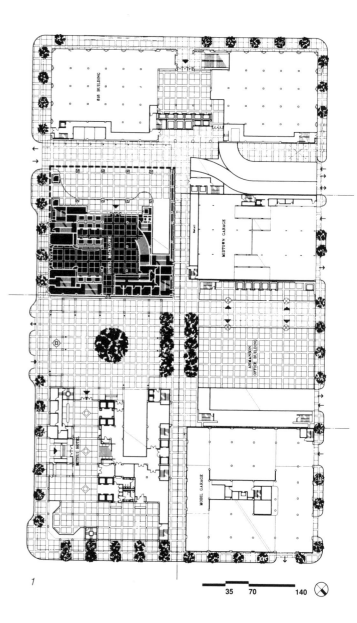

1

35 70   140

WILLIAM K.H. MAU THEATER AND DILLINGHAM HALL, THE PUNAHOU SCHOOL
Honolulu, Hawaii
Work in progress

222 The restoration of the 1929 Dillingham Hall auditorium, originally designed by Bertram Grosvenor Goodhue, expands the stage to accommodate a hundred-person orchestra and a twenty-five - member chorus. In conjunction with this expansion, the rake of the balcony seating is increased to improve sight lines. The interior improvements also include reconfiguration of the orchestra seating and restoration of the auditorium's finishes. Steel technical arches, which follow the parabolic shape of the existing roof structure, support new stage and house lighting and acoustical reflectors. The exterior restoration consists of repairing the wooden trellis and the windows and doors, as well as replacing the roof with new clay tiles. A new addition adjacent to the stage houses support spaces for theater operations and teaching. It is enclosed in a sloped tile roof, and it matches the scale and character of the existing administration building.

The new William K.H. Mau Theater provides the school with a 300-seat thrust theater with one cross aisle and an asymmetrical stage. Above the stage hangs a multilevel system of wire grids, acoustical reflectors, and a flexible lighting and rigging system made of steel and fiberglass. A new underground connection links the Mau Theater and Dillingham Hall, allowing easy access to the support facilities in both buildings.

The new construction makes use of the materials in Goodhue's original building: concrete, stucco, green clay tiles, and lava rock and coral stone for paving. Goodhue's system of walkways and lanais is continued to and around the new theater. The semicircular lanai contains seating and 1,000 square feet of decorative tiles made by faculty, students, and alumni of the school.

The Mau Theater lobby is linked to Dillingham Hall, and the two buildings share a common outdoor courtyard for school and community activities. The Patron Pavilion, also to be shared by the two theaters, is located in the eastern courtyard of the administration building.

8   16   32

1

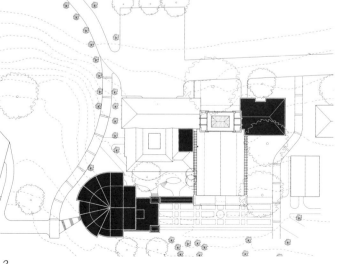

40   80   160

2

1. North elevation (left to right): Mau Theater, Dillingham Hall, and Old Schoolhouse.
2. Site plan.
3. Dillingham Hall, circa 1941.
4. Site model.

3

4

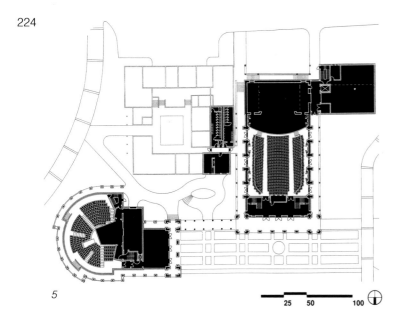

5

| 25 | 50 | 100 |

6

9200 WILSHIRE OFFICE BUILDING
Beverly Hills, California
Work in progress

The design for 9200 Wilshire emerges out of the tradition of historic structures along this premier thoroughfare of Los Angeles. It is inspired by such notable Wilshire Boulevard buildings as Bullock's Wilshire, the May Company, and the Wiltern Theater, as well as by the varied styles, colors, and devices found in much of the area's architecture. Its planned use as a contemporary office building with a flexible interior arrangement necessitates open, loftlike spaces. In response to the zoning regulations of Beverly Hills and the developer's economic requirements, the design proposes a three-story structure over three-and-a-half levels of subterranean parking, occupying a total of 97,000 square feet.

The Wilshire facade predominates, with a subtle scaling back of materials along the two side elevations of Palm and Maple Drives. On the exterior, glazed terra cotta is shaped and molded to define columns (the use of this material is characteristic of buildings on the boulevard and throughout downtown Los Angeles). Five types of clear and opaque glass are set in steel window frames reminiscent of the fenestration pattern of earlier buildings. A curtain wall of interweaving glass bands folds slightly between the columns to create bay windows, offering views up and down the street.

On the interior, the lobby features terra cotta, terrazzo, stainless steel, and pearwood. Tenant space has been designed with particular attention to clear structural spans and flexible layouts. The entrance is set asymmetrically in the facade to align with Palm Drive to the north.

The repaving and landscaping of the service alley creates a buffer between the office building and the surrounding residential neighborhood. A veranda covers most of the driveway entrance to the subterranean parking garage. At the rear, a series of stepped landscaped terraces reduces the apparent scale of the building and defers to the adjacent residential area to the south.

1

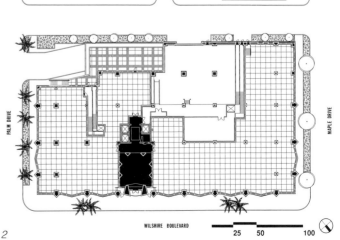

2

PALM DRIVE

MAPLE DRIVE

WILSHIRE BOULEVARD

25 50 100

1. View along Wilshire Boulevard.
2. Site plan.
3. Stepped rear facade.

3

186 EAST 76TH STREET
New York, New York
Work in progress

228 The design of this thirty-one-story residential building is part of a restoration and improvement program for St. Jean Baptiste Église, a church that is both a New York City and a National Register landmark. The critical funds needed to repair this 1910 landmark, designed by Nicholas Serracino, will be obtained by transferring air rights from the church to the adjacent development parcel.

The major elements of the program include extensive interior and exterior restoration work (cleaning and repairing the church's facade, columns, roofs, stained-glass windows, and ornamentation); the installation of two handicapped-accessible entrances; and the construction of a new 152,000-square-foot structure, including 125 apartments, medical offices, and 32 accessory parking spaces.

The site for the apartment building is directly east of the rectory on 76th Street. This new building complements the massing and Italian Renaissance style of St. Jean Baptiste by including similar geometric elements and horizontal belt courses. The volume of the new building is divided into three setbacks capped with a thirty-five-foot top containing mechanical equipment. The strong horizontals created by the belt courses identify the setbacks and recall the horizontal elements that distinguish the church and the rectory, while two-story fenestration patterns in the tower recall the large windows of the church. Vertical indentations diminish the apartment building's overall mass.

The building's base, covered in cast stone and limestone, terminates at the church's cornice height. Above it, at the first setback, the materials change to brick, a sequence typical of East Side apartment buildings. At the fourteenth floor a second setback is distinguished by turreted forms at the four corners that are reminiscent of the corner towers of the church's Lexington Avenue facade. Similar shapes join at the top to complete a faceted profile.

1

EAST 76TH STREET

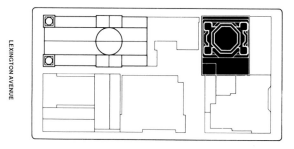

LEXINGTON AVENUE

THIRD AVENUE

EAST 75TH STREET

40   80   160

2

3

4

1. Site model, view from 76th Street and
Lexington Avenue.
2. Site plan.
3. 76th Street elevation.
4. St. Jean Baptiste Église, 1991.

CENTRAL LIBRARY,
LOS ANGELES PUBLIC LIBRARY
Los Angeles, California
Work in progress

230 The rehabilitation and expansion of the Central Library, a 1924 landmark designed by Bertram Grosvenor Goodhue, will make this the largest library in the western United States. The program includes rehabilitation of the existing main library building, construction of a new east wing, and installation of a new landscaped West Lawn over a below-grade parking structure. This expansion is intended to meet the library's programmatic needs through the year 2020.

The rehabilitation of this 210,000-square-foot landmark includes the restoration of its pyramidal roof tiles, overpainted limestone exterior sculptures, and damaged windows. In the interior of the building, major circulation patterns and entrances have been maintained; however, new environmental-control systems are installed to prevent future deterioration of significant artistic elements.

The new 330,000-square-foot east wing is inspired by the forms, materials, and interior and exterior organization found in Goodhue's building. Nearly two-thirds of this structure is below grade, and all three facades are organized asymmetrically to complement Goodhue's original composition. Directly to the east, on axis with the landmark's tower, a four-story window framed by two pylons terminates the volume of the east wing's atrium and brings light directly into the floors below. The atrium has a sloping glass-and-copper roof that reinforces the overall horizontal design. The new north facade includes the relocated and restored court of the children's wing, which maintains its original orientation and windows but has new trees and sloping tile roofs. The south facade is largely obscured or is seen only at an angle, but it continues the asymmetrical massing of the whole.

1

2

1. Fifth Street elevation.
2. West Lawn facade, circa 1928.
3. Rotunda level plan.

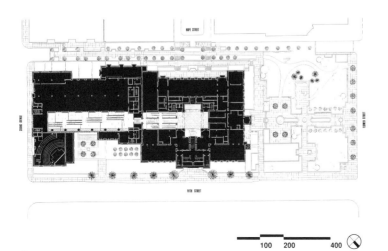

100 200 400

4

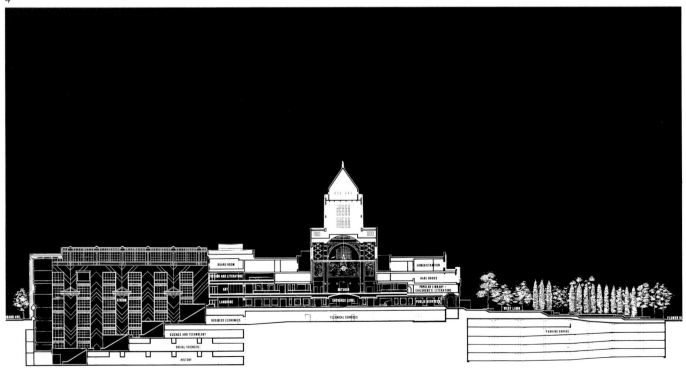

The newly landscaped West Lawn, which covers a below-grade parking structure, replaces the original Flower Street public entrance. Two landscaped courts have been created along Fifth Street, where the new building steps back to join the original. An axial circulation path of steps, fountains, and landscaping is planned from Flower Street to the reopened west entry of the building.

The existing building is reorganized to incorporate library services and administrative offices, and the new east wing houses the subject departments, with fully equipped office and library-catalogue automation systems. Sophisticated mechanical, lighting, and acoustical systems provide the appropriate environment for library patrons and for the preservation and use of books and media.

4. Model, view from Fifth Street and Grand Avenue.
5. East-west section (left to right): east wing atrium, existing rotunda, and West Lawn.
6. Atrium model.
7. Construction photo of atrium, July 1991.

6

7

APPENDICES

INGERSOLL RESIDENCE

Sharon, Connecticut, 1967
New construction
Associate Architect: T. M.
Prentice, Jr.

Saltbox forms and other interior geometric volumes are combined to produce a house whose appearance is both traditional and contemporary. The two-level plan is partially recessed into the graded site, so that the landscape embraces the house. All rooms are oriented to the south, and large picture windows provide views of the Housatonic River, as well as sunlight to warm much of the house during winter months. Small windows on the north side of the house minimize exposure. The extensive use of natural light varies the look of the house throughout the day and accentuates the sloping ceilings, which focuses attention on the river view. The study of the resident author is a distinct working environment, separate from the house.

PERFORMING ARTS CENTER, UNIVERSITY OF TOLEDO

Toledo, Ohio, 1967
Project
Associate Architect: Hahn &
Hayes

The building's site is a former parking lot, and its central location at the intersection of student and public functions helps unify the campus. Sloping roofs and landscaping visually link the center with the disparate collection of buildings that surround the site. Its two major elements are a 500-seat theater and a 500-seat concert hall, both designed with unusual shapes promoting a sense of intimacy. The theater's eight distinct seating fragments focus on a thrust-stage performance platform. In the concert hall, half the seating is in boxes surrounding the orchestra level.

HADLEY HOUSE

Martha's Vineyard,
Massachusetts, 1967
New construction

This is a year-round home whose visual and spatial complexity was designed to stimulate its resident author. A collision of three saltboxes set at 45 degrees results in a two-story, asymmetrical composition of shingled angular forms and towerlike volumes that are pitched and turned in different directions. The interior plan is aligned along three basic axes to create a fluid sequence of multifaceted spaces that range in character from large, open living areas to closed, intimate study niches. The house offers complete views around its 320-acre site, allowing daylight to constantly highlight its intricate shapes and spaces, both inside and out.

ARTS CENTER, SIMON'S ROCK OF BARD COLLEGE

Great Barrington,
Massachusetts, 1967
Conversion

The design for the reuse of three existing barns for a theater, an art studio, and music practice rooms contrasts new geometries with old farm structures, reflecting the experimental character of the school's art education program. The diagonal alignment of the 200-seat theater within the rectangular barn allows for a large, irregularly shaped stage. Two distinct seating sections are set at different angles to the stage. A rear, partially glazed addition and a large overhead skylight introduce controlled daylight into the interior and incorporate the landscape as a backdrop for performances. Studio and gallery spaces are also diagonally aligned in an adjacent two-story art barn.

CLIFF HOUSE

Cincinnati, Ohio, 1968
Project

This speculative housing plan is shaped by its sloping site along a ridge overlooking the Ohio River. The design creates an intimate residential atmosphere in a fifteen-story structure with river views for each unit and two parking spaces per apartment. The beveled, reflecting glass of the main facade (facing the river) provides the building with a distinct identity in a neighborhood composed of prosaically designed low- and mid-rise residences. The utilities and parking are shifted uphill, behind the main facade. Inside, there are no more than three apartments per floor, and public corridors are eliminated, with all units opening directly to the elevator lobby.

DOBELL RESIDENCE

Ottawa, Ontario, 1968
New construction

The elongated plan, shaped by the property's narrow dimensions, focuses on a central living space and a north-facing outdoor court. Exterior walls are built of cast concrete and are topped by clerestories that project through the roof and bring daylight into the interior. These windows are turned in several directions to grab light and reflect it off the interior walls, diffusing it throughout the house. The main living space is designed to display art and to accommodate large social gatherings. A contrast between smooth and rough-sawn concrete formwork on the exterior delineates the sequence of pavilions that define the house.

DUNCAN COMPOUND

Upper St. Regis Lake, New York,
1968
Renovation and new construction

The Duncan Compound is a lakeside vacation enclave comprising nine small buildings, each serving a specific purpose. The existing main living space is made up of two masses—a living room and a dining room—aligned on separate grids. A new, irregular hexagonal volume, prominently set in the center of the building and intersecting with the two masses, gives the enlarged kitchen a helmlike quality with a dramatic view of the lake. The expansion strengthens links between the various spaces while clearly distinguishing each one. The resulting series of geometric spaces and connections gives the building architectural presence while maintaining its vernacular appearance.

"THE GREATER NUMBER PROBLEM"

14th Triennale, Milan, Italy, 1968
Exhibition design and installation
Sponsor: Government of Italy

The theme of the exhibition is a metaphor for contemporary life: exploding population, mass production and consumption, technological obsolescence, and waste. Common elements, displayed out of context, are choreographed in this installation to demonstrate the confusion of a frenetic society always on the move and always discarding things. The exhibit is an up-close, confrontational view of contemporary consumption, including traffic lights, cars, a freestanding classical entablature, airport-runway lights, a neon Coca-Cola sign, TV sets, and Astroturf, all set in contrast to a crumpled classical column and entablature. Contemporary artifacts are displayed on two broad staircases that rise and connect at a right angle, bisected by a large two-way mirror.

JOHNSON RESIDENCE

Boston, Massachusetts, 1968
Conversion

The conversion of two adjacent commercial row structures into a home and guest house stimulated the transformation of this once deteriorated district of downtown Boston into a prime residential area. To divide and maximize the rectangular interior of both two-story buildings, two separate, diagonal plans are introduced. This creates a composition of diverse, angular spaces, each with a central living area open to a skylit roof. The roofs include sloping glass planes set into vertical walls, which admit daylight colored by the reflection from exterior brick walls. These devices expand the sense of space in an interior that does not have an exterior view. Contemporary fenestration is set within the original rough-faced brick walls, which are retained inside and out.

MUSE: BEDFORD-LINCOLN COMMUNITY CENTER

Brooklyn, New York, 1968
Conversion
Client: Brooklyn Children's
Museum

MUSE is a pilot project that envisions a network of neighborhood museums—some no more than converted storefronts—providing communities with circulating educational and cultural exhibitions. The ground floor of a former pool hall and auto showroom is reorganized around a curved entrance tunnel displaying information on cultural history, art, and animals. A two-story planetarium cuts through the mezzanine level, which is horizontally bisected by a second curved path leading to a "please touch" exhibition. Office and studio space is diagonally aligned on the second floor to create a variety of open spaces that expand into an adjacent building for drama, dance, and music activities.

NEW LAFAYETTE THEATER II

New York, New York, 1968
Renovation
Client: New Lafayette Theater and
Workshop, Inc.

By fragmenting this theater's 300 seats into three distinct sections, pitched and oriented to the stage at different angles, and by allowing actors access between these sections and along catwalks that bisect the hall, the design of this theater encourages productions that are truly dynamic for both audiences and performers. The inexpensive conversion of an old movie house into central Harlem's only performing arts theater (and the community's first black-oriented theater in more than fifty years) involved a partial renovation. Two-thirds of the seats were stripped out, and the stage and audience spaces were reconfigured. A new art gallery that doubles as a meeting hall was also created, serving as a further contribution to community activities.

ROBERT S. MARX THEATER, PLAYHOUSE IN THE PARK

Cincinnati, Ohio, 1968
New construction
Associate Architect: Robert
Habel–Hubert M. Garriott &
Associates

The final phase of HHPA's three-phase cultural plan for this section of Eden Park, the playhouse was the country's first asymmetrical thrust-stage theater, and it has superb sight lines throughout. With the audience on three sides of the stage, which actors can gain access to from twenty-four different points, the theater provides for flexibility and intimacy. The curved exterior delineates the geometry of the theater seating, which is broken by the projection of a multilevel lobby, scene shops, and backstage spaces. The project was funded exclusively by community donations and had a limited budget; air-conditioning ducts, lighting, and sound systems were left exposed as elements of the design. The same concrete-block wall both defines the facade and encloses the interior.

STRADDLE STRUCTURE

Brooklyn, New York, 1968
Project

The Straddle Structure, a response to the community-service needs of an underdeveloped area, both preserves and enhances the neighborhood's architectural character. An alternative to the destructive renewal strategies of the 1950s and 1960s, this freestanding structure rises over the community's architectural fabric, literally straddling existing buildings. It promotes the idea of the city as a conglomeration of architectural layers, encouraging juxtapositions of past and present, rather than the constant replacement of old with new.

KNOWLTON RESIDENCE

Sneden's Landing, New York, 1969
Conversion and new construction

In this conversion a carriage house and a dairy barn are unified by the insertion of a diagonal link that juxtaposes orthogonal and angled grids to create varied spaces behind vernacular facades. Space appears to be "borrowed" from adjacent areas and manipulated by changes in daylight introduced throughout the house by a network of skylights. A new diagonal corridor emphasizes the geometric tie between the two buildings.

NEWARK COMMUNITY CENTER OF THE ARTS

Newark, New Jersey, 1969
Conversion

In order to inexpensively convert this nineteenth-century carriage house into a performing arts center for local children, the original two-story plan was retained. A rehearsal room, rest rooms, and storage are located on the lower level, while performance space is on the second floor. To fit a performance hall within the narrow dimensions of a carriage house, the floor was divided diagonally, creating two equal-sized areas for stage and seating. The result is an informal, intimate theater.

ASSEMBLY HALL, PHILLIPS EXETER ACADEMY

Exeter, New Hampshire, 1969
Conversion

This redesign of a former chapel increases seating capacity, focuses views, and heightens the sense of intimacy without sacrificing the original qualities of Cram, Goodhue and Ferguson's 1914 design. A simple curved performance platform is projected in front of the original proscenium. The chapel's flat, single-level seating is replaced with a raked orchestra composed of curved upholstered benches that complement the form of the stage. A new U-shaped balcony circumscribes the room and helps expand the hall's capacity while focusing attention on the stage. Four columns are refinished in chrome, contrasting with the original plasterwork, which is painted and glazed to accentuate its classical detail.

TAYLOR THEATER, KENAN CENTER

Lockport, New York, 1969
Conversion

With the conversion of an 1850 carriage house into a contemporary thrust-stage theater, the Kenan Center has become an important cultural facility in western New York, one that can accommodate amateur and professional theater, lectures, chamber music, and films. The major elements of the redesign are the preservation of the original brick bearing walls and wood trusses, together with the reglazing of the large cupola. A new elevated thrust stage is surrounded by stepped seating on three sides, with no seat farther than five rows from the stage. Additional improvements include new backstage areas and a lobby.

ENVIRONMENTAL LEARNING CENTER, WAVE HILL

Bronx, New York, 1969
Feasibility and planning

This study for the conversion of the 26-acre historic estate and landmark Georgian mansion (built circa 1830) into a center for environmental studies takes full advantage of the site's pastoral setting within the Bronx. With the addition of three new greenhouses, a palm court, and the refurbishment of existing gardens, Wave Hill has become an important botanical center in New York, where city residents can study the natural environment. There are additional plans for an adjacent park along the Hudson and for subsequent restoration of the Perkins mansion, also on the site.

WEST SIDE MONTESSORI SCHOOL

New York, New York, 1969
Project

This open-plan school, located in a West Side urban renewal area, helps very young children to pursue their own interests in an unrestrictive environment. There are no enclosed classrooms in this two-story plan, and most learning occurs in open, interconnected spaces. These spaces are residual areas formed by nine small rectangular enclosures that contain fixed necessities such as water, storage, stairs, mechanical equipment, etc. The exterior of the rectangular building is defined by masonry curtain walls and two strips of mirrored-glass windows. A translucent, patterned three-story triangular clocktower attached to the building marks the main entrance, and a skylight provides illumination for an activity room on the ground floor.

MASTER PLAN, COOPER-HEWITT MUSEUM / NATIONAL MUSEUM OF DESIGN

New York, New York, 1970
Client: The Smithsonian Institution

The Smithsonian Institution preserved the Cooper-Hewitt's collection of decorative arts (which had been threatened with auction) by making it the core of a new museum. Housing this collection in the 1901 Andrew Carnegie mansion provided unique opportunities for exhibition and research. The necessary separation of public, semipublic, and private spaces and circulation required alteration of the building's original configuration of servant and family areas, and the new plan offers a natural sequence of public galleries in what were once private rooms. Extensive public support encourages the future development of an auditorium and a members' restaurant, and the restoration of the exceptional garden space.

SCHNEIDER RESIDENCE

Montauk, New York, 1970
New construction

The design of this four-bedroom house is based on a plan of overlapping geometric grids that create angular interior spaces to maximize the number of rooms with ocean views. While appearing two stories tall, the house actually contains four distinct levels, incorporating the upward grade of the beach away from the ocean. This configuration helps separate entertainment areas from bedroom and studio spaces, which occupy the highest, most private portion of the house. Extensive linear fenestration increases the range of views and brings direct daylight into the house.

COMMUNITY SERVICES CENTER, SHAW UNIVERSITY

Raleigh, North Carolina, 1970
New and pre-engineered construction

These pre-engineered buildings are the first phase of the university's new master plan, designed to diversify life on campus. The construction of the center was an early demonstration of the speed, economy, and flexibility of ready-made building enclosures. For use by all college departments, the center provides space for seminars, workshops, community gatherings, theater, and individual student activities. The diagonal overlapping of four units breaks up the system's rectangular appearance, creating an irregular configuration inside and out. A pedestrian network cuts in between two of the units, whose exposed structure creates a trellislike passage.

MASTER PLAN, SHAW UNIVERSITY

Raleigh, North Carolina, 1970

The purpose of this new campus plan is to introduce a college of arts into the school's curriculum. To expand and integrate academic and community activities, the plan recommends increasing building density, suggesting that the juxtaposition of old and new buildings in a geometric manner would allow the structures to visually play off one another and enliven the overall appearance of the campus. This diversification of the campus's existing organization establishes a new architectural order with formal and informal outdoor spaces. Existing buildings are altered and transient structures are introduced to provide temporary, flexible space during construction.

COMMUNITY RESOURCES CENTER

Brooklyn, New York, 1971
Study for pre-engineered construction
Client: The Ford Foundation

This project is designed for a neighborhood that is highly dependent on public assistance and lacking in basic cultural and recreational amenities. The proposal recommends pre-engineered construction and an open interior plan to reduce building costs and construction time and to increase the building's flexibility. The study surveys pre-engineered building systems and their various uses, and follows with a review of community programs for the center. The proposed activities for the center range from swimming and bowling to arts workshops and special educational programs.

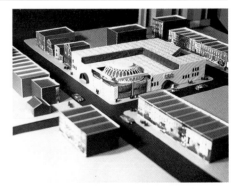

DANCE THEATRE OF HARLEM SCHOOL

New York, New York, 1971
Conversion

This internationally respected dance company offers classical ballet training of the highest caliber to the surrounding community in a space that was formerly a two-story garage. Ground-floor spaces include administrative offices, with windows fronting on the street, and dance studios with receiving areas toward the back, which allows for both natural light and privacy. The main studio occupies the upper floor, where a new skylight has been introduced. Additional space, as well as a distinctive exterior character, was gained by projecting the upper-floor plan out toward the street. The conversion of this sixty-five-year-old building was achieved within a limited budget of $350,000.

MASTER PLAN, NORTH CAROLINA SCHOOL OF THE ARTS

Winston-Salem, North Carolina, 1971

After identifying program needs, this proposal to improve the overall appearance of the campus recommends altering the school's linear, open organization through renovation, expansion, and new construction. Geometric forms are introduced to define a variety of spaces and delineate campus activities. Study, practice, and rehearsal areas are concentrated in the Work Place; a landscape plan is designed to link this with the existing Living Place (for residential and recreational activities). The new Performance Place brings a 500-seat and a 1,000-seat theater to the campus. This phased plan is flexible to accommodate the availability of funds and the evolving nature of the school's programs.

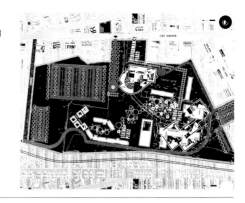

SAINT LOUIS ART MUSEUM

St. Louis, Missouri, 1971
Long-range development report

This study traces the evolution of the museum from its inception (with the 1904 St. Louis World's Fair) to the present, revealing how spatial and design alterations over the years have contrasted with the architect's original intent. A two-phase strategy reclaims Cass Gilbert's nineteenth-century Beaux-Arts plan: a sequence of formal rooms organized along a clear cross-axial corridor scheme. Key recommendations include providing additional space for new and existing uses; uniting the museum's disparate parts; reestablishing the relationship between architecture and landscape; integrating parking within the museum's overall design; and expanding the museum and providing for future activities.

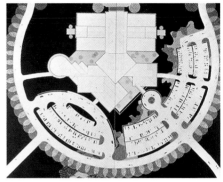

TUFTS UNIVERSITY THEATER

Medford, Massachusetts, 1971
Project
Associate Architect: Earl R. Flansburgh and Associates, Inc.

An exterior composition of curved, trapezoidal, and rectangular forms echoes the theaters on the interior. The two theaters, one directly above the other, have distinctly different floor plans and are surrounded by irregularly shaped spaces and enclosed volumes that house actors' facilities, classrooms, and shops. One indication of the building's density of uses is the fact that all public spaces double as instructional areas. Placing the building in the center of campus both strengthens the axial prominence of the hilltop location and asserts the university's commitment to the arts.

CULTURAL ETHNIC CENTER

Bronx, New York, 1972
Conversion
Client: Bronx Community School District 12

This project involves conversion of a five-story South Bronx office building, which also contains a 2,000-seat theater and six storefronts, into a progressive learning center. Movable prefabricated partitions are used to make the theater's orchestra level flexible for both large productions and smaller activities. The balcony steps, converted into larger terraces, accommodate a local heritage museum, an aquarium, a planetarium, and a six-screen amphitheater. An open-plan elementary school for 200 children occupies the redesigned second and third floors, while on the ground level, community-outreach offices are housed in former storefronts.

EMELIN THEATER

Mamaroneck, New York, 1972
New construction
Client: Mamaroneck Free Library

Constructed over a parking lot and linked to the adjacent town library, this theater reflects a commitment to developing low-cost designs that are responsive to their physical context. The building is a steel-frame box finished in two kinds of concrete block, whose ribbed and flat surfaces and smooth cornices, coping, and sills refer to the library's neoclassical facade. Inside, a curved asymmetrical seating section and balcony surround an open-end stage. Development costs were minimized by limiting backstage areas and leaving mechanical systems, catwalks, and lighting equipment fully exposed, painted in bright colors. Excellent sight lines allow for diverse presentations, ranging from intimate performances for children to professional theatrical productions.

MT. HEALTHY SCHOOL

Columbus, Indiana, 1972
New construction
Client: Bartholomew County
Consolidated School District

This elementary school is organized around two basic concepts. First, it is based on an open plan, where students are grouped by grade into three distinct semi-open clusters composed of a number of connected learning spaces, each accommodating different activities. Second, its overall organization and design are shaped by the superimposition of grids; the resulting collision of enclosed volumes generates a sequence of residual spaces and the main interior circulation path. This path, delineated by a variegated carpet, cuts diagonally through the school. To articulate their distinct uses, learning clusters, offices, and support activities are arranged on separate grids, reinforced by lighting, skylights, and exposed mechanical and structural systems painted in primary colors.

FISHER THEATER, PHILLIPS EXETER ACADEMY

Exeter, New Hampshire, 1972
New and pre-engineered
construction

This project demonstrates that although a pre-engineered, industrial (Butler) building system can be adapted to new uses with minimum cost, it requires exceptional coordination among the system's manufacturer, the structural engineer, and the architect. Five regular structural bays for the theater are integrated in an offset configuration, breaking up the system's rectangular volumes and creating spaces that are diversely shaped, both inside and out. The system's barnlike character is appropriate to both the New Hampshire countryside and the restricted site. An islandlike seating section surrounded by open space eliminates the typical fixed division between audience and stage, encouraging a variety of approaches to theatrical productions.

QUEENS COUNTY ART AND CULTURAL CENTER

Flushing Meadow, New York,
1972
Program goals and space
requirements

This proposal allows for the exhibition of important works of art currently in storage in New York's major art institutions. Three distinct galleries are designed to accommodate a wide range of works, from pre-Columbian sculpture to oversize modern canvases. The program also involves the creation of a center for local artists, including space for exhibitions, workshops, and performances. The 31,000-square-foot facility is designed for an existing building in Flushing Meadow, Queens.

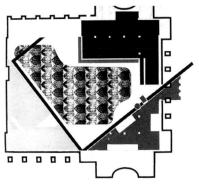

SALISBURY SCHOOL

Salisbury, Maryland, 1972
New construction

The firm's second open-plan educational facility is a return to the one-room-schoolhouse concept. Various distinct learning areas, shaped by opposing geometric grids, are used to create functional diversity. Entrance into the square one-story building (the first grid) is through a diagonal tube (the second grid). Partitioned spaces for offices, art classes, and mechanical equipment are aligned on this second grid. A third grid is defined by a central square learning area, from which small sets of stairs descend to a series of distinctly shaped classrooms. This overall configuration encourages movement from one area to another, stimulating curiosity, interconnecting different subjects, and encouraging children to advance both in terms of academics and independence.

SPAETH RESIDENCE

East Hampton, New York, 1972
New construction

The design of this modest house is based on the concept of the traditional central mass with two side pavilions. The house contains three bedrooms, a dining room, and a second-floor living room for the display of art. A diagonal central corridor intersects adjoining rooms and extends through the access drive, creating a variety of spaces inside and out. The two adjacent pavilions contain a raised screen porch, a garage, and a storage area.

WEBBER SKI HOUSE

Stratton, Vermont, 1972
New construction

This four-bedroom house is set directly on a Stratton Mountain ski slope. Its multiple pitched roofs relate to the slopes of the surrounding hills and articulate the interior plan: a layered combination of half-level spaces. Bedrooms are on the lowest level, along with a ski entrance and a kitchen; the dining room occupies the next floor up; and a living room is on top. Bold geometric lines are painted throughout the interior, accenting the forms of the house.

AMERICAN FILM INSTITUTE HEADQUARTERS AND THEATER

Kennedy Center for the Performing Arts, Washington, D.C., 1973
Conversion

This design consists of two distinct parts set within a limited, windowless space: a public film theater and the institute's offices and archives. The small film hall (40 by 150 feet) is arranged in an existing narrow space formerly occupied by the Eisenhower Theater loading dock. A raised, raked, single-tier seating area with excellent sight lines throughout focuses on a large screen that accommodates all varieties of film formats. Twelve automobile hoods and twenty-four fenders are mounted on the side walls of the hall in an alternating pattern to diffuse sound. For the windowless L-shaped office area, an open plan is devised, with freestanding diagonally aligned partitions that differentiate work spaces. These walls also form a series of portals that determine the primary circulation path.

CLOISTERS CONDOMINIUMS

Cincinnati, Ohio, 1973
New construction
Clients: Towne Properties and Irwin Management Company

The architecture of the Cloisters is rooted in the residential hillside setting of Mt. Adams, where the development is unobtrusively set on a wooded escarpment with clear views of the Ohio River. The design refers to the sloping roofs of the neighboring low-rise housing, which pitch in all directions. The wood-framed development is composed of two basic elements: one set on a ridge, the other partially stepped down the hill. Each is two stories tall and contains rectangular-plan two-bedroom apartments with balconies. The lower-level units have their own gardens.

ROBERT G. OLMSTED THEATER, ADELPHI UNIVERSITY

Garden City, New York, 1974
New construction

This 300-seat facility greatly strengthens the university's performance curriculum and programs. Developed on a limited budget, the design shows how the use of commonplace materials can yield a distinctive result. The hall provides a variety of stage and seating configurations—frontal, surround, open, and thrust—making it a flexible teaching facility as well as an intimate venue for both traditional and experimental performances. A stepped terrace amphitheater on the north side of the theater serves as an outdoor studio space.

ARTPARK

Lewiston, New York, 1974
New construction
Client: New York State Department of Parks and Recreation

Built on landfill overlooking the Niagara River, ArtPark was the nation's first publicly funded state or national park dedicated exclusively to performing and visual arts. A summer-long program provides a number of artists with residence and work spaces, and gives the public access to artists and the creative process. This interaction occurs primarily on the park's architectural centerpiece, ArtEl, a prefabricated, 500-foot-long elevated artist work space and public promenade that links the auditorium, a new 300-seat outdoor amphitheater, and parking. The success of ArtPark, which was originally conceived as a one-year experiment, has made it a permanent component in the state's park system.

COLUMBUS OCCUPATIONAL HEALTH CENTER

Columbus, Indiana, 1974
New construction
Client: Cummins Engine
Company

This health center serves Cummins Engine with a design based on a configuration of open, semi-open, and closed spaces defined by two overlapping geometric grids. Closed, private activities are set around the building's perimeter in the outer grid, which is finished in black glass. Open, public activities are set within the internal grid, whose edges delineate separate public and staff circulation; these paths are outlined above by skylights. Brightly colored mechanical and structural systems accentuate the building's various layers. The surrounding landscape can be seen from throughout the center, and at night the building's transparent walls make the interior clearly visible from the outside.

"NEW LEARNING SPACES AND PLACES"

Walker Art Center, Minneapolis,
Minnesota, 1974
Exhibition design and installation
Sponsors: The Graham
Foundation, National Endowment
for the Arts, and National
Endowment for the Humanities

This exhibition addresses the educational opportunities available in an increasingly sophisticated and "aware" world and suggests the restructuring of educational institutions to accommodate the expanding sources of knowledge. The installation occupies two galleries diagonally connected by a "wall of facts" displaying traditional educational tools. Nine separate learning modules—high-tech information/ communication centers—are constructed out of a variety of generic building materials. Visitors operate these learning centers and extrapolate how their principles could be applied in education. The exhibition recommends more flexible and less costly buildings that incorporate evolving technology in an age of constantly changing information sources.

ORCHESTRA HALL

Minneapolis, Minnesota, 1974
New construction
Client: Minnesota Orchestral
Association
Associate Architect: Hammel
Green & Abrahamson, Inc.

This new hall was designed and constructed in only sixteen months. The development of Orchestra Hall involved three basic concepts: humane urban design, superior sound, and distinctive architecture based on dual vocabularies. The hall is set back from the street to create a new sunken plaza. Together they complement the city's expanding open-space network. Inside the auditorium, plaster cubes adorn the back stage wall and ceiling, assisting in the reflection and distribution of sound. The hall itself and the support spaces (lobby, administrative, and artistic) use separate architectural vocabularies, set on distinct overlapping axes. This order articulates the building's functions and spaces, which are expressed as individual volumes finished with different materials.

PRATT RESIDENCE

Bridgewater, Connecticut, 1974
Conversion and new construction

This conversion of a tobacco barn is based on the projection of diagonal volumes into the original orthogonal form. The two diagonal elements (one on each of the building's two floors) are rectangular volumes set counter to one another. Together, they introduce a secondary grid on each floor. This overlapping of grids creates a variety of angular living rooms on the ground floor and bedrooms on the second floor. Windows cover over half the surface of the additions, dramatically increasing the amount of daylight throughout the house.

REUSING RAILROAD STATIONS

1974
Publication
Client: Educational Facilities
Laboratories
Sponsor: National Endowment
for the Arts

The goal of this publication was to promote the preservation and reuse of railroad terminals across the country, and it was one of the first documents to offer a comprehensive survey of this unique American building type. It describes the impact of certain economic forces on reuse and reveals that preservation is predicated on tax assistance and increased access to government loans and grants. It also identifies various means of acquisition and funding, including municipal zoning incentives, which can make preservation financially desirable. This work, which concludes that a strong federal involvement is critical for station reuse, led to a national symposium, legislation, and subsequent funding of station preservation.

SCHOOL FOR THE CREATIVE AND PERFORMING ARTS

*Cincinnati Union Terminal,
Cincinnati, Ohio, 1975
Programming and planning
Client: Cincinnati Board of
Education*

The vacant terminal's large open spaces, existing offices, and off-street vehicle access allow for its conversion from a commercial facility into a school for creative and performing arts. The plan respects Fellheimer and Wagner's 1933 Art Deco design, both inside and out, and preserves the terminal's basic axial symmetry and historic spaces. In adding 54,000 square feet, the design introduces two new circulation patterns that link a series of rooms arranged in an open plan across two levels. The cost of the plan is comparable to that of new construction.

MASTER PLAN FOR RESTORATION, 1894 GRAND OPERA HOUSE AND HOTEL

*Galveston, Texas, 1975
Client: Galveston County Cultural
Arts Council, Inc.*

The restoration of this grand opera house and hotel was planned to reclaim an important piece of Galveston's lost architectural and cultural heritage and to provide the city with a new arts and civic center that complements adjacent redevelopment. The plan proposes a phased restoration program and budget to expedite the reopening of the theater and to promote subsequent improvements as funds are made available. These improvements include the conversion of the hotel into commercial and cultural space and the creation of an outdoor mall in front of the theater. The study helped secure public support and financing for the restoration of the opera house, which reopened in 1982.

FIREMEN'S TRAINING CENTER

*Ward's Island, New York, 1975
New construction
Clients: New York Urban
Development Corporation and
New York City Fire Department*

The design of the center's 365-foot-long administration and education building serves as a foil to the nine training buildings, which simulate urban prototypes. Finished in metal and glass, the administration building makes use of familiar materials in unfamiliar ways. Large galvanized highway culverts serve as entrance tunnels, cutting through a landscaped berm that faces the training area. A large red tank forms the main entrance; two others, protruding through the roof, hold offices. The semi-open interior plan contains freestanding classroom and office structures, each finished in different materials.

MASTER PLAN, MADISON CIVIC CENTER

*Madison, Wisconsin, 1975
Client: City of Madison*

By siting the civic center along Madison's most significant urban axis (which connects the state capitol with the University of Wisconsin campus), this plan reinforces State Street's commercial and cultural importance. The street's scale and texture are maintained by blending new, contextual structures with existing buildings. The program recommends the renovation of the 2100-seat Capitol Theater and the creation of a 400-seat thrust theater, a new home for the Madison Arts Center, and an extensive pedestrian network linking the civic center's multiple levels with adjacent streets. With the subsequent execution of this plan, the civic center served as an anchor for redevelopment in downtown Madison.

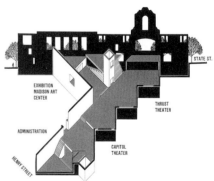

AGNES DeMILLE THEATER, NORTH CAROLINA SCHOOL OF THE ARTS

*Winston-Salem, North Carolina,
1975
Conversion
Associate Architect: Newman
VanEtten Winfree Associates*

When the North Carolina School of the Arts was established on the site of an existing high school, the tall ceilings of the 17,500- square-foot gymnasium made the building ideal for conversion into the campus's first theater. Combining features of both a traditional and an experimental hall, this semicircular theater is the home of drama, dance, and opera productions. A flexible orchestra pit allows for thrust expansion of the stage or for additional seating. A narrow walkway rings the hall along the second level and provides primary access to all seats. To take advantage of the breadth of the building, a second floor that accommodates three dance studios is inserted adjacent to the theater.

VON BERNUTH RESIDENCE

Dobbs Ferry, New York, 1975
New construction

This two-story house is intimately scaled and designed to accommodate an extensive collection of nineteenth-century antiques. Its composition is based on a separation of public areas from private spaces with an entrance at the center of the L-shaped plan. Two shingled gables, symmetrically placed on either side of the entry access, define the front. Various types of fenestration introduce substantial daylight to the interior and reinforce major elements of the plan.

246

BASKERVILLE HALL AND WINGATE GYMNASIUM, CITY COLLEGE OF NEW YORK

New York, New York, 1976
Renovation

The alterations for the renovation of Wingate Gymnasium are designed to increase the safety of its pool for small children and handicapped swimmers, while new construction introduces facilities for handball and fencing, physiological laboratories, and offices. Baskerville Hall's renovation provides new offices for counseling, evaluation, research, testing, and guidance, and a variety of classroom spaces.

COOPER-HEWITT MUSEUM / NATIONAL MUSEUM OF DESIGN

New York, New York, 1976
Conversion
Client: The Smithsonian Institution

The conversion of the Andrew Carnegie mansion was the foundation for the firm's extensive record of interpretative restorations. The landmark's extraordinary variety of period rooms and the fact that it is a freestanding structure in a garden setting provide a remarkable environment for the permanent exhibition of the Cooper-Hewitt's collection of decorative arts. The axial plan of the Georgian-style mansion is maintained and reinforced on the second floor, where a collection of small rooms is unified into one extended gallery. Additional improvements include new public circulation spaces and new lighting and environmental systems.

TERRY DINTENFASS GALLERY

New York, New York, 1976
Conversion

This economical conversion of a two-story recording studio into an art gallery provides a large yet intimate exhibition space, along with appropriate support facilities.

BROOKLYN CHILDREN'S MUSEUM

Brooklyn, New York, 1977
New construction

For the first time since it was founded in 1899, the museum now occupies flexible spaces specifically designed for its programs. Rather than creating a new building to replace the original house-museum, the design called for a submerged facility that allows Brower Park to expand over the museum's roof. The museum's design involves a continuous juxtaposition of forms, materials, and spatial experiences. The process of discovery begins as one enters through a kiosk (which formerly served the Queensboro Bridge), passing by grain silos and highway signs that evoke and define the museum's presence below. A 180-foot-long ramp breaks at each of the museum's four exhibition floors to provide access to a diverse, multilevel changing space.

FELD BALLETS/NY HEADQUARTERS AND STUDIOS

New York, New York, 1977
Conversion

The complete redesign of this 17,000-square-foot commercial loft space reflects the informal, colorful character of the ballet company. It also marked the initial phase of the conversion of this building into a dance center. (The address is now home to other dance companies, including the headquarters of the American Ballet Theater, also designed by HHPA.) An open office plan in the front portion of the space minimizes the separation of activities, facilitating interaction between administrators and performers, and allows for future growth. The floor's large structural bays delineate the orthogonal layout of the four studio spaces in the back of the building.

KLEINWORT BENSON McCOWAN, INC. OFFICES

New York, New York, 1977
Renovation

This redesign of the thirty-fifth floor of a lower Manhattan office building introduces a semi-open office plan configured around U-shaped circulation. The stepped corridors are aligned with offices, whose fenestration of punched windows and doorless frames suggests a row of small residential units. This configuration echoes the building's jagged exterior and creates a variety of office spaces, maximizing access to the view and creating movement patterns with changing focal points.

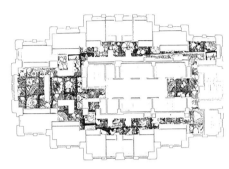

NEWARK SYMPHONY HALL

Newark, New Jersey, 1977
Feasibility and planning
Clients: Newark Economic Development Corporation, Mayor's Policy and Development Office, and Newark Community Center of the Arts
Sponsors: National Endowment for the Arts and The Schumann Foundation

This study outlines a plan for the rehabilitation and expanded reuse of Symphony Hall. It suggests a phased schedule of improvements for the hall, evaluates user demand and public interest in additional performance space, and reviews adjacent public and private development projects. The plan includes the commercial reuse of vacant spaces, the modernization of stage and mechanical equipment, overall building renovation and landscaping, and the acquisition and rehabilitation of small adjacent structures for recital, rehearsal, and theatrical activities. The development of a neighborhood center and an outdoor amphitheater is also recommended.

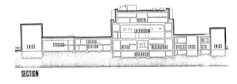

SCULPTURE HALL AND EAST WING, SAINT LOUIS ART MUSEUM

St. Louis, Missouri, 1977
Restoration and renovation

The extraordinary character of Cass Gilbert's 1904 Beaux-Arts design was revealed by this interpretive restoration. In stripping away years of insensitive alterations, the museum's original cross-axial plan was restored, the sequence of diverse exhibition spaces was repaired, and original details were reclaimed. Interior walls are refinished in a contemporary palette, and new environmental control and lighting systems, along with reglazed windows and skylights, improve the appearance and the operation of the museum. Connections between the museum and its park setting are improved by the restoration of original views and the creation of new exterior vistas.

"WARBURTON AVENUE: THE ARCHITECTURE OF A NEIGHBORHOOD"

Hudson River Museum, Yonkers, New York, 1977
Exhibition design and installation

This exhibition surveyed neighborhood change in Yonkers between the Hudson River and Warburton Avenue—the development and subsequent decline of nineteenth-century residences, twentieth-century industrial structures, and contemporary commercial buildings. Open-forum workshops provided local residents with the opportunity to shape neighborhood planning. The exhibition was organized around an armature of reconstructed building facades and a continuous photomural illustrating both sides of Warburton Avenue. Additional displays included archival photographs, drawings, and proposals for the avenue. The exhibition helped create a stronger link between the museum and the community.

ANNAPOLIS PERFORMING ARTS CENTER

Annapolis, Maryland, 1978
Analysis and statement of needs
and potential
Client: State of Maryland
Prepared with: American Council
for the Arts

This study, developed at a time when Annapolis was lacking in professional performance space, promotes the development of a flexible center to accommodate dance, theater, and concerts. The major spaces proposed are a 1,500-seat auditorium and a 300-seat theater; also recommended is a 5,000-square-foot gallery to add to the center's role as a major cultural facility. The preliminary plans suggest solutions for maximizing lobby views, minimizing the bulk of the stage houses, providing visitor access and parking, and reinforcing the architectural quality of the Annapolis Historic District.

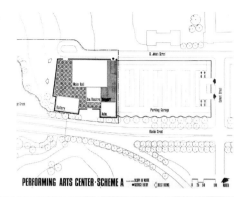

BOETTCHER CONCERT HALL

Denver Center for the Performing
Arts, Denver, Colorado, 1978
New construction
Clients: City and County of
Denver, Denver Center for the
Performing Arts, and Denver
Symphony Orchestra

The inspiration for this project, which was the first concert hall in America whose seating completely surrounds the stage, was the desire to re-create the intimacy and informality of outdoor summer performances. Part of a four-square-block master plan (prepared by Kevin Roche) for a performing arts center, the hall breaks with the belief that good sound can come only out of a "shoebox" design. A fragmented, circular configuration minimizes the distance between the seats and the stage and introduces sight lines that establish a strong sense of intimacy between the audience and the performers. In addition to giving the hall a layered, sculptured look, the asymmetrical, multibalcony plan increases the number of front-row seats.

THE EYE INSTITUTE, PENNSYLVANIA COLLEGE OF OPTOMETRY

New construction
Philadelphia, Pennsylvania, 1978

The design of the institute expresses concern for bringing light, space, color, and comfort into the educational environment. The low-rise, glass-enclosed, sawtooth forms of the exterior complement existing buildings. The primary enclosed spaces—offices and examining rooms—are set askew to the diagonal plan, creating a variety of irregularly shaped open areas that define the major circulation path. The jagged exterior walls maximize the number of offices with windows, and brightly painted ductwork, striped carpeting, and ribbed-tile walls enhance the naturally lit open plan.

AMERICAN CENTER FOR STUDENTS AND ARTISTS

Paris, France, 1979
Proposal for restoration and
future expansion
Associate Architect: J. P. Jouve,
Architecte

The goal of this three-phase plan is for the American Center to become the primary focus of American performing and visual arts in France. Improving the cultural and educational activities necessitates the rehabilitation of the center's exterior, its mechanical systems, and its auditorium; the reorganization and remodeling of existing interior space; and the underground construction of a flexible theater/hall/conference space, backstage support facilities, and classrooms. A landscape plan, which devises new entrances and permits special outdoor activities, strengthens the building's relationship to its residential setting in Montparnasse.

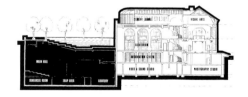

CENTRAL PARK VISITORS CENTER

New York, New York, 1979
Proposal
Client: City of New York,
Department of Parks and
Recreation

This proposal to renovate the boathouse and the Bethesda Terrace into an informal visitors' center was an early effort to reverse the deterioration of Central Park caused by years of minimal maintenance. The plan has two major goals: the creation of educational and recreational activity points along the east side of the lake, which would reduce congestion, increase use, and improve the appearance of the boathouse, the Bethesda Terrace, and the space in between; and the development of year-round uses for the boathouse and the terrace, with activities and spaces that would change with the seasons, including a center for learning about the park's landscape and wildlife. All of the improvements were designed in the spirit of Olmsted and Vaux's original plan.

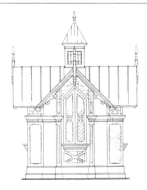

"DRAWINGS BY MICHELANGELO FROM THE BRITISH MUSEUM"

Pierpont Morgan Library, New York, New York, 1979
Exhibition design
Sponsors: Philip Morris Incorporated and National Endowment for the Arts

McKim, Mead & White's 1907 library was the site for the first major exhibition of Michelangelo drawings outside Europe. In preparation for one of the library's most significant exhibitions, three permanent improvements were made to the landmark's interior: the main exhibition hall and the second-floor music room were brightened and made warmer by replacing the dark-green damask wall panels with beige linen-covered panels; flexible exhibition stands with cast-iron legs and Plexiglas covers were introduced that permitted both the flat display of art objects and the two-sided vertical display of drawings; and new lighting was installed that improved viewing conditions and the overall appearance of the interior.

14TH STREET REVITALIZATION PLAN

New York, New York, 1979
Clients: 14th Street Task Force and 14th Street Local Development Corporation
Sponsors: New York State Council on the Arts and The J. M. Kaplan Fund

This plan, a response to the deterioration of a major commercial strip bordering several distinct communities, focuses improvements on the portion of 14th Street around Union Square—the core of the area's development. After reviewing historical trends and other street-revitalization projects in New York, the plan inventories existing conditions: land and transportation uses, streetscape features, lighting, and security. The design objectives include improved pedestrian movement and the redesign of the streetscape to reflect the area's diverse architectural character, as well as its current occupants and users. The report suggests improved street maintenance, better signage, the creation of mural paintings for blank walls and storefronts, and the restoration of the block's facades.

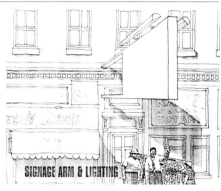

LANGWORTHY RESIDENCE

New York, New York, 1979
New construction

The original row house on this Greenwich Village street was accidentally blown up in 1970 by the Weathermen, the political-activist group. The new house knits the block back together while acknowledging that its history is quite different from that of the other houses in the row. A diagonal plan creates spatial and visual diversity inside and projects through the flat, continuous facades of the surrounding Greek Revival structures. At the same time, the house is integrated with adjacent structures by reproducing their stoops, rusticated bases, and cornices. The Langworthy house was the first new design in an historic district to be approved by the New York City Landmarks Preservation Commission.

MANHATTAN THEATER CLUB AND EASTSIDE PLAYHOUSE

New York, New York, 1979
Architectural survey and renovation design

Two adjacent theaters are integrated into one unified theatrical center in this plan. It evaluates the building conditions of the Manhattan Theater Club and the Eastside Playhouse (located directly behind the club) and develops a feasible internal link that enables the 299-seat theater of the playhouse to become the new center's main performance hall; the consolidation of the two sites eliminates redundant spaces. An enlarged common lobby is linked with the new ground-level connecting corridor that provides access throughout the site. The plan also recommends improvements in egress and fire safety, as well as the renovation of the exterior facades.

SOUTHWEST HANGAR STABILIZATION

Gateway National Recreation Area, Miller Field, Staten Island, New York, 1979
Client: U.S. Department of the Interior–National Park Service

Miller Field stands as one of the country's first airports. The Southwest Hangar, a historic two-story-tall double hangar, was designed by the American Bridge Company in 1920. This project involves the structural and surface stabilization of the hangar, along with new landscaping to protect its oceanfront location from erosion. These improvements are necessary for the airfield to be included within the Gateway National Recreation Area, a park system along New York City's waterfront.

SYMES TOWNHOUSE

New York, New York, 1979
Restoration

Designed in 1948 by Philip Johnson as a guest house for Mr. and Mrs. John D. Rockefeller III, this International Style single-family residence is a distinctive structure for midtown Manhattan. This restoration of the house's wood, brick, and plaster surfaces and the improvement of its mechanical systems (including the introduction of air-conditioning) preserves the house's period design. The novel central atrium plan—in which a pool separates the two-story living and entertaining section in front from the single-story rear bedroom—is also retained.

250

ARTHUR KILL GENERATING STATION

Staten Island, New York, 1980
Visual impact study
Client: Consolidated Edison
Company of New York, Inc.

Part of a comprehensive environmental-impact study of the plant's proposed fuel conversion from oil to coal, this report identifies a variety of visual effects resulting from the delivery of coal by railroad and barge, a new coal conveyance system, and several 100-foot-tall structures. The study recommends that new features be integrated into the existing industrial fabric, aided by a detailed landscape plan involving layers of berming and tree planting. A paint plan is also suggested to further minimize the impact of the tall structures within the landscape.

BEST PRODUCTS COMPANY, INC. HEADQUARTERS, PHASE I

Richmond, Virginia, 1980
New construction

The effectiveness of this corporate design relies on the strength of a two-story curved glass-block facade, and on the intersection of a corresponding curved interior circulation path with an otherwise orthogonal plan. The building is filled with historic imagery and allusions: a watercourse set in front of the diaper-patterned facade, large Art Moderne eagles astride the main entrance, and classical-style moldings. The glass-block facade filters daylight throughout the interior. A diverse, unexpected sequence of intersections and residual spaces provides open work areas in addition to traditional closed offices. Muted wall colors and a lively carpet based on a design by Jack Beal provide a backdrop for the company's extensive art collection.

BUNKER HILL: LOS ANGELES MUSEUM OF MODERN ART AND MUSEUM PLAZA

Los Angeles, California, 1980
Competition
Client: Maguire Partners

The Museum of Modern Art is a small but key element of a major downtown improvement plan that seeks to strengthen the area as the region's cultural and commercial hub. The museum and its plaza occupy the primary corner of the new four-block-long Grand Avenue. Museum Plaza is a terraced garden, shared by an adjacent luxury hotel, that holds an outdoor café and visual- and media-arts displays while serving as an access point to a new public-transit network. The building is a deeply notched glass cube six stories high that cantilevers over the plaza. Its exterior finish—transparent, translucent, and opaque glass—varies the quality of daylight throughout the museum's diverse gallery types, which range from one to three stories in height.

CHARLESTON VISITOR RECEPTION CENTER

Charleston, South Carolina, 1980
Programming and planning
Client: City of Charleston
Prepared with: Economic
Research Associates, David H.
Katzive, and Alan M. Voorhees &
Associates

The impetus for this project was the desire for an information clearinghouse and visitor center for the city that would serve as a catalyst for neighborhood improvement. Located on the edge of historic Charleston, the center encourages visitors to take a shuttle bus downtown, thus reducing traffic and parking congestion. The proposed site for the center is the William Aiken House and Associated Railroad Structures, a historic property that enjoys high visibility and adequate access to both the town and the region.

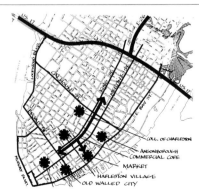

FINE ARTS MUSEUM OF LONG ISLAND

Hempstead, New York, 1980
Programming and planning

This plan demonstrates that a 1950s suburban department store can be redeveloped into an effective museum. The two-level rectangular shell is converted into a pattern of gallery and public spaces that radiate from a circular core. The four-phase program includes space for exhibition, research, art education, and conferences, as well as a 240-seat theater. Other improvements include the creation of a winter garden and an outdoor sculpture court.

FLOYD BENNETT FIELD

Gateway National Recreation Area, Brooklyn, New York, 1980
Proposal for improvements
Client: U.S. Department of the Interior–National Park Service
Prepared with: M. Paul Friedberg

This interdisciplinary study seeks to improve access to the water surrounding three sides of a national recreation area and to increase the presence of water throughout the site. Three land-use plans are considered. The first dedicates nearly half the site to a series of man-made canals and islands that establish special wildlife and vegetation zones. An elevated walkway minimizes human interference in the environment. A second proposal converts the runways into canals for recreational purposes by creating berms along their edges. The third plan encompasses a portion of the bay by adding floating piers, boardwalks, and jetties to develop marine-related activities. Each scheme reuses airfield structures and introduces new buildings for community use.

MADISON CIVIC CENTER

Madison, Wisconsin, 1980
Renovation, conversion, and new construction
Client: City of Madison

One of the first urban-revitalization projects to weave a major arts facility into an underutilized commercial corridor, this civic center simultaneously preserved and improved the character of State Street. New infill construction connects the exteriors of two different structures: Rapp and Rapp's Moorish-inspired Capitol Theater (designed in 1928) and the somewhat Georgian Montgomery Ward department store (built in 1941). Inside, an extensive pedestrian network integrates the center's four levels with the two diverging streets that border the site.

MASTER PLAN, THE MUSEUM OF MODERN TIMES

Birmingham, Alabama, 1980
Reuse of Sloss Furnace buildings and grounds
Client: City of Birmingham

A plan to preserve two great blast furnaces as the centerpiece of a new thirty-seven-acre educational and cultural complex symbolizes the past, present, and future of Birmingham. Conceived as a regional attraction, the museum highlights the interdisciplinary nature of human development; it includes exhibitions such as historical "Corridors of Time" and pavilions for American and Afro-American cultures, finance, law, biology, and medicine. Also part of the restoration plan is a re-creation of the great blast furnaces in operation, a demonstration of the industrial strength that built Birmingham.

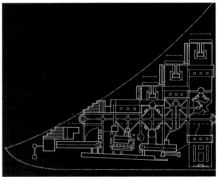

NATIONAL VIDEO CENTER RECORDING STUDIOS

New York, New York, 1980
Renovation

The reuse of the former West Side Airlines Terminal Building is part of the redevelopment of West 42nd Street. The design of the center's two main floors displays their primary functions. An irregularly shaped lobby is largely defined by the curvilinear side of one of two twenty-one-foot-tall studios. On the third level, sound-sensitive editing and production rooms are grouped in the center of the floor, buffered from outside noise. These rooms are aligned on a 45-degree angle to the building's grid, creating a variety of corridors and residual spaces. Functions that are less sound-sensitive—offices, library, stairs, and mechanical operations—are set along the perimeter of the building.

MUSIC AND DANCE BUILDING, ST. PAUL'S SCHOOL

Concord, New Hampshire, 1980
New construction

The goal of this design is to relate the performing arts facility to its sloped wooded setting and to the rustic, Gothic, and contemporary architectural forms of the campus. Instead of calling for a single large structure, the design splits the program into three volumes. Two are set perpendicular to one another; the third is attached to a separate building, Memorial Hall. This reduces the facility's mass and puts it in scale with other small structures on the campus. Pitched roofs help to integrate the buildings into the steeply graded site. The interior combines modern and traditional materials and forms: exposed mechanical systems, gabled roofs, wood paneling, and clerestories. An underground level, containing lockers and rehearsal rooms, links the music and dance spaces.

SPIRIT SQUARE ARTS CENTER

Charlotte, North Carolina, 1980
Restoration, conversion, and new construction
Associate Architect: Ogburn and Steever Architects

This center, Charlotte's first major downtown reuse project, reflects a major commitment to the local arts community and a significant contribution to the stabilization and improvement of the central city. The plan for a visual- and theatrical-arts center integrates four disparate structures—a Baptist church, a Sunday school, a multistory administrative building, and a factory. The most important aspect of the program is the restoration and conversion of the 1908 neo-Byzantine church into a 675-seat thrust-stage performance hall. An adjacent new building—People Place—provides a lobby for the hall, linking it with the rest of the complex. The brick and glass design of the addition complements the finish and texture of the former church, and the original baptismal font is employed as a box office.

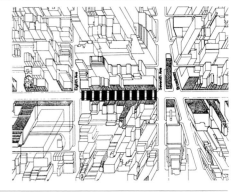

10 THEATERS ON 42ND STREET

1980
Publication
Client: City at 42nd Street, Inc.

This study analyzes the feasibility of renovating ten theaters along West 42nd Street. Two types of reuse are proposed: commercial, in which unequipped renovated theater space is rented out; and institutional, in which a nonprofit organization maintains a fully equipped theater for various productions. Preliminary construction budgets were prepared for each theater and both types of uses to assist public and private sectors in evaluating the study's recommendations.

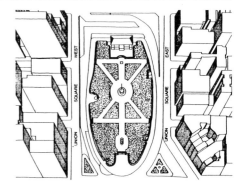

UNION SQUARE ZONING STUDY

New York, New York, 1980
Clients: 14th Street Local Development Corporation and Union Square Local Development Corporation
Sponsor: The J. M. Kaplan Fund

Concerned with preserving and reinforcing the existing sense of neighborhood while encouraging future development, this study recommends the creation of a special zoning district. This would upzone the area while encouraging builders to respond to the neighborhood's specific land uses and architectural character. Development would be linked to builder-supported public improvements. Three specific goals of the study are the partial reclamation of the area's historic residential character, the improvement of the 14th Street retail corridor, and the focusing of development and improvement around the transit hub at the southeast corner of the square.

AMERICAN BALLET THEATER OFFICES AND STUDIOS

New York, New York, 1981
Renovation

This design for one of the world's foremost dance companies divides two levels into distinct plans to create a variety of unexpected spaces resulting from the building's trapezoidal configuration. In the front portion two geometric grids overlap. One aligns with the building's long, parallel sides and is juxtaposed to the smaller grid, which is aligned with the building's frontage along Broadway. This creates a sequence of unusually shaped office, lounge, and lobby spaces connected by an open stair. In contrast, the back two-thirds of the headquarters is orthogonally organized to accommodate the rectangular dimensions necessary for the large dance studios.

"ARTISTS & ARCHITECTS COLLABORATION: BRYANT PARK RESTAURANTS"

New York, New York, 1981
Centennial project of The Architectural League
Prepared with: Jack Beal and Sondra Freckelton

On the occasion of the Architectural League's centennial, this theoretical project revived the tradition of collaboration between artists and architects to generate more spirited design. A precursor to the firm's actual restoration plan for Bryant Park, this proposal was for a new restaurant pavilion along Sixth Avenue to help reclaim the park for safe public use. Responding to the symmetry of both the park and the New York Public Library's west elevation, the design is a balanced composition of classical and modern fragments that creates a formal entrance to the park. In the center of the building, Jack Beal's rococo-style pillars support a pergola that shelters the Lowell Fountain and anchors the overall design. The celebration of nature is the theme of the wall murals Sondra Freckelton designed for the project.

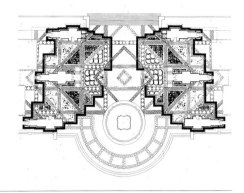

253

COOPER-HEWITT MUSEUM / NATIONAL MUSEUM OF DESIGN

New York, New York, 1981
Proposal for expansion
Client: The Smithsonian Institution

The popular success of HHPA's conversion of the Carnegie mansion into the National Museum of Design spawned plans for additional space. This proposal recommends restoration and expansion of an adjacent town house (presently used by the museum) and the construction of a new wing connecting the mansion and the town house. It establishes the permanent collection in the mansion and relocates changing exhibition space to the town house. Major departments and the library are expanded. A 299-seat auditorium and classrooms are spread across a single floor in the town house and new wing, serving the museum's master's program in decorative arts. A new central entrance and improved circulation paths reduce visitor congestion by providing direct access to the museum's various functions.

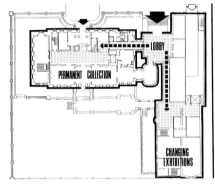

DESIGN GUIDE FOR MUSIC AND DRAMA CENTERS

1981
Publication
Client: U.S. Department of the Army

The Army commissioned these guidelines in response to the need for high-quality performance centers in its bases throughout the U.S., Western Europe, and the Pacific. The study defines basic planning and design criteria and describes the nature and order of the decision-making process. It points out the interdependence of all the various design factors, and promotes successful design by stressing early understanding of site conditions, program needs, and key logistical requirements. The study also discusses various stage and seating configurations and their effect on acoustics, sight lines, access, and overall ambience. The guide includes program descriptions organized by theater type and size, and provides a full range of built examples.

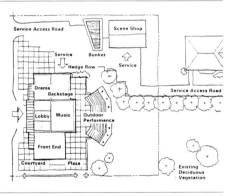

UNDERGROUND PEDESTRIAN NETWORK, GRAND CENTRAL TERMINAL

New York, New York, 1981
Report
Client: New York Metropolitan Transportation Authority
Sponsor: National Endowment for the Arts

The first comprehensive study of Grand Central's extensive underground pedestrian network (connecting local and regional transit systems and twenty-one adjacent buildings) led to the terminal's first master plan. To strengthen the terminal as a major transportation hub and retail center, the study calls for adding first-class retail operations, establishing a spatial hierarchy of these operations that responds to the use and character of the network, adopting graphic standards, creating a north concourse as a new circulation and retail area, building new links north of the terminal, and transforming the main concourse into a special-activities center during non-rush hours. The report emphasizes that tax incentives are essential to induce private investment.

MASTER PLAN, LOS ANGELES COUNTY MUSEUM OF ART

Los Angeles, California, 1981

This master plan is for the functional and aesthetic unification of new development within the existing 5½-acre museum site. The phased plan, which doubles the square footage of the museum, remains one of the most comprehensive plans devised for an American cultural institution. The goals identified by the plan are creation of a central arrival and orientation space; integration of new buildings into the complex; improvement of circulation between existing buildings, the central arrival space, and all additions; identification of future on-site development parcels; reorganization and expansion of exhibition and support space; and strengthening of the design relationship between the complex and Wilshire Boulevard.

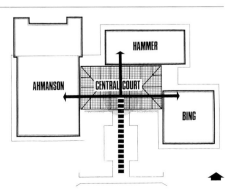

MAGIC MOUNTAIN

Los Angeles, California, 1981
Physical improvement plan
Client: Six Flags, Inc.
Prepared with: Lawrence Halprin
and Harvey Perloff

The emphasis of this study for the Magic Mountain theme park is on the intense initial experiences that are required to promote a more vigorous definition of place and to encourage return visits. It proposes the creation of eight distinct theme areas set in a large, circular plan that would diversify the site and utilize its natural resources. The focus of each area is defined by a distinctive use of water, landscape, lighting, and architectural elements.

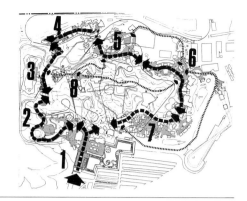

CURRIER GALLERY OF ART

Manchester, New Hampshire,
1982
New construction

This addition, which expands gallery space for touring exhibitions and introduces handicapped access throughout the complex, complements the design and plan of Edward L. Tilton's 1929 Beaux-Arts museum. Flanking a sloping courtyard are two new pavilions, whose brick columns and cornices, large punched openings, and central Palladian entrance are both contemporary and in keeping with the neoclassical character of the original building. The addition also reinforces the existing interior central court as the focus of circulation. The new large galleries are topped with sloping translucent roofs and open steel trusses that diffuse daylight throughout the galleries.

DEVELOPMENT MASTER PLAN, FORT WORTH CULTURAL DISTRICT

Fort Worth, Texas, 1982
Client: City of Fort Worth

The existing concentration of art, commercial, and medical institutions just beyond downtown Fort Worth provides a context for the creation of a cultural district to stimulate further private and public development. The goal of redeveloping the extensive network of parking lots and other underutilized parcels is to promote economic growth, expand cultural programs, and allow for the creation of an overall architectural image. Major aspects of the plan are the alignment of new buildings along two existing axes, the development of new residential uses around the district's edges, the consolidation of surface parking lots, and the creation of an open-space network to link the district and an adjacent park.

"GRAND CENTRAL TERMINAL: CITY WITHIN THE CITY"

New-York Historical Society, New York, New York, 1982
Exhibition design and installation
Client: Municipal Art Society of New York
Sponsors: Philip Morris Incorporated, National Endowment for the Arts, and National Endowment for the Humanities

This exhibition featured films, walk-through models, original architectural renderings, and archival photographs to increase public appreciation of the historic and architectural qualities that justify the terminal's landmark status. It traced the simultaneous evolution of the city and the terminal and described the contributions of the Vanderbilt family—the force behind railroads in New York and the creation of Grand Central. Design and construction processes were documented in photographs and sketches. Also illustrated was Grand Central's influence on adjacent growth. The show concluded with a prognosis for the terminal's future, identifying threats to the landmark and recommending the creation of a public and private partnership to ensure the terminal's survival.

VIADUCT AND UPPER ROADWAY, GRAND CENTRAL TERMINAL

New York, New York, 1982
Study
Clients: New York City Urban Development Corporation and The Trump Organization

This study evaluates the deteriorating condition of the viaduct and upper roadway—perhaps the most ingenious component of Reed and Stem's 1903 Beaux-Arts design for negotiating traffic on Park Avenue around the two-block terminal. It reviews the terminal's street-level features that are not presently being renovated and identifies needed improvements: the rehabilitation of the viaduct's eroding stone balustrade, the removal of the New York Convention and Visitors Bureau from under one of the support arches, the replacement of the sidewalk, and the restoration of the terminal's entrances.

HUDSON HIGHLANDS

*Hudson River Valley, New York,
1982
Investigation of land usage and
guidelines for development
Client: The Rockefeller
Foundation*

This project maps a wide range of planning strategies conceived by foundations and private interests for the Hudson River Valley to help develop a coordinated vision of the region. The study, which identifies major issues and proposes development guidelines for the area between Riverdale and Albany, reflects a balance between preservation and development concerns.

HULT CENTER FOR THE PERFORMING ARTS

*Eugene, Oregon, 1982
New construction
Client: City of Eugene
Associate Architect:
Lutes/Sanetel Architects*

This multipurpose complex is the centerpiece of a $50 million two-block master plan. The two-theater plan accommodates diverse community interests, and the center's dual architectural vocabulary accentuates the disparate spaces and uses. The large, open, floral-carpeted lobby is composed of a series of gabled volumes supported by wood columns, all enclosed by a patterned-glass curtain wall. This translucent, multigabled lobby is a primary feature, both inside and out. The two theaters are wrapped in cast concrete. The larger, two-tiered hall is horseshoe-shaped to allow for greater intimacy between audience and performers. The smaller, asymmetrical proscenium theater is a flexible space, encouraging experimental productions by local performing arts groups.

THE JOYCE THEATER

*New York, New York, 1982
Conversion
Client: Elgin Theater Foundation,
Inc.*

The conversion of this former movie house into a fully equipped dance theater was in direct response to the recent growth of small and mid-size New York dance companies. The interior was entirely gutted, and a steeply raked single level was inserted, offering excellent sight lines throughout the theater. The stage is built to the site's full width, with support facilities located below. Two slightly elevated rows are introduced along both side walls of the hall, enclosing the new seating plan and permitting patrons to view both the stage and each other, increasing the theater's sense of intimacy. A new illuminated marquee on the exterior announces attractions, and former storefronts are filled in with a patterned masonry wall that extends the facade's original design.

OLD EXECUTIVE OFFICE BUILDING

*Washington, D.C., 1982
Existing conditions report and
recommendations for
improvement
Client: The White House*

Generations of interior alterations have disfigured much of the original plan of this building, designed by Alfred B. Mullett and built in 1888 as an office annex to the White House. The study seeks to heighten interest in this national landmark, one of the country's best examples of Second Empire architecture, and raise support for its restoration. Proposed improvements include reopening corridors and foyers, restoring access to windows and balconies that terminate the ends of each vista, stripping paint from skylights above domed stairwells, and relocating unsightly mechanical and support equipment. These changes would reclaim much of the building's original character, reintroducing exterior views, improving lighting, and providing better visitor orientation.

MASTER PLAN FOR PERFORMANCE USE, ST. ANN AND THE HOLY TRINITY

*Brooklyn, New York, 1982
Clients: Diocesan Church of St.
Ann and the Holy Trinity and
Episcopal Diocese of Long
Island*

The accommodation of both performing arts and religious services was the primary concern in restoring this 1847 Gothic Revival–style church. The improvements are designed to refine audience focus, expand sight lines, and improve acoustics, lighting, and access. The spatial conflict arising from use for religious and performance activities is resolved by replacing the pews with a flexible seating system that uses hydraulically controlled platforms. This allows for variations in audience focus and permits myriad uses. Two new chapels near the entrance reestablish a sense of religious intimacy. On the exterior, the projection of four laser lights at night visually re-creates the church's original spire.

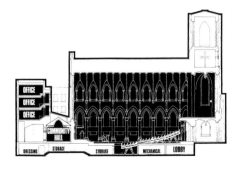

SOUTHERN THEATER

Columbus, Ohio, 1982
Restoration and improvement
plan
Client: Columbus Association for
the Performing Arts

The revitalization of the city's oldest existing theater, designed by Yost and Packard in 1896, would provide an anchor at the southern end of a new downtown retail district. Proposed improvements to the landmark theater (modeled after the Chicago Auditorium and Carnegie Hall) include the restoration of the auditorium and lobby and the modernization of lighting, stage equipment, and performance and public-support spaces. New mechanical systems allow for the comfortable accommodation of drama, dance, music, and film within the 1,000-seat theater.

TOLEDO MUSEUM OF ART

Toledo, Ohio, 1982
Renovation and new entrance

The haphazard expansion of Edward B. Green's 1912 Greek Revival design and the subsequent growth of visitor parking have altered public access routes and the original classical plan of the museum. Along with reorganizing the building's central two-story core, this scheme creates a formal axis between the new entrance (serving visitors parking at the rear of the museum) and the original front door, highlighted by the reconfiguration of the central stair into a new grand stair hall. Equally important are the installation of new environmental systems and the conversion of a former auditorium into a gallery, which increases temporary-exhibition space by 7,000 square feet.

TWYLA THARP DANCE COMPANY STUDIO

Brooklyn, New York, 1982
Study

To convert the abandoned Strand Theater, a three-story movie palace originally designed by Thomas Lamb in 1919 and subsequently altered, this study recommends a three-phase renovation plan. The third floor is divided into two parts, one for use by Twyla Tharp and the other for a TV production studio. Building access is redesigned to provide each organization with its own separate ground-floor lobby fronting different streets. The renovated ground floor accommodates additional rental space, and the second floor is converted into rental studios.

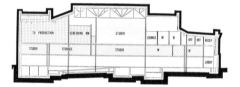

UNIVERSA CORPORATION OFFICES AND STUDIOS

New York, New York, 1982
Renovation

The upper floors of the West Side Airlines Terminal Building are expanded with the addition of a new two-story volume. The design, which features an interior atrium, is defined on one side by a long, curving wall that intersects the structure's basic rectangular form and is surmounted by two levels of clerestory windows. Adjacent work stations are grouped in a radial configuration focusing on the daylit portion of the atrium. Executive offices on the mezzanine level are arranged like small houses, with arched entrances and French doors, around a central square—the reception area. The largest offices further the residential imagery by opening onto balconies that overlook the atrium.

WILLAMETTE CIVIC CENTER ARCADE AND PARKING STRUCTURE

Eugene, Oregon, 1982
New construction
Client: City of Eugene
Associate Architect:
Lutes/Sanetel Associates

This garage was the first component of HHPA's master plan for downtown Eugene. Together with the Hult Center for the Performing Arts, it occupies a full block. The garage provides parking for the center, an adjacent hotel and block-long retail mall, and surrounding offices. The five-story, precast-concrete freestanding structure is surrounded by a four-foot landscaped berm that softens its appearance along the street. A pedestrian bridge connects the garage to the Hult Center, reinforcing a significant visual axis that extends through that facility's lobby to the new convention center and hotel. The walls of the bridge are finished with glazed, colored-glass panels designed by Ed Carpenter.

WILLARD HOTEL

Washington, D.C., 1982
Design for restoration and new construction
Clients: Stuart S. Golding Co. and The Oliver T. Carr Company
Agency: Pennsylvania Avenue Development Corporation
Associate Architect: Vlastimil Koubek

The rehabilitation and expansion of the Willard Hotel is the centerpiece of an ongoing plan to revitalize Pennsylvania Avenue. This scheme restores much of Henry J. Hardenbergh's original 1901 design, while a 250,000-square-foot addition introduces the retail and office space needed to finance the project. The design of the addition is a composite of masses, each finished with elements found in the original Willard. Since the addition is set back in consecutive steps away from Pennsylvania Avenue, primary attention remains focused on the original hotel. A three-story classical stone portal links the new and the old, holding the property line and helping define the street wall.

257

AMERICAN FILM INSTITUTE

Los Angeles, California, 1983
Campus plan and renovation

This renovation of three existing structures of Immaculate Heart College transforms the staid interiors of the former girl's school into a home for an international film center whose goals are to help sustain the country's film heritage as well as advance the art of film and television. The three-story central building is redesigned to provide production and editing space, classrooms, the 350-seat Ted Ashley Theater, and administrative offices. A second, smaller building is converted into the Louis B. Mayer Library. The Sony Corporation financed the conversion of a third building into a state-of-the-art video center.

AVONDALE TOWN CENTER

Cincinnati, Ohio, 1983
New construction
Client: Oscar Robertson Company

The Town Center is the cornerstone of a redevelopment plan proposed to revive this downtown neighborhood. Occupying a key intersection, the curved, arcaded structure introduces twenty new retailers to an area that is lacking in basic shopping facilities.

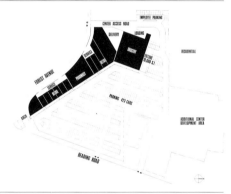

CIRCLE REPERTORY COMPANY

New York, New York, 1983
Feasibility study for relocation

The proposed 350-seat two-tier proscenium theater provides the company with a flexible space as part of the renovation of the Old Federal Archives Building. Doubling the capacity of the group's current house, this theater offers the configuration the company requires to produce a wide range of new plays. There are unobstructed views throughout and sufficient support space for performance- and audience-related activities. Administrative space is available on the upper floors of the building.

MILLS MANSION AND HOYT HOUSE

Mills-Nouvrie State Park, Staatsburg, New York, 1983
Proposal for reuse
Client: MPM Partnership Group
Agency: New York State Office of Parks, Recreation and Historic Preservation

In this proposal, a reuse strategy is outlined for the preservation of two large nineteenth-century country estates that occupy 400 acres along the Hudson River south of Rhinecliff. This plan, an outgrowth of the state's need to maintain the properties, has three basic objectives: to enhance the site's historic qualities; to maximize public access and use; and to minimize costs while increasing local and regional economic benefits. Two basic programs are proposed: an executive conference center and a resort hotel with conference facilities. The design guidelines suggest that the mass, scale, proportions, rhythm, textures, and colors of existing buildings be synthesized to help create new contextual designs that would be neither indifferent to nor imitative of the historic structures.

PINGRY SCHOOL

Bernards Township, New Jersey, 1983
New construction

This high school's diverse activities are reflected in the building's appearance and layout. The front masonry facade, finished in smooth and red split-face concrete block with minimal fenestration, encloses large activity areas that require little daylight (gyms, an auditorium, a pool, and a library). The back half of the school is defined by white metal panels and a linear, shaded fenestration that give light and air to the classrooms. A central space links these two distinct sides and is marked on the front by a three-story terra-cotta portico, the school's main entrance. The abstract form of the entry recalls the school's previous clocktower; it also responds to a nearby church that lies on axis with the school.

RUSSELL LIBRARY

Middletown, Connecticut, 1983
Renovation and new construction
Client: City of Middletown

To house the future library needs of this community, an addition was designed that triples the existing space and connects a 1950s bank with the original 150-year-old landmark. The 26,000-square-foot addition links the two structures in a composition made of old and new elements. A new central entrance provides direct access to all parts of the expanded complex. Other improvements include the renovation of the landmark, the introduction of a media facility and a community center, the expansion of all departments, and the creation of an outdoor courtyard.

SCHOLASTIC, INC. OFFICES

New York, New York, 1983
Conversion and new construction

To consolidate Scholastic's operations (formerly spread out on eight unconnected floors in an office building) into the top three floors of the former Wanamaker warehouse, this conversion provides a loosely structured corporate environment characterized by a variety of spaces, colors, and light sources. An open skylit central staircase links the three floors. Each level has its own palette and its own plan, organized along a distinct diagonal corridor that cuts across a grid of cubicles and offices to create a diversity of intersections. The plan emphasizes perimeter light throughout by leaving the exterior edges of each floor open with circulation or low-partitioned spaces. Overall unity among the floors is achieved through a common treatment of circulation paths, cubicles, and offices.

30 THEATERS

1983
Publication
Clients: The Shubert Organization, Nederlander Productions, and Jujamcyn Theaters

This study, a response to upzoning of the Theater District and a moratorium on theater demolition, promotes a balanced policy of development and preservation. A historic and architectural catalogue of thirty theaters, the study identifies the qualities of configuration and enclosure geometry that characterize the Broadway theater. It concludes that a judicious preservation approach would allow for alterations that are necessary to ensure the theaters' commercial viability.

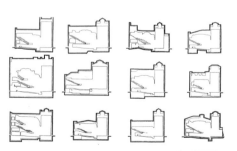

WCCO-TV COMMUNICATION CENTER AND HEADQUARTERS

Minneapolis, Minnesota, 1983
New construction
Client: Midwest Communications, Inc.

The design of this building is a challenge to the traditionally high-tech character of most television stations. It takes into account its prominent location in downtown Minneapolis and makes use of familiar materials in unusual ways. Large windows offer pedestrians views of the activities inside the station. The exterior's Minnesota stone veneer (cut in a unique manner to reveal its special variegated character) visually anchors the station at the corner of the block and encloses office and administration space. The two stone facades then step back along both public sides of the lot, giving way to the large copper-clad studio (an original application of copper shingles) that extends the building's street wall.

BAYLES APARTMENT

New York, New York, 1984
Renovation

Two identical apartments located on the seventh and eighth floors of a Fifth Avenue apartment house were consolidated by inserting a new stair that fits within the building's structure while complementing existing design and circulation. To minimize alterations, the stair is located so that it eliminates only services that were already provided elsewhere. The cherry-wood stair becomes the central unifying feature of this Greenwich Village duplex, with the lower, entrance floor transformed into the public living space and the upper level redesigned for personal use.

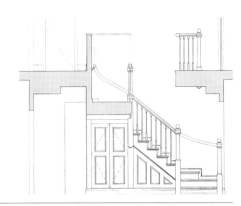

259

GALBREATH PAVILION AT THE OHIO THEATRE

Columbus, Ohio, 1984
New construction and renovation
Client: Columbus Association for the Performing Arts
Associate Architect: Phillip Markwood Architects Inc.

Thomas W. Lamb's grand 1928 movie palace (a National Historic Landmark) was facing demolition before plans were devised for its preservation and expansion into a cultural center. To allow for a wide variety of performances, the renovation calls for doubling the size of the stage, adding rehearsal rooms, and increasing lobby and office space. A new pavilion, an extension to the theater, is designed in the spirit of the original structure, but its abstraction of historic details announces its contemporary nature. A two-story curvilinear glass wall encloses the pavilion's colonnaded side. Sketched against this brightly colored space is a two-story double-staircase lobby, which recaptures the opulence of past theatergoing and highlights the fascination of watching people gather.

GRAND CENTRAL POST OFFICE TOWER

New York, New York, 1984
Competition
Client: Harry Macklowe Real Estate Company, Inc.
Associate Architect: Schuman Lichtenstein Claman Efron Architects

The concept for this proposed thirty-six-story skyscraper is based on Warren and Wetmore's design scheme for Grand Central Terminal. The new building's footprint, along with its traditional fenestration and masonry finishes, is sympathetic to the six-story limestone post office (which would be restored), while its details, profiles, and overall composition convey a contemporary character. The project supplements Grand Central Terminal's pedestrian network, which links more than twenty buildings to local and regional transit, and includes a two-story lobby with a coffered ceiling and chandeliers, inspired by designs of Warren and Wetmore. A sky lobby on the seventh floor serves as a transitional space between the old and new volumes.

HARRISON-ERICKSON APARTMENT

Brooklyn, New York, 1984
Renovation

This apartment was renovated as if it were still two completely different residences, reflecting a separation of entertainment and personal spaces that involves a shift from formality to near fantasy. The formal area, called the Main House, includes a large living room, a dining room, and a study finished with parquet floors and Oriental rugs. A graffiti-patterned carpet extends from the double parlor doors that separate the two sides of the apartment, leading through to the Backyard, which contains bedrooms and a second study area. The master bedroom includes numerous garden allusions: trelliswork, a floral-design carpet, and a sky-blue ceiling. The closets have garage-style doors, the bathroom resembles a porch entrance, and the mirrors are treated like windows.

NEW AMSTERDAM THEATER ROOF GARDEN, NATIONAL THEATER CENTER

New York, New York, 1984
Renovation plan
Client: 42nd Street Development Corporation

The New Amsterdam Theater, designed in 1903 by Herts and Tallant, is the most architecturally significant of the 42nd Street theaters. The existing rooftop theater was a supper club with tiers and tables. This renovation reconfigured the space into a thrust-stage "auditorium" with rows of seats. The new stage configuration increases the sense of intimacy between performer and audience. Additional changes include the overall renovation of public spaces and the improvement of mechanical systems, egress, and service access. This project is part of the civic effort to revitalize 42nd Street.

NEW-YORK HISTORICAL SOCIETY

New York, New York, 1984
Project
Clients: Walker, Malloy &
Company, Inc. and New-York
Historical Society

A plan to erect a twenty-three-story residential tower atop this 1908 landmark (designed by York and Sawyer and expanded by Walker and Gillette in 1938) would finance the improvement and maintenance of a unique New York City institution. With new construction providing the structural support necessary for new floors in the original building, the tower's development both expands the society's archival and support spaces and improves environmental systems throughout. Several levels of stack spaces are incorporated into the new building. The tower's exterior consists of a series of setbacks that echo the formal tripartite composition of the historical society; its profile complements existing residential structures and adds to the street wall of Central Park West.

CULTURAL CENTER, UNIVERSITY OF CALIFORNIA AT DAVIS

Davis, California, 1984
Programming and planning

The purpose of this development program is to alleviate the shortage of performing and fine arts facilities on campus. It identifies functional, visual, acoustical, and capacity requirements for all new spaces. The advantages and disadvantages of square, "shoebox," fan, thrust-stage, and hybrid configurations are reviewed in a prototype study of theater and concert hall designs. Four development sites are then examined, with attention given to physical context, vehicular and pedestrian access, and the cultural center's overall relationship to the campus and the city of Davis. The study concludes with a visual reference section outlining various design ideas, suggesting a general configuration for the center.

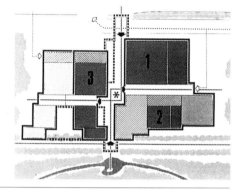

CHURCH OF ST. LUKE IN THE FIELDS

New York, New York, 1985
Reconstruction and new
construction

The reconstruction of this landmark Greenwich Village church, which was extensively damaged by fire, preserves its original spirit. The most significant change of this interpretive restoration is the relocation of the altar from the apse to the center of the building. An arch colonnade announces the new altar, naturally illuminated from above by an oculus. The translucency of handmade glass windows in mullioned frames is graduated, with the darkest at the center of the church to dramatize the altar's importance. The former high altar is transformed into a chapel, lit by diffused daylight, and the baptismal font is moved to the entrance. The original vaulted ceiling is restored, and the original featureless western wall of the exterior is replaced by a bay containing the new chapel.

RETAIL DEVELOPMENT PLAN, GRAND CENTRAL TERMINAL

New York, New York, 1985
Client: New York Metropolitan
Transportation Authority

Grand Central is a multilevel complex of passageways and public spaces, including waiting rooms, balconies, and concourses. The design guidelines outlined in this study integrate existing and proposed retail activities with the terminal's improvement programs; the overall recommendation is for the codification of a unified terminal plan that accommodates public and private interests. To avoid the visual conflict that retail operations often impose on the station, the distinct character of each occupied space is taken into consideration. The terminal's preservation and restoration is stressed above all, and the most significant proposed improvement is the reuse of the main waiting room, which no longer serves its intended purpose.

IBM INFOMART SHOWROOM

Dallas, Texas, 1985
New construction

IBM's first diversified showroom is divided into an offset plan composed of various asymmetrical learning and sales areas. The entry-corner reception area provides access to a presentation theater and to product-display and sales-information areas. Separate from these spaces are rooms for the demonstration of product use in a number of different office contexts. Profiled maple walls, oak and ash detailing, colorful fabrics, patterned carpets, and epoxy paint enrich the showroom, which is designed to accommodate 500 to 1,000 visitors a day.

RIZZOLI INTERNATIONAL 57TH STREET BOOKSTORE

New York, New York, 1985
Conversion

The renovation of this old piano showroom and office re-creates the ambience of Rizzoli's original flagship store on Fifth Avenue. The spatial reorganization of the entire three-story shop introduces a progression of sales areas, which are finished with cherry-veneer bookcases. A restored groin-vault plaster ceiling surmounts the entrance; this element is echoed throughout the second floor by simple abstractions of the form. Like the atmosphere of the original store, the effect here is of a traditional European library, but the design also fulfills the requirements of contemporary commerce.

261

SKYLER RESIDENCE

Bridgehampton, New York, 1985
New construction

This house is a composite of vertical masses with distinct profiles on all four sides and varying geometric fenestration throughout. The most open areas front the beach and ocean, reflecting the home's orientation. The interior is staggered to create four distinct half-levels, a plan that separates the living and eating areas on an elevated first floor and provides the master bedroom with greater privacy and more commanding views on the second floor. The interior is expressed on the exterior by an asymmetrical composition of small, medium, and large windows. This fenestration creates a variety of natural light conditions and controlled views from room to room.

WEST WING, VIRGINIA MUSEUM OF FINE ARTS

Richmond, Virginia, 1985
New construction

The museum's acquisition of two major art collections prompted construction of the new West Wing. While distinct in design, the addition blends with the facade and plan of the original building. The patterns of Peebles and Fergusen's 1936 facade inspired the design of smooth and ribbed blocks of limestone that runs throughout the exterior of the addition. The museum's original axial plan is referred to in the new wing's central hall. However, the addition's plan then diverges with a series of small-scale traditional spaces and large-scale galleries that complement the character of each collection.

MASTER SITE PLAN AND THEATER, WARNER PERFORMING ARTS SQUARE

Woodland Hills, California, 1985
Client: The Cultural Foundation

This project is for a square that serves as the focal point of performing arts in the new 164-acre Arts Park L.A. as well as the center of theatrical activity in the region. The diagonal, multilevel plan integrates three distinct theaters: a 1,200-seat concert hall, a 650-seat multipurpose theater, and a 150-seat experimental theater. The well-defined hipped roofs and stage houses of the three halls are set in geometric contrast to one another. Extensive terracing exploits views of the surrounding park and provides a variety of vantage points to watch visitors gather.

WELLESLEY COLLEGE SPORTS CENTER

Wellesley, Massachusetts, 1985
New construction and renovation

Introducing this 140,000-square-foot recreational center (including a short-course Olympic pool and a multipurpose field house) into Olmsted's picturesque campus required extensive and sensitive site review. To minimize the sports center's mass and to integrate it with existing facilities, the design calls for two new low-rise structures that linked to an existing recreational building. The courtyard configuration of the new center complements the existing network of well-defined courtyards and paths. The facades, composed of brick and steel panels, accented with a ceramic stringcourse, and topped with gabled roofs, are a response to the collegiate Gothic context.

CENTER FOR ARTS AND CULTURE, YERBA BUENA GARDENS

San Francisco, California, 1985
Study
Client: Olympia & York Cos.
(USA)
Agency: City Redevelopment
Agency of San Francisco

This is a program for cultural facilities to be located at the center of San Francisco's major multiuse urban development, the Yerba Buena Gardens. The proposal includes two buildings, housing a 600-seat multipurpose theater; a video and film center, including a 100-seat screening room; a flexible art gallery with museum-quality exhibition space; a public "forum" space with collapsible seating; and administrative and support areas. The buildings are aligned along an interior central garden and also define a small garden along the street, attracting visitors to the site.

BEST PRODUCTS COMPANY, INC. HEADQUARTERS, PHASE II

Richmond, Virginia, 1986
New construction
Associate Architect: Marcellus
Wright Cox & Smith

The second phase of this corporate headquarters enlarges HHPA's initial design (completed in 1980) from two to three stories. A portion of the new exterior—a two-story, curved, and diaper-patterned glass-block wall—clearly refers to the earlier portion. However, the wall abruptly gives way to an entrance portico that leads into a three-story central atrium, asymmetrically splitting the addition into two distinct, open floor plans. The atrium cuts across the building, revealing a wide view of the woods behind the complex. Finished in a variety of materials (marble, drywall, and Tectum panels), the atrium is topped with a gabled skylight and bisected by two bridges that connect its two sides.

CATHEDRAL OF ST. JOHN THE DIVINE SHOPS AT EQUITABLE CENTER

New York, New York, 1986
New construction

To give this uptown landmark church greater public visibility, the Equitable Life Assurance Company has provided the cathedral with midtown retail spaces in the company's new corporate headquarters. Two small stores are set on either side of the main Avenue of the Americas entrance of the Equitable Center. The stores strike an architectural balance between retail and ecclesiastical styles, expressed in an abstract Gothic manner with delicate oak arches and ribbing. The design creates a sophisticated place of commerce consistent with the cathedral's ambitious civic goals.

CORAL GABLES BILTMORE HOTEL

Coral Gables, Florida, 1986
Competition
Client: Worsham Brothers
Company, Inc.

The winner of a national competition, this proposal restores the building to its position as the glamorous focal point of the city and one of south Florida's premier hotels. Before its slow demise, the Biltmore was the original symbol of Coral Gables' cultural aspirations, and this redevelopment creates a new and vital cultural, social, and recreational center. The purpose of the restoration is to eliminate inconsistent alterations and to reinstate original spaces, finishes, and landscapes. New construction serves to re-create structures that had been razed and to provide hotel rooms that meet today's standards of quality.

HARDY HOLZMAN PFEIFFER ASSOCIATES OFFICES

902 Broadway, New York, New
York, 1986
Renovation

Many of the firm's design principles are brought together in this two-floor office. Each of the building's two oblique sides generates a distinct plan grid. Where the grids collide, a sequence of residual spaces is created, defining a portion of the circulation. In addition to providing informal meeting and waiting areas, these spaces offer visual and spatial contrast to the more formal work spaces, offices, and conference rooms. Circulation is delineated by a variegated carpeted path that directs visitors from the lobby through a variety of open and enclosed spaces. Paths terminate with large windows that serve as clear focal points. Muted colors define each of the office's basic elements: partitioned spaces, offices, the central core area, mechanical systems, and structure.

MEMORIAL HALL, HARVARD UNIVERSITY

Cambridge, Massachusetts, 1986
Proposal for reuse

Taking into consideration the overall campus, the specific site, and the conditions of Memorial Hall, this study develops seven basic design solutions to demonstrate how the Great Hall could be restored and reused. The study assesses the architectural impact of each approach on this landmark, modeled after Westminster Hall in London, and suggests two specific reuse schemes, both involving administrative and educational activities. One proposal inserts new floor levels into the Great Hall with an open terrace plan; the second scheme expands the building below grade, retaining the hall in its present configuration for ceremonial uses.

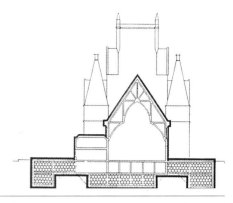

263

ROBERT O. ANDERSON BUILDING AND TIMES MIRROR CENTRAL COURT, LOS ANGELES COUNTY MUSEUM OF ART

Los Angeles, California, 1986
New construction

This addition integrates 115,000 square feet of gallery, support, and office space into a three-building plaza complex, redefining the museum's exterior presence on Wilshire Boulevard. The Anderson Building was shaped by three basic decisions: to maintain a portion of the original central plaza as a common entrance to the complex; to create a multistory atrium entrance that draws visitors into the plaza; and to begin with a first phase of construction that allows for future expansions. A network of pedestrian bridges has been designed to cross over the central court, connecting the various buildings. Inside Anderson, three levels of open, flexible galleries are distinguished by varied spaces, materials, and lighting. Office spaces are centralized on the ground floor.

MART 125

New York, New York, 1986
New construction
Clients: Harlem Urban Development Corporation and New York City Economic Development Corporation

Mart 125, a new urban retail mall, offers space at low rent to dozens of street vendors who had been obscuring local merchants' retail operations with their outdoor stands along the sidewalks of 125th Street. The two-story masonry-and-steel structure provides a variety of retail stalls in a large, open, skylit space. Vendors are offered free instruction in the retail business to help them manage their operations and, ultimately, to encourage commercial growth in Harlem.

NEW WORLD CENTER FOR THE PERFORMING ARTS

Miami, Florida, 1986
Programming and planning
Clients: City of Miami, Dade County, and Miami Dade Community College
Prepared with: Deloitte & Touche

This improvement plan outlines the creation of a professional performing arts center to encourage major new development. The study recommends a three-phase program: the improvement of an existing movie palace; the development of a 500- to 600-seat dance/drama theater and a 2,600-seat Grand Theater for opera, ballet, and major musical productions; and the construction of a new 2,200-seat symphony hall. The recommended sites, located near existing commercial and educational activities, are highly visible, with access to all modes of transit, substantial infrastructure, and support services already in place. Developers would be offered benefits in return for construction of the performance facilities in accordance with design guidelines.

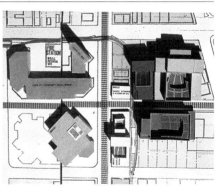

SOUTH FERRY PLAZA

New York, New York, 1986
Competition
Client: Related Properties
Associate Architect: Hooker/Siskind & Associates

The design of this proposed sixty-three-story glass-and-masonry tower is a response to a variety of urban design opportunities at a prime development site on the tip of lower Manhattan. The building's inland facade is a nearly flat masonry wall intended to effectively terminate Whitehall Street while preserving the harbor view through a fifteen-story-high pedestrian opening cut through the tower's lower level. The sculpted, bow-shaped elements of the facade, which is set back from the bay, make reference to the harbor and to the contours of the lower Manhattan skyline. The project includes a new transportation plaza (on and below grade), which integrates access to buses, subways, ferries, cars, and taxis while ensuring public use of the waterfront.

ALBUQUERQUE PERFORMING ARTS CENTER

Albuquerque, New Mexico, 1987
Programming and planning
Client: City of Albuquerque
Prepared with: Hoshour &
Pearson, Architects

264

The purpose of this study is to outline a program for a new performing arts center and to promote its development. After reviewing the requirements of music, theater, and dance groups that may use the facility, the study concludes that three theaters are needed: a 1,600- to 2,000-seat traditional hall, a 450-seat playhouse, and a 150-seat experimental theater with a flexible stage. Several organizational schemes are examined, and the recommended plan is one configured around single-loaded public and support spaces.

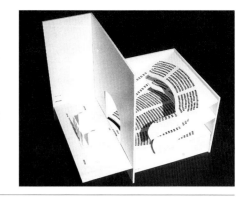

ALICE BUSCH OPERA THEATER

Cooperstown, New York, 1987
New construction
Client: Glimmerglass Opera
Company

As a response to the rural site of this seasonal opera house in upstate New York, the design uses barnlike forms, accented by extended eaves and roof monitors. Sliding barn doors offer the audience views of the surrounding landscape before performances and during intermission. The interior of the hall is an abstraction of a small Italian opera house. Its intimate acoustics and scale (all seats are within seventy feet of the stage) help make the theater a major proving ground for young musicians. A patterned-wood ceiling, inspired by domestic quilts, complements the hall's sprightly interior.

BAM MAJESTIC THEATRE

Brooklyn, New York, 1987
Reconstruction
Client: Brooklyn Academy of
Music
With: Peter Brook and Chloe
Obolensky

This reconstruction of the Majestic revived the theater for new uses without the expense of an architectural restoration. At the suggestion of director Peter Brook, the project was designed to incorporate the transformations of time: crumbling, water-stained, frost-damaged plaster and brick establish the primary character of the theater. The original orchestra level is eliminated, and the first balcony descends forward onto the foot of the new raised stage, now projected twenty-one feet toward the audience.

BAYLES HOUSE

Tannersville, New York, 1987
New construction

The exterior of this three-story house projects a predominantly rustic New England profile, with a gable roof, an attached single-story shed, and an Italianate tower topping a hipped roof. The uncoursed facade of local stone is divided by modern fenestration. Offering controlled views of the rustic landscape, the windows are framed by stone load-bearing lintels. Inside, activities are arranged within an open plan that features a number of vernacular elements, including wide pine floorboards, fir posts and beams, loggias, and a balcony.

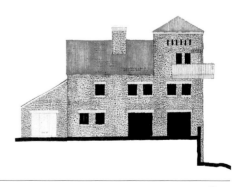

BROADWAY THEATERS: REFINING LANDMARK DESIGNATION AND REGULATION PROCESSES

1987
Report
Clients: The Shubert
Organization, Nederlander
Productions, Jujamcyn Theaters,
and New York City Landmarks
Preservation Commission

This study develops architectural review criteria to assist the New York City Landmarks Preservation Commission in its preservation of Broadway theaters. It critically focuses on the architectural elements that make these theaters unique and identifies specific architectural characteristics and relationships that justify landmark status (i.e., spatial geometry, the configuration of stage and seating). It further distinguishes between the scenic and the historic elements of these buildings, advocating the adoption of regulations that will not hinder their current use.

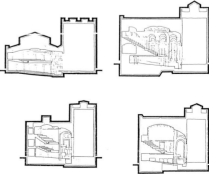

THE CAROLINA THEATER

Durham, North Carolina, 1987
Project
Clients: City of Durham, Durham Arts Council, and Carolina Cinema Corporation of Durham

The Carolina was designed in the late 1920s as a segregated movie house, with multiple entrances and separate seating. The renovation and expansion transform it into a multipurpose center for drama, dance, music, and film that accommodates 1,200 people. The redesign enlarges the orchestra pit, the proscenium, and backstage areas. Seating in the balcony is significantly improved, with better sight lines. On the exterior, the original Beaux-Arts facade is restored. Symmetrical side wings, added in phases, double the size of the facility: the first phase is the addition of three new cinemas; the second is the creation of a new lobby and additional support spaces.

GURWIN EDUCATIONAL RESOURCE CENTER, LONG ISLAND JEWISH MEDICAL CENTER

New Hyde Park, New York, 1987
Project

A new auditorium, office spaces, and library—which expand the hospital's public research, lecture, and conference facilities—are integrated around a skylit lobby. On the exterior, these uses are separated into distinct volumes, wrapped in two types of stone, copper shingles, and glass. Future improvements adjacent to the medical center include a new public entrance and elevator core (which permits separate circulation for staff and visitors) and additional expansion of the main building. A new public galleria links these spaces and the Gurwin Center with the main building.

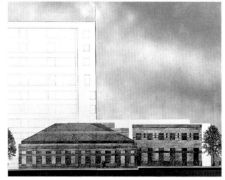

MADISON HOUSE

New York, New York, 1987
Project
Client: Madison 65th Associates

The initial twenty-two-story design for this Madison Avenue site, in one of the city's most fashionable residential and commercial quarters, is a composition of irregular massing whose patterned brickwork and multiple setbacks generated a highly articulated facade. Masonry colonnades line the edge of each setback, which is accented by copper finials. A Minnesota stone base contains two levels of retail. Objections to the demolition of two on-site brownstones led to a subsequent redesign.

MASTER PLAN, MIDDLEBURY COLLEGE

Middlebury, Vermont, 1987

This master plan, the seventh prepared by the college in this century, maintains and enhances the essential features of the Middlebury campus: the organization of buildings around greens; the predominance of freestanding masonry and wood architecture; the use of a variety of styles; and the distinct articulation of buildings' fronts and backs, which are linked to pedestrian and vehicular networks. The first phase of development involves the consolidation of fine arts facilities in a new 100,000-square-foot building and the conversion and expansion of McCullough Gymnasium and Brown Pool into a student activities center. Several building renovations make up the master plan's second phase.

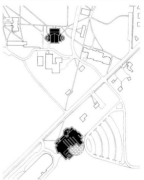

PARK PLAZA HOTEL

Toronto, Ontario, 1987
Competition
Client: The Bristol Group

The redesign of this block-long complex serves to visually and functionally unify the original 1920s building and a 1950s addition, and to restore the hotel's five-star status. The mass of the original, south tower is modestly altered to more closely reflect the symmetry of H. G. Holman's 1920s design. The modern, north tower, built in 1956 on the opposite end of the block, is entirely refinished to incorporate stepped massing, establishing a relationship between the towers. A new stone retail colonnade and a serpentine three-story glass pavilion set behind the colonnade provide a new lobby, along with a reception area, a ballroom, and commercial spaces.

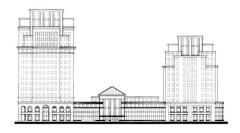

RAINBOW ROOM AND ROCKEFELLER CENTER CLUB

New York, New York, 1987
Restoration and renovation
Client: Rockefeller Center
Management Corporation

The top two floors of Rockefeller Center's tallest building were completely gutted (except for the Rainbow Room) to strip away layers of arbitrary alterations, and a variety of distinct new spaces and circulation areas was created. Geometric patterns inspired by the architectural vocabulary of Rockefeller Center are executed in mahogany, milled aluminum, polished bronze, etched and cast glass. Clear access to previously ignored views shapes much of the reconfiguration of corridors and rooms. The sixty-fifth floor is now a sequence of unique spaces, culminating in the restored Rainbow Room. The sixty-fourth floor is a series of distinctly designed private suites, featuring period furniture from Radio City Music Hall as well as new pieces that pay homage to Donald Deskey, the hall's designer.

RIVERBANK WEST

New York, New York, 1987
New construction
Client: Harry Macklowe Real
Estate Company, Inc.
Associate Architect: Schuman
Lichtenstein Claman Efron
Architects

This project announces the redevelopment of West 42nd Street at the Hudson River. Its base, containing retail stores and a health club, maintains the street walls along both West 42nd Street and Eleventh Avenue. The tower above is set back symmetrically, rising forty-five stories. The building's two-colored brick facade is reminiscent of the patterning of 1930s high-rise buildings along 42nd Street, while its massing and the bold horizontal concrete lines in the four-story brick mechanical penthouse recall those of the McGraw-Hill Building. A half-acre entrance garden along West 43rd Street is formally appointed with a sculptural fountain and a vine-clad redwood pergola.

SANTA ANA MUSEUM DISTRICT

Orange County, California, 1987
Architectural, economic, and
implementation guidelines
Client: Santa Ana Community
Redevelopment Agency

The purpose of this special development district is to spur cultural and commercial growth, expand the city's economic base, and provide a formal entry into Santa Ana. A mix of cultural and private activity reinforces their mutual development, reducing the replication of some infrastructure (i.e., parking and public space) while making for a more lively, integrated environment. The plan encourages the city to assemble sites, streamline the review process, offer financial benefits for buildings that provide space for cultural activities, and set aside land for the construction of three new museums. Proposed design guidelines encourage the creation of a gateway park, an arts plaza, a formal promenade, and a retail arcade, and call for both diversity and continuity in development.

ALASKA CENTER FOR THE PERFORMING ARTS

Anchorage, Alaska, 1988
New construction
Client: Municipality of Anchorage
Associate Architect: Livingston
Slone, Inc.

This complex is the centerpiece of the city's $165 million development program for the 1980s. Its design springs from the distinct character of its three theaters and its open, multilevel lobbies. The impact of the stage houses is diminished by setting them perpendicular to surrounding streets, behind the sloping roofs of the lobbies and auditoriums. This configuration creates a collage of rectangular, triangular, and curvilinear forms, giving each side of the building a different appearance. A fragmented portico imparts a sense of "front" to the center's three main sides. In the interior, each hall has its own character, but a common thread of regional art and design runs through all.

MASTER PLAN, BASS MUSEUM OF ART / MUSEUM SQUARE

Miami Beach, Florida, 1988
Client: City of Miami Beach

The expansion of this 15,500-square-foot museum is linked to a transformed Museum Square—a nine-acre, mixed-use site with direct access to the ocean—to create a new public focal point. Additional space for temporary and permanent exhibitions, as well as educational and revenue-producing activities, augments the museum's current program and enlarges its former quarters in Russell Pancoast's 1940 library. More than 68,000 square feet of new space is wrapped around the T-shaped museum, converting the plan into a rectangle and framing the main Art Deco facade. Two new outdoor courtyards and a new central corridor reinforce the site's primary axis, connecting the original main door to a new drop-off entrance on the museum's west side.

CHARLES W. BOWERS MUSEUM

Santa Ana, California, 1988
Project
Client: City of Santa Ana

In response to Orange County's rapid growth and broadening cultural interests, the area's leading decorative-arts museum plans an expansion to increase the flexibility of its exhibition space, relieve administrative congestion, and consolidate and improve its fractured architectural image. The study recommends a linear expansion that organizes space along a single axis and extends the front courtyard, introducing a new central entrance. The two-phase plan preserves the original Bowers Museum building (built in 1936), replaces a 1960s addition, and adds a third, adjacent structure. The contemporary design of the new buildings makes reference to the museum's Spanish Mission architecture.

COMMUNITY THEATER OF MORRISTOWN

Morristown, New Jersey, 1988
Project
Client: U.S. Land Resources

The creation of a Broadway-type theater not far from Manhattan provides an experimental theater company an affordable means to produce Broadway-bound musicals. In this renovation, a former 1,200-seat movie house is significantly altered and expanded. The lobby is nearly tripled in area to enhance the ambience and to strengthen the visitors' sense of arrival. The character of the hall itself is improved by reducing its size, adding side boxes, and expanding the balcony; the rakes of the orchestra and balcony are increased to create better sight lines. The stage and backstage areas are enlarged and the stage house rebuilt to accommodate new rigging.

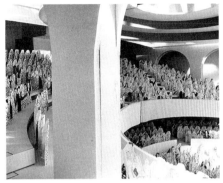

"GLORIOUS PAST– FABULOUS FUTURE"

Municipal Art Society, New York, New York, 1988
Exhibition design and installation
Clients: 42nd Street Development Project, New York State Urban Development Corporation, and New York City Economic Development Corporation
Prepared with: Robert A.M. Stern Architects

Home to more theaters than any other street in the world, 42nd Street has been the intense focus of redevelopment plans that seek to regain its once celebrated past. This month-long exhibition was the initial collaboration of the architects and public agencies involved in the project. It offered a vision of redevelopment in which the lost historic and aesthetic qualities of the block between Seventh and Eighth Avenues were revived.

LIBERTY AND VICTORY THEATERS

New York, New York, 1988
Study for nonprofit reuse
Client: New York State Urban Development Corporation

As part of the billion-dollar 42nd Street Development Project, this study provides guidelines for the U.D.C. in its negotiations with developers of improvements in two theaters. The Liberty and Victory theaters are two of Broadway's oldest standing theaters, designed at the turn of the century by Herts and Tallant and J. B. McElfatrick, respectively. Plans to extend the theaters into the lower floors of proposed adjacent development would remedy the problem of insufficient lobby, support, rehearsal, and administrative spaces without significantly altering existing interior or exterior conditions of either theater.

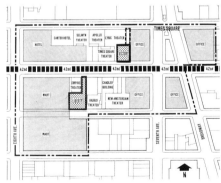

LILLIAN VERNON CORPORATION DISTRIBUTION CENTER

Virginia Beach, Virginia, 1988
New construction

The introduction of architecture into a building type that is normally treated only as a functional structure reflects the client's concern for employees. This commitment can be seen in the landscaped areas that adjoin the building, a common entrance and cafeteria for all employees, a skylit atrium where internal circulation converges, and a lively, diverse color scheme, in which walls, railings, and light and heavy machinery in the distribution facility are distinguished by vivid hues. The multifaceted glass of the office component provides a distinctive facade for this otherwise rectangular building, and its grid of red mullions increases the scale of the structure, suggesting that it contains more than its two floors.

MADISON HOUSE II

New York, New York, 1988
Project
Client: David Frankel Realty

The site for this apartment house is reduced to a single parcel (a two-story "taxpayer") by utilizing the air rights of two adjacent brownstones. After extensive review by the New York City Landmarks Preservation Commission, unanimous approval was given for construction of the project, the first new apartment house to be built in the Upper East Side Historic District. The fifteen-story building appears to be an integration of three smaller structures. The lower portion of the building responds to the five-story town houses along Madison Avenue, using setbacks to articulate the two-story retail base and the fifth-story cornice line.

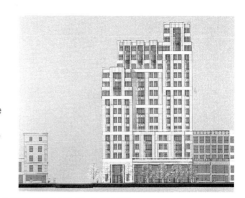

MASTER PLAN, MARKET SQUARE MIXED-USE DEVELOPMENT

Manchester, New Hampshire, 1988
Client: Market Square Associates
Associate Architect: Lavallee/ Brensinger Professional Associates

Planned as a private project to revitalize downtown Manchester, this master plan centers a half million square feet of commercial, residential, and civic development around a new pedestrian space, redefining the area's image and delineating a variety of access points and controlled views. Design guidelines recommend the use of brick and limestone facades, tripartite massing with well-articulated fenestration, and the creation of street walls and enclosed spaces. Rooftop areas, accented with pergolas and gardens, are developed to offer open views of the city. A portion of a secondary road (Market Street) terminates in the square and is converted into a landscaped pedestrian mall.

McCOWAN ASSOCIATES OFFICE

New York, New York, 1988
Conversion

By converting a town house into their corporate offices, this investment-management company retained the building's residential character. Each floor is designed for specific use: the basement is divided to house the technical staff, the computer system, and all records; the second floor has been extended over a first-floor wing to accommodate the partners' offices. The stepped alignment of the offices along the corridor, along with the punched windows and doors, suggests individual facades within a streetscape. Many of the original interior conditions—the staircase, the mantel, the trim—have been restored.

NORMAN ROCKWELL MUSEUM

Stockbridge, Massachusetts, 1988
Competition

The acquisition of the Linwood Estate by the museum offered the opportunity to relocate the nation's primary collection of Rockwell works from a small eighteenth-century house (where only a fraction of them could be displayed) to a new, larger exhibition hall. The new museum retains the intimacy of the original, as well as its separation of the galleries from the main circulation. A multi-terraced landscape plan takes advantage of the site's grade change, which is also used to subtly alter the appearance of each gallery, reflected in a shifting fenestration pattern.

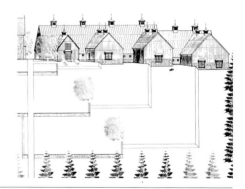

PALACE WEST / ORPHEUM THEATER

Phoenix, Arizona, 1988
Programming and planning
Client: City of Phoenix
Associate Architect: Architecture One, Ltd.

The central improvement of this plan is the restoration of the 1,700-seat, Spanish Revival–style Orpheum Theater (designed by Lescher & Mahoney in 1927) and the modernization of its acoustical, mechanical, and electrical systems. New office, retail, and production space is configured within the existing structure, and a 10,000-square-foot addition expands lobby areas, support space, and the stage, allowing for a greater diversity of productions. With the preservation of this rare theater type for film, theater, dance, music, and civic and community activities, the Orpheum is playing a critical part in the area's redevelopment.

PARAMOUNT THEATER AT THE COMMONWEALTH CENTER

Boston, Massachusetts, 1988
Project
Client: F. D. Rich Company of Boston

The revitalization of one of the city's most significant historic theaters, designed in 1932 by Arthur H. Bowditch, is a key component of Boston's new downtown Cultural District. The interior reconfiguration of this Art Deco theater creates two new halls. The original proscenium stage becomes part of a mid-size dance theater, which also occupies the orchestra level and the front portion of the balcony. Halfway up the balcony, a stage is raised above the steep rake of seats, and the balance of this level is converted into a multiuse theater. The Art Deco lobby is restored and new public elevators are introduced to improve access throughout the building. On the exterior, the restoration of the landmark marquee and sign marks the revival of this important district.

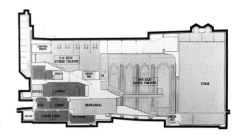

THE PLAZA HOTEL

New York, New York, 1988
Competition
Client: The Trump Organization

The restoration of the original detailing and overall look of the exterior of Henry J. Hardenbergh's 1907 French Renaissance–inspired landmark involves improvements to the cast-iron canopies, window awnings, marblework, period lighting fixtures, and roof decoration. The hotel's relationship to the adjacent plaza is strengthened with new landscaping, pavements, and street lighting. The conversion of the underutilized top floors into luxury suites and the replacement of mechanical rooms and work sheds with a new penthouse level take advantage of the hotel's prominent views while restoring the building's original, clean roofline.

SEELBINDER RESIDENCE

New York, New York, 1988
Renovation

This addition to a mid-nineteenth-century town house is an interpretive design that re-creates the feeling of the original. All mechanical equipment has been replaced and a fifth story, with a new master bedroom, has been added. The bedroom features a double-height ceiling and French doors opening onto front and rear terraces that provide views of the east midtown neighborhood. The new floor introduces a sense of Victorian grace to an otherwise nondescript building.

JAMES H. DONOVAN HALL, STATE UNIVERSITY OF NEW YORK

Institute of Technology, Utica/ Rome, New York, 1988
New construction
Client: State University Construction Fund

The institute's extensive scientific and technological curricula are consolidated in this one specialized facility, which houses classrooms, laboratories, lecture halls, and office space to serve the divisions of Electrical, Mechanical, and Industrial Engineering Technology; Arts and Sciences; Business Management; and Nursing. The design meets the state's exterior skin-to-floor ratio requirements, but the plan serves to diminish the appearance of the building's 300-foot-long dimensions. It maximizes the number of labs and offices with windows and minimizes the length of the four main corridors. Skylit atriums appear where the corridors intersect, and each is distinctly designed to orient students, faculty, and visitors.

MASTER PLAN, VILLAGE AT SQUAW VALLEY

Olympia Valley, California, 1988
Client: Squaw Valley USA

The focus of this plan is a village of urban density that actively complements the existing ski resort. It is anchored to the east and west by two existing facilities, and in between are "places" linked by retail and residential corridors. Phased development is directed along a primary view corridor—a pedestrian way—that connects the eastern anchor to a new village center. Limited construction is planned along a secondary development axis, which runs between the center and the western anchor.

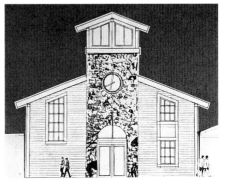

TSAI PERFORMANCE SPACE, BOSTON UNIVERSITY

Boston, Massachusetts, 1989
Conversion

The conversion of this lecture hall, located in a major campus building designed by Cram and Ferguson in 1940, into a performance space required significant improvements to the stage, the seating, and the acoustics. The proscenium has been acoustically reconstructed, and a flexible orchestra pit has been added, which extends the stage by ten feet when raised. Curved rows of seating focus on the stage, improving sight lines and creating a strong sense of contact between performers and audience. Four acoustical arches frame the hall, and bold forms embellish the balcony fascias. Once accessible only from the lobby, the balcony is now connected to the main orchestra level by new stairs inside the hall.

BRIDGEMARKET

New York, New York, 1989
Project
Client: Bridgemarket Associates

The creation of this new food market involves the renovation and public reuse of the sixty-foot-high landmark terra-cotta vaults underneath the Manhattan approach of the Queensboro Bridge. The conversion of the space, originally built as a market in 1908 and most recently used for city parking and storage, preserves the architectural integrity of the vaults, designed by Rafael Guastavino. A single level is excavated and a mezzanine added, resulting in a three-level center that maximizes the dramatic vistas. Terra-cotta pilasters, granite-trimmed terra-cotta arches, and walls of glass-and-steel windows are restored. The design creates an open, multilevel daylit volume of space ideal for a market and associated retail activities.

INTERNATIONAL CULTURAL AND TRADE CENTER/FEDERAL OFFICE BUILDING COMPLEX

Federal Triangle, Washington, D.C., 1989
Competition
Client: Prentiss Properties, Ltd.
Agency: Pennsylvania Avenue Development Corporation

The competition required the organization of a 3.1 million-square-foot, mixed-use program on an odd-shaped, eleven-acre lot that is surrounded by neoclassical architecture. To avoid a monolithic solution, this proposal divides the program into several formal geometric masses. The main axis, diagonally aligned to Pennsylvania Avenue, is defined by a succession of rotundas that draw pedestrians into the project's centerpiece—a 150-foot-wide Geosphere. This atrium links a variety of government and international trade activities and is designed to be one of Washington's grand halls.

JACOB RIIS PARK

Gateway National Recreation Area, Brooklyn–Queens, New York, 1989
Redevelopment plan
Clients: U.S. Department of the Interior–National Park Service, P. Wallenberg Development Company, and Halper Associates Management Company

This rehabilitation plan for the 300-acre park—a designated historic district on the National Register of Historic Places—recommends the restoration of the landmark bathhouse, the mile-long boardwalk, and the concession stands. It also simplifies and increases access to the park, creates additional picnic and rest areas, improves athletic facilities, relocates an existing twenty-six-acre golf course, develops a new fifteen-acre aquatic theme park, and develops new stage areas for performing arts and children's activities. The study also examines the feasibility of a year-round restaurant, an additional swimming pool, and a 15,000-seat amphitheater.

AHMANSON THEATER, LOS ANGELES MUSIC CENTER

Los Angeles, California, 1989
Competition

This study investigates the theater's strengths and deficiencies and outlines a series of improvements to enable the effective production of a wide variety of theater and musical events. An efficient, phased improvement program is outlined, based on prioritized needs. Suggestions include the installation of a suspended fabric ceiling, and the alteration of side walls and seating to enrich the acoustics and character of the hall, transforming it into a more intimate space. New ornamentation is proposed to improve the room's acoustics, scale, and warmth. The study also recommends redesigning the outside plaza and the interior lobbies to sharpen their focus and to refine the theater's image and highlight the sense of arrival.

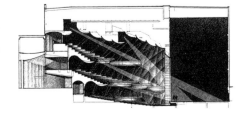

MASTER PLAN, BRONX MUSEUM OF THE ARTS

Bronx, New York, 1990
Clients: Bronx Museum of the Arts and New York City Economic Development Corporation

This master plan provides for the museum's evolution into a dynamic and distinguished institution that would broaden its reach as a cultural and educational center and serve as a catalyst for the economic revitalization of the Grand Concourse. A fivefold increase in existing floor space is called for to accommodate an expanded arts program, a new performance center, additional exhibition and classroom space, a new restaurant/banquet facility, and a parking structure. The plan treats various site, reuse, public circulation, and functional requirements in three alternate schemes; a budget analysis helps to clarify the approaches to phased development.

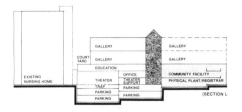

FINE AND PERFORMING ARTS CENTER, CREIGHTON UNIVERSITY

Omaha, Nebraska, 1990
Programming and planning

This study recommends a site and an overall image for the university's new 57,000-square-foot fine and performing arts center. The building consolidates and improves the university's theater, music, and visual arts programs, reaffirming their importance to students and the public. It introduces the university's first professional performing arts space, a 400-seat proscenium theater. The center also creates a strong architectural focus on campus, highlighting the role of the arts at the university, marking a new entrance to campus, and strengthening the central pedestrian walk.

FOX THEATRES ENTERTAINMENT CENTER

Wyomissing, Pennsylvania, 1990
Project

This cineplex is designed to make the moviegoing experience into more than just watching a film. A 500-foot-long shed enclosing a pedestrian boulevard descends the sloping site. This open public space is lined with kiosks that sell a variety of refreshments and movie-related items. It provides access to the fourteen theaters, which are contained in clusters of barrel-vaulted spaces. The interiors of the different-sized theaters are finished in diverse materials, colors, and patterns. All are distinctively lit. They offer a variety of settings recalling the grandeur of old movie palaces.

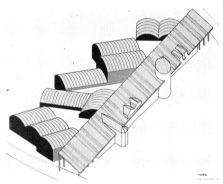

MASTER PLAN, FRANCISCAN UNIVERSITY OF STEUBENVILLE

Steubenville, Ohio, 1990

The master plan for Franciscan University shows how incremental changes in building and landscape will, in time, lead to a more coherent, responsive place. Among the recommendations contained in the plan are the creation of courtyards, the separation of pedestrian and vehicular circulation, and the strengthening of visual corridors to exploit the hilltop location. New buildings are designed to reinforce primary pedestrian axes and existing uses. Roads are realigned to remove cars from the center of campus. Several outdoor focal points are established, around which new development is organized.

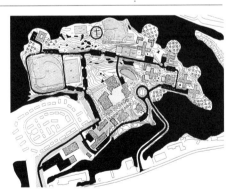

MASTER PLAN, JOHN MICHAEL KOHLER ARTS CENTER

Sheboygan, Wisconsin, 1990

This three-phase expansion plan triples the floor area, provides separate delivery and support spaces for the galleries and the theater, and establishes a new front door with circulation that integrates the center's distinct volumes. The expansion incorporates an adjacent library building and a landmark Italianate house relocated from an adjacent site. Other elements of the plan include the improvement of environmental conditions throughout the galleries, the enlargement of the existing theater, the reinstitution and expansion of original educational programs, and the consolidation of administration spaces.

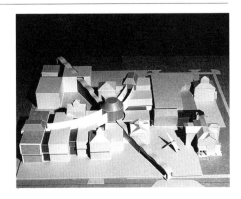

LIBERTY S.PA.C.E.: SUPER PERFORMING ARTS CENTER FOR EVERYONE

New York, New York, 1990
Proposal for reuse
Client: Hospital Audiences, Inc.

As part of the billion-dollar redevelopment of 42nd Street, this proposal converts the Liberty Theater into the first professional performance hall with complete handicapped access on *both* sides of the footlights, accommodating physically impaired actors and stagehands as well as spectators. Space for an enlarged lobby, circulation areas, and elevators is provided by reconstructing the original orchestra level (the stage is relocated to the mezzanine level) and annexing the stage house of the adjacent Empire Theater (the remainder of which is converted into a multipurpose auditorium). Other improvements include the restoration of the proscenium arch, boxes, decorative ceiling, balcony fascias, and stage curtain.

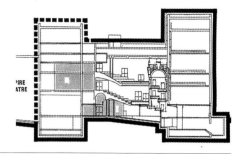

NEW CITY HALL

Culver City, California, 1990
Competition
Client: Culver City
Redevelopment Agency

This competition design uses indigenous Mission features and details inspired by the original City Hall to resolve the program's division of public and private spaces and a large parking requirement (two-thirds of all floor space). Light wells penetrate the below-grade parking levels to provide orientation and access to the central courtyard above. The three-story exterior, faced in stucco and terra-cotta tiles, features a central clocktower and a circular City Council Chamber embellished with regional motifs designed by local artists. The landscaped courtyard gives the building a strong internal focus and eliminates the concept of rear office space. Pedestrian arcades on three levels circumscribe the courtyard and function as interior circulation.

MAIN LIBRARY, NEW HAVEN FREE PUBLIC LIBRARY

New Haven, Connecticut, 1990
Renovation and new construction
Client: City of New Haven
Associate Architect: Office of
Felix Drury

The restoration and expansion of Cass Gilbert's 1910 Georgian-style library doubles the floor area on a constricted site and reorganizes its plan from a closed-stack to an open-stack system. The L-shaped addition wraps around the library's less public sides, deferring to Gilbert's main facades. To the west, it rises to the same height as the library, abstracting its basic elements and extending the library's dominant horizontal lines. The addition's new masonry finish is muted in comparison with Gilbert's high-contrast brick-and-marble composition. Inside, the original building and the addition are horizontally linked along a central axis and vertically integrated by a new elevator and stair core.

NEW YORK BOTANICAL GARDEN "SPRING 90" IMPROVEMENTS

Bronx, New York, 1990

This series of scenic improvements strengthens access to, orientation within, and understanding of the botanical garden's major displays. A nonvehicular entrance is established; large graphic pylons orient visitors to the garden, while banners direct them to the museum building and information center. Two small, temporary lattice pavilions in front of the museum building sell refreshments and create new public space. A tram connects six major sites in the garden, each marked by similar pavilions and information pylons. These new features graphically unify the network of gardens, providing a stronger overall sense of place.

NEW YORK CENTRAL TERMINAL

Buffalo, New York, 1990
Proposal for reuse

Built in 1929 and designed by Alfred Fellheimer and Steward Wagner in the tradition of the grand railroad terminal, this vacant Art Deco transportation complex is now listed on the National Register of Historic Places. This interpretative restoration transforms the terminal, on the outskirts of the central business district, into a major commercial center. Its large vaulted passenger and train concourses are converted into a retail center and market. The adjacent seventeen-story, setback tower is transformed into a hotel, and the four-story baggage building is redesigned to contain offices. Most of the terminal's historic elements are restored.

RAINBOW BRIDGE U.S. TOLL PLAZA

Niagara Falls, New York, 1990
Competition
Client: Niagara Falls Bridge Commission

As the first phase of a $30 million improvement program, this reconstruction and expansion modernizes the approaches to the fifty-year-old Rainbow Bridge, allowing a heavily traveled point of entry to nearly double its capacity. The competition-winning design emphasizes the efficient processing of people and vehicles, yet it also blends aesthetically with the natural grandeur of the site. An expanded plaza is provided, distinguished by a curving row of faceted-glass customs booths and an open network of exposed trusses that support the main building—a sweeping structure that houses customs and immigration space, toll facilities, and administrative offices.

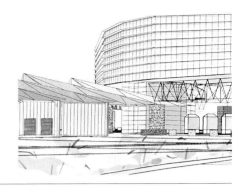

25 EAST 65TH STREET

New York, New York, 1990
Project
Client: Cugini Development Company

Based on the same footprint used in Madison House II, this more pragmatic development retains the basic volume that secured previous municipal approval. It uses an articulated retail base, patterned brickwork, and integrated massing, but it minimizes the number of setbacks and distinct apartment plans. While maintaining the same number of units as in Madison House II, the redesign increases apartment size by 10 percent and reduces development costs.

B. ALTMAN'S MIDTOWN CENTRE

New York, New York, 1991
Project
Client: Olshan-Kazis Realty Corporation and Mall Properties, Inc.
Associate Architect: Emery Roth & Sons Architects

The vertical expansion of Altman's represents only the second time the New York City Landmarks Preservation Commission has approved significant new construction atop a major landmark building. This addition uses elements of the original fenestration to create a sympathetic new composition. The expansion of six floors on Madison Avenue, the consolidation of retail space on five floors, and the conversion of 350,000 square feet into office space are part of an overall redevelopment strategy aimed at preserving Fifth Avenue's first department store. In the process, much of Trowbridge and Livingston's thirteen-story Renaissance Revival design (built in three phases between 1905 and 1913) is restored.

42ND STREET ENTERTAINMENT CORPORATION OFFICES

New York, New York, 1991
Renovation

The design premise for these corporate offices is the spirited character of 42nd Street itself. The palette of forms, materials, light, and color developed for the offices is meant to reinforce this famous thoroughfare's most striking quality: variety. Cabinetry and millwork are in black matte and the desk veneers are stained pink; the waferboard walls are angled; and the Tectum ceiling panels and sisal carpeting provide a rich texture and a neutral color complement. Clusters of partitioned office cubicles divide the rectangular plan and encourage interoffice communication and the sharing of ideas. The only enclosed spaces are the director's office and the adjacent boardroom, positioned to overlook the activity of 42nd Street.

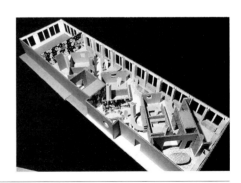

LOS ANGELES UNION STATION

Los Angeles, California, 1991
Study
Client: Catellus Development Corporation

Los Angeles Union Station was the last of the great urban train stations to be built in the United States. This comprehensive survey of the station's existing spaces and historic features, supported by archival research, was compiled to ensure the preservation of the building's many historic elements. Intended as a resource to guide the station's maintenance, the upgrading necessary to comply with codes, the identification of historic materials, and the definition of historic priorities, the study also proposes a detailed plan for Union Station's restoration, rehabilitation, and potential for adaptive reuse.

ARTS CENTER, MIDDLEBURY COLLEGE

Middlebury, Vermont, 1991
New construction

Middlebury's fine and performing arts activities are consolidated and expanded in this center. Its siting and materials are typical of the college's buildings—a freestanding structure situated on a through-campus street, with a distinctive front and back finished in masonry and wood. The design involves the juxtaposition of internal elements. Portions of the major components, each finished with distinct materials, textures, colors, and fenestration, project through the building's facades. They articulate the building's various functions and provide scale and focus to the long exterior walls.

McCULLOUGH STUDENT CENTER, MIDDLEBURY COLLEGE

Middlebury, Vermont, 1991
Renovation and new construction

The conversion of McCullough Gymnasium and Brown Pool into the college's primary student activities center calls for the expansion of the building by more than 50 percent. The original structure's architectural integrity is maintained by dividing the program into two parts (located on the east and west sides of the gym) to diminish its apparent size, to preserve the importance of McCullough's symmetrical main north facade, and to obscure the negative visual effects of the previous Brown Pool addition. The two sides, finished in stone and wood, are composed of a series of octagons that incorporate a number of the gym's architectural features—prominent exterior walls, steeply pitched roofs, and cupolas.

DOWNTOWN FACILITY, SEATTLE PUBLIC LIBRARY

Seattle, Washington, 1991
Programming and planning

The library's central facility, completed in 1960 in the International Style by Bindon and Wright, occupies a full block in the center of downtown Seattle. No major changes to the building and its systems have been implemented since it was built. The plan develops a realistic, long-range expansion of the library and suggests upgrading options to make existing space more efficient and flexible. Also considered for introduction are "public benefits" such as a 3,000-square-foot parcel park, wider sidewalks, overhead weather protection, the enclosure of mechanical equipment, a performing arts theater, a visual arts museum, and a 5,000-square-foot public atrium with additional outdoor areas.

SUNDANCE INSTITUTE AMPHITHEATER

Sundance, Utah, 1991
Project

This new open-air theater provides a public outlet for Robert Redford's educational center for American filmmakers, writers, directors, producers, and actors. A technically sophisticated stage allows for a variety of experimental and traditional productions, including musicals, children's plays, solo concerts, and orchestral performances. The theater utilizes the surrounding landscape as part of the overall design, emphasizing the natural setting. A two-tiered, raked seating plan is integrated into the grade of the site. A pair of parallel arches support lighting, rigging, and video equipment, and can also accommodate a stage backdrop when required. The orchestra pit, which holds thirty musicians, can be covered to increase the depth of the stage.

COLGATE DARDEN GRADUATE SCHOOL OF BUSINESS, UNIVERSITY OF VIRGINIA

Charlottesville, Virginia, 1991
Project

The goal of this site improvement and expansion plan is to unify the Darden School and the adjacent Sponsors Hall. The relocation of the existing approach road and service access, which now separates the two buildings, allows for the creation of a new common courtyard and vehicular drop-off point. Two new entrance lobbies provide access to both buildings from the central courtyard. The addition to the main building, a series of multistory masses containing offices and instructional spaces and finished in brick and stone, creates a dynamic architectural presence that recasts the school's image.

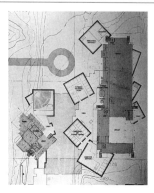

LILLIAN VERNON RESIDENCE

New York, New York, 1991
Renovation

The redesign of this Fifth Avenue duplex apartment, located on the fifteenth and sixteenth floors, separates entertainment areas from the owner's personal space. It exploits the magnificent views of Central Park and provides a backdrop for a collection of fine art and furniture. Guests enter on the top floor and descend a circular staircase into a large living/dining space that is unified by two diagonal elements: a partially dropped ceiling and a patterned terrazzo floor. Textured walls, illuminated niches, rich veneers, and dramatic lighting distinguish the interior. Outside, a fifty-foot-long terrace is modulated by a vine-clad lattice, pergolas, and a greenhouse/dining room.

WILMA THEATER

Philadelphia, Pennsylvania, 1991
Project
Associate Architect: Alesker Reiff and Dundon, Inc.

The relocation of the Wilma Theater Company from an old side-street garage to a prominent site on Broad Street's "Avenue of the Arts District" marks a decade of remarkable growth by this avant-garde theater. The new thrust-stage facility is set within the base of a new parking garage. Audience and performers are accommodated in one open space, which retains the intimate character of the theater's previous home. The single-level hall is composed of a curved seating section to provide superior sight lines throughout. Although primarily designed for theater, the Wilma can accommodate a variety of performing arts activities.

BRYANT PARK RESTAURANTS

New York, New York, 1992
New construction
Client: Bryant Park Restoration Corporation

The purpose of this restoration and new development is to re-create the splendor of the Beaux-Arts–inspired park and to reclaim the area for public use. The number of entrances has been doubled, handicapped access has been provided, and new paths have been created to encourage increased use by local workers. The park's overall redevelopment is anchored by two symmetrical restaurant pavilions (each 5,250 square feet) on the library's West Terrace and by four food kiosks at the edges of the park. The pavilions' facades are adorned with weathered-wood trellises supporting wisteria.

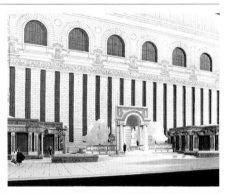

888 MADISON

New York, New York, 1992
Facade redesign and new construction
Client: Larstrand Corporation
Associate Architect: Tudda, Scherer & Zborowski

The redesign and expansion of this two-story "taxpayer" transforms an underutilized structure into a more substantial piece of architecture that better defines the intersection of Madison Avenue and 72nd Street. Located in one of the city's prime retail and residential quarters, this four-story building makes reference to both the height and the geometric divisions of adjacent town houses along 72nd Street, as well as to the distinctive storefronts along Madison Avenue. The new fenestration recalls the dimensions of standard town-house windows and is accented by alternating bays of polychrome terra cotta and limestone. Ground-level storefronts are designed, with minimal architectural treatment, to emphasize window displays.

FINNEGAN FIELD HOUSE, FRANCISCAN UNIVERSITY OF STEUBENVILLE

Steubenville, Ohio, 1992
New construction

The current athletic program of the university will be greatly expanded by this new building, which is divided into three distinct volumes: gymnasium, racquetball courts and weight room, and office and support spaces. The field house is sited in close relationship to the existing J. C. Williams Center and a future convocation center and is directly accessible to adjacent playing fields. This reflects the idea that sports are participatory and an integral element of student life. Sloping roofs give the building a distinct shape that complements the undulating topography. A four-story, vertical architectural element, introduced to help define the entrance and orient users, is reminiscent of the bell towers found in Assisi, home of the Franciscan Order.

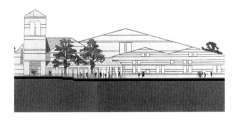

HIGHLAND HOUSE

Madison, Wisconsin, 1992
New construction
Clients: Robert Horowitz and
Susan B. King

Highland House symbolically expresses the theories of contemporary physics. The volumetric elements correspond to the six flavors of quarks: up, down, top, bottom, strange, and charmed. The asymmetrical plan, with no obvious center and a non-Cartesian organization, reflects Einsteinian relativity. The temporal dimension is symbolized by the use of granite and limestone. While the forms are Euclidean, they are connected by meridians to allow for a flexible and expanding living environment, a visual metaphor for a universe expanding in a Big Bang and, perhaps, little bangs.

LOS ANGELES CITY HALL

Los Angeles, California, 1992
Rehabilitation; Phase I
Client: Project Restore

This master plan focuses on improving the public circulation spaces, the most heavily utilized portion of this twenty-seven-story landmark. The major element of the plan is the restoration of the building's original elegance through surface cleaning and decorative painting, removal of superfluous elements, re-creation of lost or damaged elements, execution of deferred improvements, and sympathetic integration of modernized functions for lighting, signage, staff services, and safety. The master plan includes historic research along with drawings and models that review existing conditions, leading to specific recommendations and a proposal for a phased budget. A demonstration project involves the Main Street lobby and garage entry, City Hall's most significant public spaces.

MARKET SQUARE

Pittsburgh, Pennsylvania, 1992
New construction
Client: Urban Redevelopment
Authority of Pittsburgh
Associate Architect: LaQuantra
and Bonci Associates

This project refines the appearance and use of Market Square to ensure its better integration into a redeveloping neighborhood. The square is redesigned as an open pedestrian area rather than a traditional pastoral park. The purpose of the redesign is to make the square a symbolic focus of downtown, linking several pedestrian axes; to preserve and restore adjacent buildings; to stimulate retail activity and private investment in and around the square; to reduce the conflict between pedestrian and vehicular traffic; to provide space for a variety of public events; and to introduce major landscape elements into the heart of the city.

MASTER PLAN AND RECREATION BUILDING, MONAGHAN FAMILY COMPOUND

Ann Arbor, Michigan, 1992
New construction
Client: Domino's Farms
Development

The master plan for this fifty-acre estate outlines locations for four 4,000-square-foot houses, a recreational center, and access roads. Reforestation is used to increase the privacy of the houses. The plan of the recreational center, located on the southern edge of the property, is a slightly skewed cross that creates subtle visual tension between its interior and its exterior spaces. The stepped configuration of two-story volumes enclosed in a series of pitched roofs generates massing that is sympathetic to the contours of the site.

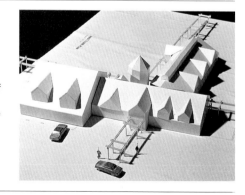

MEMORIAL CHURCH, STANFORD UNIVERSITY

Stanford, California, 1992
Rehabilitation

Memorial Church, the focal point of Stanford University's main quadrangle, was significantly damaged in the 1989 Loma Prieta earthquake, adding to several preexisting structural inadequacies discovered after the famous 1906 earthquake. Because of its unreinforced exterior and inadequate lateral bracing, the church was judged to be unsafe and was closed to use. This structural evaluation and restoration report includes recommendations for structural repair; the protection and enhancement of the architectural, mechanical, and acoustical characteristics of the building; and the preservation and re-creation of all artwork and artifacts.

FINE ARTS EDUCATION BUILDING, UNIVERSITY OF NEBRASKA AT OMAHA

Omaha, Nebraska, 1992
New construction
Associate Architect: The Schemmer Associates, Inc.

This design creates a new focus for the arts at the university and emphasizes their importance. The building is architecturally distinctive—it is finished in three different masonry materials—yet it is also compatible with the existing character of the campus. The central classroom/laboratory component is a four-story brick mass whose undulating facade foreshortens and articulates the 300-foot length. The art gallery and the experimental theater, both one story high and distinguished by granite facades and gabled roofs, are connected to the north and west ends of the central structure, respectively, to define a courtyard/sculpture garden. The building is designed to accommodate future south and east additions for the radio and television departments and a new proscenium theater.

CLEVELAND PUBLIC LIBRARY

Cleveland, Ohio, Future
Renovation and new construction
Client: Cleveland Public Library Board of Trustees
Associate Architect: URS Consultants, Inc.

The organization of the new library is derived from that of the original building, which was an innovative departure from the traditional municipal library design of the time. Monumental spaces are largely replaced with an efficient layout that emphasizes the library's function as, first, a place for readers and books. The addition expands the library's open-shelf network of departments, with stacks set toward the center of the building and reading areas arranged around the perimeter, allowing for natural lighting. Primary public circulation paths are kept distinct from internal department routes. Eastman Garden serves as a constant point of orientation throughout. Each subject department is contained on its own level, and administrative areas and remote stacks are located on top floors.

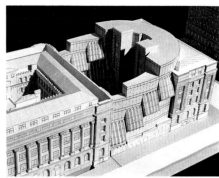

DANCE THEATRE OF HARLEM SCHOOL

New York, New York, Future
Renovation and new construction

This major New York City cultural institution has become an internationally respected performing arts organization. Its present school occupies a space that was formerly a two-story garage, converted by HHPA in 1971. The rapid growth of the school now necessitates expansion to accommodate new faculty offices, conference rooms, lounges, and rehearsal space. To help generate funds for these improvements, the new plan outlines the development of a three-story, 12,000-square-foot building next to the existing one. It also proposes a vigorous streetfront scheme that juxtaposes dissimilar elements and materials to create a lively appearance and a strong presence for the school in this residential neighborhood.

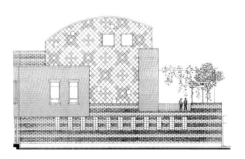

HAWAII THEATRE CENTER

Honolulu, Hawaii, Future
Restoration and new construction

A key component in the redevelopment of downtown Honolulu's historic Chinatown is the revitalization of the landmark Hawaii Theatre as a performing arts center. This plan calls for the 1,400-seat Beaux-Arts theater, designed by Emory and Webb in 1923, to be restored, with significant improvements in lighting and performance technology. The second phase of the plan introduces a new grand stair and handicapped access, and enlarges the lobbies, rehearsal rooms, banquet facilities, and offices. Low-rise buildings adjacent to the theater will be acquired and converted for related activities, and a new park will be developed to serve as an outdoor lobby for the theater and a focal point for the surrounding area.

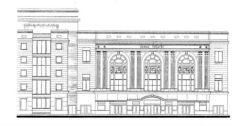

HOTEL MACKLOWE

Los Angeles, California, Future
New construction
Client: Harry Macklowe Real Estate Company, Inc.
Associate Architect: Langdon Wilson Architects

A refined, glass-and-aluminum curtain-wall design distinguishes this major commercial development in the heart of the Los Angeles Business District. The forty-three-story building complements the city's downtown master plan, responding to municipal concerns about land use, open space, pedestrian circulation, transit connections, and historic context. A ten-story convention center defines the base of the tower. Five levels of underground parking also serve the adjacent Barker Brothers Building, a landmark structure connected to the tower by a new skylit motor court.

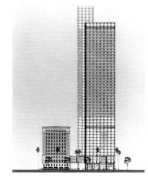

CULTURAL CENTER, LEE COUNTY ALLIANCE OF THE ARTS

Fort Myers, Florida, Future
New construction

The selected development of a ten-acre site is planned to enhance the function and presence of the Lee County Alliance of the Arts, transforming it into a significant focal point for the community. To establish a campus-type plan, first-phase improvements include the reuse of an existing farmhouse for children's programs and the building of a new structure for art education, administration, and a gallery. An outdoor performance facility and a parking area are developed as parts of a series of half-acre green spaces. Second-phase improvements include new indoor performance spaces and additional visual arts spaces.

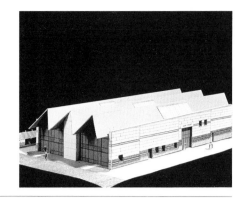

CENTRAL LIBRARY, LOS ANGELES PUBLIC LIBRARY

Los Angeles, California, Future
Rehabilitation and new
construction
Client: City of Los Angeles:
Board of Library Commissioners
and Community Redevelopment
Agency

The rehabilitation of Bertram Goodhue's 1924 landmark library corrects years of minimal maintenance and substantial damage caused by arson fires. Modernization and expansion also address the growing demands that have rendered the original building inadequate. This addition more than doubles the size of the library and enables its conversion from a closed-stack to an open-stack system, while state-of-the-art technology is used to update operations. Architecturally, the addition is a contemporary interpretation of Goodhue's design, sympathetic in finish, fenestration, and proportion. Its scale, circulation, and physical orientation further focus attention back to the original building.

9200 WILSHIRE OFFICE BUILDING

Beverly Hills, California, Future
New construction
Client: Columbia Development
Partners

The dimensions of this three-story building are shaped by its zoning envelope and the requirements of a speculative office plan. Its internal column bay is articulated in the facade, which blends ceramic building elements with a modern glass curtain-wall system. Glazed terra-cotta pilasters and arches join with the tricolor undulating glass curtain wall to establish an architectural cadence that extends the full length of the block-long front along Wilshire Boulevard.

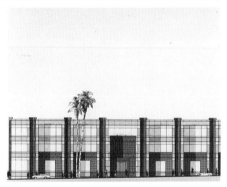

186 EAST 76TH STREET

New York, New York, Future
New construction
Client: Brodsky-Quinlan
Development Corporation

The design of this thirty-one-story residential building is in direct response to the financial difficulties of a landmark church, St. Jean Baptiste Église, which raised critical funds by transferring its air rights to the adjacent development parcel. The new tower is set back above the base to correspond to the massing of the church and the rectory. Rusticated stone and brickwork, turreted corners, and the division of the facades into horizontal sections further relate the new building to the church.

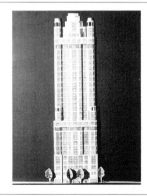

WILLIAM K.H. MAU THEATER AND DILLINGHAM HALL, THE PUNAHOU SCHOOL

Honolulu, Hawaii, Future
New construction and renovation

The creation of the Mau Theater, together with the renovation and expansion of Bertram Goodhue's Dillingham Hall, improves the school's performing arts programs and increases their presence on campus. The concentric arrangement of the 300 seats in the Mau Theater generates a clear focus for this educational thrust-stage facility. A new common outdoor entrance plaza and a network of lanais link the two buildings in a manner consistent with Goodhue's 1921 master plan. The proscenium stage in Dillingham Hall is enlarged to accommodate the school's 125-member orchestra and choir, and seating is reconfigured to improve sight lines.

WILSHIRE/LAPEER OFFICE BUILDING

Beverly Hills, California, Future
New construction
Client: Columbia Development Partners

The city's zoning and landscape requirements shaped the basic mass of this speculative office building, delineating a three-story envelope set back from the sidewalk, with three levels of below-grade parking. The exterior is finished with a conventional curtain wall, which is accented with wide spandrels to give horizontal emphasis. Two-story metal-panel pilasters divide the building's base into bays, a reference to storefronts along the older portions of Wilshire Boulevard.

279

RUNDEL MEMORIAL BUILDING, ROCHESTER PUBLIC LIBRARY

Rochester, New York, Future
Renovation and new construction

The redesign and expansion of Rochester's central library take full advantage of the building's riverfront location. Interior vertical and horizontal circulation is reoriented to maximize views of the water. An existing lower service level is reconstructed and extended over the river, accommodating new services and several major departments, which now have clear river views. Historic rooms of the library are restored in an interpretive manner. Library operations and environmental systems are modernized, and these functional improvements allow for direct public access to 70 percent of all materials (up from 30 percent). An improved street-level plaza circumscribes the building, creating a major downtown public space with riverfront access.

SPECIAL ATTRACTION THEATER

Universal City, California, Future
New construction
Client: ION Pictures

Situated at the focal point of Universal City's Citywalk project, this new 1,200-seat Special Attraction Theater is aimed at those who are inspired by the history and technology of the motion picture industry. Engineered to facilitate future developments in moviemaking well into the twenty-first century, the 45,000-square-foot theater is distinguished by a twenty-story sphere modeled after the historic trylon and perisphere of the 1939 World's Fair in New York. The theater features a domed ceiling, IMAX technology, and one of the largest projection screens in the world.

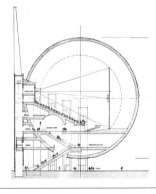

TIFFANY PLAZA OFFICE BUILDING

New York, New York, Future
New construction
Client: Continental Development Corporation

The design of the forty-story Tiffany Plaza is shaped by zoning and the desire to integrate it with the Tiffany Building (designed by McKim, Mead & White and built in 1906), located next door. The symmetrical setbacks of the new building are sculpted by an interpretation of sky-exposure regulations and result in massing suggestive of 1930s skyscraper design. The tower's precast-concrete-and-glass base extends the landmark's three major cornices along Fifth Avenue and replicates the older building's two-story window bays with glass, rather than stone, spandrels. The new base is further divided vertically with paired concrete pilasters that recall the Tiffany Building's coupled columns.

SECRETARY-GENERAL'S RESIDENCE

The United Nations, New York, New York, Future
Rehabilitation

Originally built in the late 1930s by J. P. Morgan for his daughter Ann, this Sutton Place town house was acquired by the United Nations in 1972 as the residence for the secretary-general. This plan surveys the structural, mechanical, and architectural conditions of the five-story Georgian-style home, and recommends a series of aesthetic and environmental improvements.

SELECTED BIBLIOGRAPHY

280 **GENERAL**

Chorneau, Tom. "Architect Pfeiffer Reflects on Adorning L.A. Landmarks." *The Los Angeles Business Journal*, 26 October 1987, pp. 1, 24.

Cohen, Stuart E. "Hardy Holzman Pfeiffer on America." *Progressive Architecture*, February 1975, pp. 54–58.

Davis, Douglas. "Mixed Marriages of Art." *Newsweek*, 16 March 1981, p. 71.

———. *The Museum Transformed: Design and Culture in the Post-Pompidou Age*. New York: Abbeville Press, 1990, pp. 68, 133–36, 164.

Dean, Andrea O. "An Evocative Approach to Adaptive Use." *AIA Journal*, June 1976, 38–40.

———. "Hardy Holzman Pfeiffer Associates: Winner of the 1981 AIA Architectural Firm Award." *AIA Journal*, February 1981, pp. 40–49.

Diamonstein, Barbaralee. *American Architecture Now*. New York: Rizzoli International Publications, 1978, pp. 79–102.

———. *American Architecture Now II*. New York: Rizzoli International Publications, 1985, pp. 185–93.

———. *The Landmarks of New York*. New York: Harry N. Abrams, 1988, pp. 279, 370.

———, ed. *Collaboration: Artists and Architects*. New York: Whitney Library of Design, 1981.

Ellis, Russell, and Dana Cuff, eds. *Architects' People*. New York: Oxford University Press, 1989, pp. 65, 69–73, 93, 96, 97, 99.

Forsyth, Michael. *Buildings for Music: The Architect, the Musician, and the Listener from the Seventeenth Century to the Present*. Cambridge, Mass.: MIT Press, 1986, pp. 15, 294, 306, 307.

Freidman, Mildred S., ed. "Learning Spaces and Places." *Design Quarterly* 90/91 (1974).

Goldberger, Paul. "Brash, Young and Post-Modern." *New York Times Magazine*, 20 February 1977, pp. 18–31.

Green, Kevin W., ed. *The City as a Stage: Strategies for the Arts in Urban Economics*. Washington, D.C.: Partners for Livable Places, 1983, pp. 35, 71, 76, 80–82.

Hardy, Hugh. "Acts of Conscious Choice." *The Canadian Architect*, April 1976, pp. 45–54.

———. "An Architecture of Awareness for the Performing Arts." *Architectural Record*, March 1969, pp. 117–21.

———. "Architecture and the Psychology of Aesthetic Distance." *Theatre Design and Technology*, October 1970, pp. 21–28.

———. "Designing Random Focus." *The Drama Review*, vol. 12, no. 3 (Spring 1968), pp. 121–26.

———. "Flexible Theater of Performance." *Theatre Design and Technology*, December 1967, pp. 6–11.

———. "The 'Greater Number' Problem." *Spazio e Società* (Italy), January/March 1991, pp. 8–19.

———. "Hardy Holzman Pfeiffer Associates," in *Encyclopedia of Architecture: Design, Engineering and Construction*, vol. 2. New York: John Wiley & Sons, 1988, pp. 693–96.

———. "Total Design and the Architect." *Progressive Architecture*, October 1965, pp. 198–203.

———. "Towards an Architecture of the Valley." *Places* (The Design History Foundation, Journal of Environmental Design), vol. 6, no. 3, pp. 28–31.

———. "What Time Is It?" *OZ* (Kansas State University College of Architecture and Design Journal), vol. 12, pp. 30–35.

Hardy, Hugh, Malcolm Holzman, and Norman Pfeiffer. "Architecture as Environment." *Design Quarterly* 90/91 (1974), pp. 11–12.

———. "The Movie Palace in Context." *Architectural Record*, July 1980, pp. 86–87.

———. *Reusing Railroad Stations*. New York: Educational Facilities Laboratories, 1974.

———. "Saving Grand Central Terminal or the Future of Midtown Manhattan." *Journal of Architectural Education*, November 1976, pp. 16–21.

———. *30 Theaters*. New York: Hardy Holzman Pfeiffer Associates, 1983.

Heyer, Paul. *Architects on Architecture: New Directions in America*. New York: Walker and Company, 1978, p. 407.

Holzman, Malcolm. "The Play's the Thing in Educational Theater Design." *American School and University*, December 1968, pp. 64–68.

———. "Precursors: Thomson's Glasgow." *Progressive Architecture*, June 1982, pp. 90–95.

Hughes, Robert. "Doing Their Own Thing: U.S. Architects, Goodbye to Glass Boxes and All That." *Time*, 8 January 1979, pp. 52–59.

Jensen, Robert, and Patricia Conway. *Ornamentalism*. New York: Clarkson N. Potter, 1982, pp. 114, 139, 153.

Klotz, Heinrich. *New York Architektur 1970–1990*. Frankfurt: Deutsches Architekturmuseum, 1989, pp. 142–47.

Matousek, Mark. "The Thespian Touch." *Metropolis*, March 1985, pp. 16–19, 26.

Morgan, Ann Lee, and Colin Naylor, eds. *Contemporary Architects*, 2d ed. Chicago: St. James Press, 1987, pp. 383–85.

Pfeiffer, Norman. "Older Buildings Compete." *Office Market Journal of Greater Los Angeles*, January 1988.

———. "Right Side of the Tracks: An Investigation Into the Economics of Redeeming America's Old Train Depots." *Architectural Forum*, November 1973, pp. 66–73.

———. "A Non-Esthetic Alternative." *Casabella* (Italy), August/September 1973, pp. 27–32.

"The Recycling of America: Old Buildings Make New Landmarks." *Time*, 11 June 1979, pp. 82–85.

"Restoration of Things Past." *Newsweek*, 23 March 1981, pp. 84–86.

Schmertz, Mildred F. "Design for Learning: Work of Hardy Holzman Pfeiffer Associates." *Architectural Record*, April 1972, pp. 109–18.

"The Shell Game: Filling the Shells of Old Buildings Scores Points for Architects." *Progressive Architecture*, June 1969, pp. 94–99.

Smith, C. Ray. *Supermannerism: New Attitudes in Post Modern Architecture*. New York: E.P. Dutton, 1977.

Sorkin, Michael. *Hardy Holzman Pfeiffer Associates*. New York: Whitney Library of Design, 1981.

Stephens, Suzanne. "It's Not Graphic Design Exactly. Nor Is It Architecture. And It Probably Isn't 'Art'. What Is It? Graphitecture." *Print*, November/December 1972, pp. 23–31.

———, ed. "Art and the Walls Within: Currier Gallery of Art, Virginia Museum of Fine Arts, Los Angeles County Museum of Art," in *Building the New Museum*. New York: Architectural League of New York, 1986, pp. 38–51, 56–62.

Stern, Robert A.M.. "Forty Under Forty." *Architecture + Urbanism* (Japan), January 1977, pp. 42, 99–101.

"Technology: Some Young Architects Take a Fresh Look at Pre-Engineered Metal Building Systems." *Architectural Forum*, April 1971, pp. 52–55.

Truppin, Andrea. "Pure Theater: Profile of Hardy Holzman Pfeiffer." *Interiors*, July 1987, pp. 161–81.

Wright, Sylvia Hart. *Sourcebook of Contemporary North American Architecture: From Postwar to Postmodern*. New York: Von Nostrand Reinhold, 1989, pp. 137–43.

Zasada, Marc. "The Man Redrawing the Central Library: Norm Pfeiffer and His New York Firm Have Been Taking Los Angeles By Storm." *Downtown News* (Los Angeles), 16 February 1987, pp. 6, 7.

ALASKA CENTER FOR THE PERFORMING ARTS
Eng, Rick. "Jewel On Ice." *Designers West*, June 1989, pp. 114–21.

LaRue, Michelle. "Alaska Center for the Performing Arts: The House That Drama Built." *Theatre Crafts,* November 1989, pp. 34–43.

Schmertz, Mildred F. "Northern Lights." *Architectural Record*, April 1989, pp. 96–110.

ALICE BUSCH OPERA THEATER
Anderson, Grace. "Open-Air Opera." *Architectural Record*, August 1988, pp. 90–93.

Hoelterhoff, Manuela. "Glimmerglass Opera Gets New House." *Wall Street Journal*, 3 July 1987.

Porter, Andrew. "Glimmerglass." *The New Yorker*, 13 July 1987, pp. 72–73.

BAM MAJESTIC THEATRE
Andersen, Kurt. "Best Design of 1987: Echoes of the Past, Visions for the Present." *Time*, 4 January 1988, pp. 74–75.

Anderson, Susan Heller. "Restoring a Theater to Its Decrepit State." *New York Times*, 13 October 1987, pp. B1, B4.

Breton, Gaelle. *Architecture Thématique: Théâtres*. Paris: Editions du Moniteur, 1989, pp. 84–87.

Murphy, Jim. "A Celebrated Dissolution." *Progressive Architecture*, April 1988, pp. 100–103.

BEST PRODUCTS COMPANY, INC. HEADQUARTERS
"Best of All." *Corporate Design*, March/April 1982.

Knight, Carleton, III. "Building Collections/Collecting Buildings." *Portfolio*, September/October 1981, pp. 82–87.

"Le Siège Social de BEST à Richmond." *Architecture Intérieure* (France), November 1981, pp. 120–25.

Morton, David. "Best Bets." *Progressive Architecture*, February 1981, pp. 66–73.

———. "Best Laid Plans." *Progressive Architecture*, March 1987, pp. 108–13.

BOETTCHER CONCERT HALL
"Rocky Mountain High." *Time*, 20 March 1978, pp. 22–23.

Saal, Hubert. "Symphony in the Round." *Newsweek*, 20 March 1978, p. 78.

Schmertz, Mildred F. "Denver's Boettcher Concert Hall." *Architectural Record*, March 1979, pp. 99–110.

Schoenberg, Harold C. "Listening in the Round in Denver." *New York Times*, 19 March 1978, pp. 21, 25.

BROOKLYN CHILDREN'S MUSEUM
"The Best in Exhibition Design: Brooklyn Children's Museum." *Print Casebooks*, no. 4 (1980/81), pp. 16–19.

"Esprit Grows in Brooklyn." *Progressive Architecture*, May 1978, pp. 62–67.

Smith, C. Ray. "The Great Museum Debate." *Progressive Architecture*, December 1969, pp. 76–85.

———. "Museum Goes Underground." *Contract Interiors*, June 1978, pp. 116–19.

CLOISTERS CONDOMINIUMS
"A Cincinnati Condominium." *House Beautiful*, June 1972, pp. 50–55.

Murphy, Jim. "Outcrop on Mt. Adams." *Progressive Architecture*, May 1971, pp. 86–91.

"Seven Multi-Family Winners." *House and Home*, August 1973, pp. 70–71.

282 **COLUMBUS OCCUPATIONAL HEALTH CENTER**
Drexler, Arthur. *Transformations in Modern Architecture*. New York: Museum of Modern Art, 1979.

Hardy, Hugh, Malcolm Holzman, and Norman Pfeiffer. "Machine, Man, and Architecture." *Architectural Record*, October 1975, pp. 95–102.

Schmertz, Mildred F. "An Industrial Medical Center Designed for Human Beings." *Architectural Record*, April 1972, pp. 112–13.

COOPER-HEWITT MUSEUM/NATIONAL MUSEUM OF DESIGN
"A New Splendour." *New York*, 20 September 1976, pp. 50–51.

Hardy, Hugh, Malcolm Holzman, and Norman Pfeiffer. "Recycling Architectural Masterpieces—and Other Buildings Not So Great." *Architectural Record*, August 1977, pp. 81–92.

Lynes, Russell. *More than Meets the Eye: The History and Collections of the Cooper-Hewitt Museum*. Washington, D.C.: Smithsonian Institution, 1981.

Osman, Mary E. "Honor Awards: Cooper-Hewitt Museum Restoration." *AIA Journal*, mid-May 1978, p. 139.

FIREMEN'S TRAINING CENTER
Goldberger, Paul. "Crossing Signals." *Progressive Architecture*, February 1976, pp. 64–68.

GALBREATH PAVILION AT THE OHIO THEATRE
Schmertz, Mildred F. "Lobby for a Landmark." *Architectural Record*, September 1985, pp. 114–19.

HADLEY HOUSE
"A Collision of Forms." *Progressive Architecture*, May 1968, pp. 104–9.

Sverbeyeff, Elizabeth. "A House Built to Savor Them All: Summer Sky, Summer Sea, Summer Breeze." *House Beautiful*, July 1968, pp. 22–25.

HULT CENTER FOR THE PERFORMING ARTS
Porter, Andrew. "How it Played in Peoria (and Elsewhere)." *The New Yorker*, 18 October 1982, pp. 163–70.

Schmertz, Mildred F. "Art for Art's Sake." *Architectural Record*, May 1983, pp. 120–33.

Schoenberg, Harold C. "Electro-Acoustic Concert Hall Opens in Oregon." *New York Times*, 27 September 1982, p. C13.

Tims, Marvin, and Dana Tims. *The Hult Center: From Dreams to Reality*. Eugene, Oregon: Northwest Cultural Information Associates, 1987.

THE JOYCE THEATER
Armstrong, Leslie, and Roger Morgan. *Space for Dance*. Washington, D.C.: Design Arts Program and Dance Program of the National Endowment for the Arts, 1984, pp. 101–5, 151.

"For Dancers Exclusively." *Architectural Record*, November 1984, p.. 102–5.

Sommers, Michael. "The Joyce Theater." *Theatre Crafts*, December 1988, pp. 40, 59–61.

LANGWORTHY RESIDENCE
Asbury, Edith Evans. "Architect Pleads for a 'Village' Design." *New York Times*, 10 March 1971, pp. 45, 86.

Huxtable, Ada Louise. "Compatibility Called Key to Building Plan." *New York Times*, 10 March 1971, p. 45.

Knight, Carleton, III. "A Disruption in Greenwich Village: An Interview with Hugh Hardy." *Historic Preservation*, July-September 1972, pp. 36–42.

"Modernism Exploding Onto The Streets." *Building Design*, 25 February 1983, pp. 16–17.

ROBERT O. ANDERSON BUILDING AND TIMES MIRROR CENTRAL COURT, LOS ANGELES COUNTY MUSEUM OF ART
Goldberger, Paul. "New Wing Conquers the Los Angeles County Museum of Art." *New York Times*, 7 November 1986, Arts and Leisure Section, pp. 35, 38.

Hardy, Hugh. "Adding Consistency to LACMA." *Spazio e Società* (Italy), January/March 1988, pp. 20–27.

Schmertz, Mildred F. "A Gathering of Fragments." *Architectural Record*, February 1987, pp. 110–19.

Tuchman, Mitch, ed. *The Robert O. Anderson Building*. Los Angeles: Los Angeles County Museum of Art, 1986.

CENTRAL LIBRARY, LOS ANGELES PUBLIC LIBRARY
Chandler, John. "Four City Panels Agree on Revised Central Library Design." *Los Angeles Herald Examiner*, 22 April 1988.

Hall, Mark. "Los Angeles Central Library." *L.A. Architect*, April 1987, pp. 1, 3.

Harris, Scott. "Architect's Plan Accepted." *Los Angeles Times*, 22 April 1988, Section II, pp. 1, 3.

Nairn, Janet. "The New Los Angeles Central Library Complements Bertram Goodhue's Original Historic Structure." *Sun/Coast Architect/Builder*, June 1988, pp. 12–14.

MADISON CIVIC CENTER
Dolan, Jill. "Oscar Mayer Theatre." *Theatre Crafts*, December 1988, pp. 44, 68–71.

Schmertz, Mildred F. "The New Madison Civic Center." *Architectural Record*, July 1980, pp. 77–86.

ARTS CENTER, MIDDLEBURY COLLEGE
Masur, Randy. "Mastering the Fine Arts." *Architecture*, January 1991, p. 34.

Prud'homme, Alex. "Building in a Landscape." *Middlebury College Magazine*, Autumn 1989, pp. 44–51.

MT. HEALTHY SCHOOL
"Open Planning in Columbus." *Progressive Architecture*, February 1971, p. 72.

Schmertz, Mildred F. "An Open Plan Elementary School." *Architectural Record*, September 1973, pp. 121–28.

NEW-YORK HISTORICAL SOCIETY

Hardy, Hugh. "New York Historical Society: HHPA Proposal." *Oculus* (New York Chapter/AIA), March 1984, pp. 14–17.

Horsley, Carter B. "Save the Museum, Improve Our Skyline." *New York Post*, 22 September 1988.

Wiseman, Carter. "Taking on the Towers." *New York*, 23 January 1984, pp. 62, 63.

ORCHESTRA HALL

Goldberger, Paul. "Orchestra Hall's Design: A Rebuke to Red Velvet." *New York Times*, 23 October 1974.

Morton, David. "Orchestra Hall." *Progressive Architecture*, October 1974, pp. 50–53.

ASSEMBLY HALL, PHILLIPS EXETER ACADEMY

"New Life for Old Buildings." *Architectural Record*, December 1971, pp. 124–25.

"New Places in Old Spaces." *Progressive Architecture*, December 1970, pp. 62–64.

PINGRY SCHOOL

Dean, Andrea Oppenheimer. "School with a Stony Front and Shiny Rear." *Architecture*, May 1985, pp. 193–97, 370.

Morton, David. "Upscale School." *Progressive Architecture*, August 1984, pp. 65–73.

ROBERT S. MARX THEATER, PLAYHOUSE IN THE PARK

"Cincinnati's New Playhouse: Uncommon Architecture from Common Materials." *Architectural Record*, March 1969, pp. 122–28.

Morton, David. "Cincinnati One-Ups Lincoln Center." *Progressive Architecture*, May 1967, pp. 161–63.

Robbins, William. "New Theater a Production in Itself, With Audience Adding to the Decor." *New York Times*, 13 October 1968.

"Settings for a New Stage Shape." *Theatre Crafts*, January/February 1971, pp. 16–21, 34–35.

RAINBOW ROOM AND ROCKEFELLER CENTER CLUB

Brenner, Douglas. "Change Partners and Dance." *Architectural Record*, June 1988, pp. 110–21.

Cohen, Edie Lee. "Rainbow." *Interior Design*, June 1988, pp. 240–51.

Conway, John A. "David Rockefeller Builds His Dream Club in the Sky." *Manhattan, Inc.*, December 1987.

Goldberger, Paul. "The New Rainbow Room: S'Wonderful." *New York Times*, 20 December 1987, Arts and Leisure Section.

RIZZOLI INTERNATIONAL 57TH STREET BOOKSTORE

Slavin, Maeve. "Literate Renaissance." *Interiors*, August 1985, pp. 176–81.

SCHOLASTIC, INC. OFFICES

Geran, Monica. "Invisibile Diversity." *Interior Design*, May 1984, pp. 304–13.

SCULPTURE HALL AND EAST WING, SAINT LOUIS ART MUSEUM

King, Mary. "Respect for the Past." *Artnews*, February 1978, pp. 119–21.

Overby, Osmund. *The Saint Louis Art Museum: An Architectural History*. St. Louis: Saint Louis Art Museum, 1987.

"Restoration of Saint Louis Art Museum." *AIA Journal*, mid-May 1979, pp. 197–99.

Schmertz, Mildred F. "HHPA Re-Establishes the Formal Themes of a Great Beaux-Arts Building." *Architectural Record*, October 1978, pp. 85–96.

MUSIC AND DANCE BUILDING, ST. PAUL'S SCHOOL

Stephens, Suzanne. "Raising the Roof." *Progressive Architecture*, February 1981, pp. 74–77.

WEST WING, VIRGINIA MUSEUM OF FINE ARTS

Arts in Virginia: Building the West Wing. Richmond: Virginia Museum of Fine Arts, 1982.

Knight, Carleton, III. "Virtuoso Performance in Stone." *Architecture*, January 1986, pp. 40–45.

Rastorfer, Darl. "Putting It All Together." *Architectural Record*, June 1986, pp. 154–63.

Searing, Helen. *New American Art Museums*. New York: Whitney Museum of American Art, 1982, pp. 114–21, 131–32.

WCCO-TV COMMUNICATION CENTER AND HEADQUARTERS

Baymiller, Joanna. "Solid and Spare Urban Geometry." *Architecture*, May 1984.

Gustafson, Karen. "The Satellite's the Limit for WCCO-TV." *Corporate Design and Realty*, March 1985, pp. 58–63.

WELLESLEY COLLEGE SPORTS CENTER

Dietsch, Deborah K. "A Picture of Health." *Architectural Record*, August 1987, pp. 90–95.

WILLARD HOTEL

Forgey, Benjamin. "Willard Hotel: Well Worth the Wait." *Washington Post*, 9 August 1986, pp. D1-2.

Goldberger, Paul. "On Pennsylvania Avenue, a Restoration with Wit." *New York Times*, 22 September 1986.

"Hardy Holzman Pfeiffer's Design Wins Willard Hotel Competition." *AIA Journal*, February 1979, p. 21.

Hardy, Hugh. "The Willard Hotel." *Design Quarterly* 113/114 (1980), pp. 38–39.

MAJOR FIRM HONORS AND AWARDS

Since 1967 Hardy Holzman Pfeiffer Associates has received more than one hundred awards recognizing the work of the firm as a whole as well as individual projects. Among the outstanding firm honors and individual project awards are the following:

Firm Award
American Institute of Architects
1981

Medal of Honor
New York Chapter/American Institute of Architects
1978

The Bartlett Award
President's Committee on Employment of the Handicapped and
American Institute of Architects
1976

Arnold W. Brunner Prize in Architecture
National Institute of Arts and Letters
1974

BEST Products Company, Inc. Headquarters
1983 Honor Award for Excellence in Architectural Design
American Institute of Architects

Madison Civic Center
1981 Honor Award for Extended Use and Excellence in Architectural
Design
American Institute of Architects

Saint Louis Art Museum
1979 Honor Award for Extended Use and Excellence in Architectural
Design
American Institute of Architects

Cooper-Hewitt Museum/National Museum of Design
1978 Honor Award for Extended Use and Excellence in Architectural
Design
American Institute of Architects

Columbus Occupational Health Center
1976 Honor Award for Excellence in Architectural Design
American Institute of Architects

BIOGRAPHIES

Hugh Hardy

Malcolm Holzman

Norman Pfeiffer

Victor H. Gong

HUGH HARDY, FAIA

Hugh Hardy was born in Mallorca, Spain, in 1932. He received his B. Arch. in 1954 and his M.F.A. in Architecture in 1956 from Princeton University, where he was a D'Amato Prizeman. He served as a construction-drafting instructor in the Army Corps of Engineers from 1956 to 1958 and as the architectural liaison between Jo Mielziner and Eero Saarinen during design of the Vivian Beaumont Theater at Lincoln Center from 1958 to 1962. Before establishing a partnership with Malcolm Holzman and Norman Pfeiffer in 1967, Hardy was the principal of Hugh Hardy & Associates (1962–66).

Hardy has served as Chairman of the Design Arts Advisory Panel of the National Endowment for the Arts, and currently serves as Vice President of the Municipal Art Society and as a Vice President for Architecture of the Architectural League of New York. He is a member of the board of trustees of the Glimmerglass Opera Company, the New York City Historic House Trust, the Isamu Noguchi Foundation, and the McCarter Theatre Center at Princeton University. He is also an associate of the National Academy of Design and a fellow of the American Institute of Architects.

He has been an instructor at Harvard University's Graduate School of Design and has held both the Saarinen and Davenport Visiting Professorships at Yale University. He has lectured widely and chaired a number of design award juries. He has served as a member of the American Institute of Architects' "Star Firm" roundtable and as an IBM fellow at the International Design Conference in Aspen. His writings have been published in a number of professional and scholarly publications, including *Architectural Record*, *Spazio e Società*, the environmental journals *OZ* and *Places*, and the *Encyclopedia of Architecture*.

MALCOLM HOLZMAN, FAIA

Malcolm Holzman was born in Newark, New Jersey, in 1940. He received his B. Arch. from Pratt Institute in 1963. Before he became a partner in Hardy Holzman Pfeiffer Associates in 967, he was an associate of Hugh Hardy & Associates (1964–66), a designer with John Graham & Company (1963), and a draftsman at various New York City firms.

Holzman is a fellow of the American Institute of Architects and has held several academic appointments throughout the United States,

including the Saarinen and Davenport Visiting Professorships at Yale University in 1987 and 1976, respectively; the Eschweiler Professorship at the University of Wisconsin-Milwaukee's School of Architecture and Urban Design, 1977–79; and, in 1991, a Visiting Professorship at the Lawrence Technological University's College of Architecture and Design. In recognition of his many contributions to the fields of architecture and education, Holzman received Pratt Institute's Distinguished Alumni Achievement Award for 1988; and in 1991 he was named a trustee of the institute. Holzman also serves on the board of trustees of the Amon Carter Museum, Fort Worth, Texas.

A frequent lecturer at professional and public events in the United States and Canada, Holzman has also participated in academic and professional juries and symposia. He has contributed articles to *Smithsonian*, *Architecture*, and *Progressive Architecture* on topics ranging from Michelangelo's Campidoglio to the work of the Scottish architect Alexander Thomson. He has also directed research for the book *Movie Palaces: Renaissance and Reuse*, published by the Academy for Educational Development.

NORMAN PFEIFFER, FAIA

Norman Pfeiffer was born in Seattle in 1940. He received his B. Arch. cum laude from the University of Washington in 1964. In 1965 he received his M. Arch. from Columbia University. Before becoming a partner in Hardy Holzman Pfeiffer Associates in 1967, Pfeiffer was an associate of Hugh Hardy & Associates (1965–66). In 1986 he returned to the West Coast to establish HHPA's Los Angeles office.

An active participant in the profession throughout the western United States, Pfeiffer was appointed to the Architectural Commission of the University of Washington in 1989 and since 1987 has served as Visiting Professor of Architectural Design at U.C.L.A. He also served as Davenport Visiting Professor of Architectural Design at Yale University in 1976, and in the late 1960s was a Visiting Professor of Architecture at the University of Cincinnati. He is a fellow of the American Institute of Architects and a member of the Central City Association of Los Angeles, the Los Angeles Conservancy, and the Los Angeles Historic Theater Foundation.

Pfeiffer is a frequent contributor to discussions on the issues of architecture and urbanism,

including the 1990 American Library Association Conference and L.A. Architect's 1989 "Critics & Cranes" symposium, which featured newsmakers in the development of downtown Los Angeles. He has also written several articles on preservation, including "Saving Grand Central Terminal or the Future of Midtown Manhattan," in the *Journal of Architectural Education,* and "Older Buildings Compete," in the *Office Market Journal of Greater Los Angeles,* as well as co-authoring (with Hugh Hardy and Malcolm Holzman) the book *Reusing Railroad Stations.*

VICTOR H. GONG, AIA

Victor H. Gong was born in San Francisco in 1946. In 1969 he received his B. Arch. with honors from the University of California at Berkeley, and in 1971 he received his M. Arch. from the University of Pennsylvania, where he studied with Louis I. Kahn.

Gong joined Hardy Holzman Pfeiffer Associates in 1976 and was named an associate in 1979. In 1981 he was named a partner of Hardy Holzman Pfeiffer Associates; he is responsible for project management and the firm's daily operations. Before joining HHPA, Gong worked as an architect with several New York City firms, including Skidmore, Owings & Merrill and Gruen Associates.

Gong is a registered architect in Alaska, New York State, and Ohio and is NCARB certified. He is also a member of the American Institute of Architects, the New York Chapter of the American Institute of Architects, and the New York State Association of Architects, among various other professional organizations.

COLLABORATORS SINCE 1967

286 The nature of this volume precludes appropriate mention of all the individuals whose aesthetic, technical, and administrative talents have contributed to Hardy Holzman Pfeiffer Associates. In the following list we have credited those who have participated for six months or more in the HHPA collaboration.

Partners
Hugh Hardy
Malcolm Holzman
Norman Pfeiffer
Victor H. Gong

Associate Partner
Stephen Johnson

Senior Associates
Harris Feinn
Kalavati A. Somvanshi

Associates
Robert T. Almodóvar
Donald Billinkoff
Diane R. Blum
Evan Carzis
Kenneth Drucker
Darlene O. Fridstein
Alec W. Gibson
Stewart B. Jones
Kurt W. Kucsma
Robin Kunz
Don A. Lasker
Pamela J. Loeffelman
Raoul Lowenberg
John J. Lowery
Jack Martin
Cleo Phillips
David W. Rau
Conrad D. Schaub
Craig A. Swanson
Mark Tannin
Marvin Wiehe
Peter Wilson

Design and Production Staff
R. Cleveland Adams, Jr.
James W. Akers
Ron Albinson
Dorothy Alexander
Robert Allen
Gerd Althofer
Eric Anderson
David D. Arnold
Tracy Aronoff

Vivian Awner
Reed M. Axelrod
Richard L. Ayotte
Nili Baider
Thomas Baio
Curtis R. Bales
Elizabeth P. Barnhill
Thomas A. Bauer
Kim Beeler
J. Anne E. Bell
Ann Benson
Christopher Lee Bercel
Carol Berens
Caroline Bertrand
David E. Biscaye
Anthony Scott Blanchard
John P. Bohan
William David Boling
John Bossung
Nestor Bottino
François Bourdin
Stephanie A. Bower
Joseph A. Briggs
Scott W. Briggs
James Brogan
Mark A. Buchalter
Paul Buck
George F. Buckmann
Susan E. Butcher
Jerome Buttrick
Mary Buttrick
David Cagle
Benjamin Caldwell
Brian Carey
Tom Casey
Joan Won Yee Chan
Hung Vi Chau
John Chimera
Joseph.N. Chou
Jean S. Chu
Woo-Hun Chung
Preston Scott Cohen
Jonathan Cohn
Nathaniel K. Coleman
John B. Collins
Vivien P. Coombs
Tracy A. Conrad

Donal Timothy Coyne
John R. Crellin
H. Hobson Crow III
Donald D'Avanzo
Richard D. Davis
David R. Defilippo
Alphonso Delaney
Mark DeMarta
Steven A. Derasmo
Anthony V. DeSimone
James DeSpirito, Jr.
Edward Dickman
Neil Dixon
Robert David Eisenstat
Milton Ewell
David E. Exline
Foad Farahmand
Maurice Farinas
Sandra R. Ford
Glenn Forley
Jaime A. Fournier
Jacob Frumkin
John Fulop, Jr.
Alan M. Gershon
Charles A. Gifford
Robert P. Goesling
Jacob J. Goldberg
Ira Goldfarb
Michael B. Gordon
Leslie W. Gould
Henry Grabowski
Theron E. Grinage
David Earl Gross
Theodore J. Grunewald
Perry Hall
Mark J. Harari
Michael Hardiman
John C. Harris
Lee Harris
Patrick Hayden
Dave Hoggatt
Stephen Horvath
Tony Hsiao
Nancy E. Humphreys
Yuh-Hwa Hung
Violeta Dumlao Jacobson
Gary Jacquemin

Vincent B. James
John G. Janco
Raul Jara
David B. Johnson
David S. Johnson
Peter Johnston
William Jordan
Elionora Kachka
Michael Kaplan
Alfred Katz
Stephen F. Keller
Mark Kessler
Stephen E. Kirk
Patricia J. Knobloch
Tore Knudsen
Jeffrey W. Kusmick
Anthony Lafazia
Diane K. Lam
Woon Yui Lam
Daniel J. Lansner
William S. Leeds
John B. Leggett
Michelle Lewis
Daniel Wardwell Lincoln
Thomas A. Little
Hilda Lowenberg
Leslie Lam Lu
Joanne I. Maddox
Leah Madrid
Jaime Margulies
John T. Mariani
Todd C. Martin
Carol Maryan
Amy Masters
Jerry McDonnell
Bobby Michael McGlone
Thomas J. McNamara, Jr.
Douglas W. Mehl
Yann Mellet
Brian Martin Melnik
Manuel Mergal
David Mohney
David G. Morin
Monica Morrow
Douglas Moss
Marty Munter
Charles Muse

*Left: New York office, August 1991.
Right: Los Angeles office, August 1991.*

John Thomas Newman
Paul O'Callaghan
Noreen G. O'Carroll
Laura Oh
Setrak Ohannessian
Susan K. Oldroyd
Rachel Claire O'Neill
Margie O'Shea
Hyeshin Park
Karin Payson
Clint Howard Pearson
Rafael Pelli
Daniel A. Perry
W. Scott Perry
Susan Marie Petit
Andrew L. Pettit
Carolle Philippon
Stephen Pickard
Michele Piva
Jeffrey Poorten
Andreas Odysseus Pournaras
Frank J. Prial, Jr.
Brian Principe
Greg Radford
Lynn S. Redding
Lindsay Laird Reeds
John M. Reimnitz
Candace Rosaen Renfro
Robert S. Reno
James Rhodes
Victor Rodriguez
Alison B. Roede
Richard Rose
Michael Ross
Albert J. Rotundo
Ronit Rubin
Stephen Alexander Saitas
Gilbert R. Sanchez
James Sarfaty
Steven Schenker
Alan L. Schwartz
David J. Senninger
Michael C. Sharlow
Ted M. Sheridan
Natalie W. Shivers
Ruey-Bin Shyu
Todd Sklar

Gary Slutzky
Clark O. Smith
George Snead
Steven Solomon
Bruce Spenadel
Sheila Spencer
Patrick Stanigar
M. Herbert Staruch
Douglas A. Stebbins
David Stein
Jonathan Bernard Strauss
Abby P. Suckle
R. Scott Sullivan
James Charles Susman
Peter Szego
Matthew Tendler
Lynne Thurmond-Brandt
John Tittmann
Michael J. Tobin
Steven Tonelson
Samuel Christopher Tonos
Dale Turner
Alex Twining
John A. Van Mulders
John Peter Varsa
Claudio Veliz
Bernard Vernon
Amelia C. Wagenbach
Kristina Walker
Robert Wallace
John Way
Barbara Weinstein
John Wender
Catherine Louise Whalen
Havilande B. Brown Whitcomb
Thomas H. Wittrock
Amy S. Wolk
Joseph S. Woo
Brian T. Wurst
Thomas Yeung
Robert E. York
Steven Zalben
Sergio Zori
Katarzyna Zwierko-Hausbrandt

Administrative Staff

Janet D. Alling
Linda Atkinson
Maria Bauza
Joanna Baymiller
Johnna K. Beeson
Lucrecia M. Beza
Sandra Bryant-Scott
Charles Buchanan
Karen Burden
Claudia Burgess
Julie Carlson
Louisa Chan
Michael Anthony Clay
Edilberto J. Cruz
Annie Doris David
Leonora Davis
Evadney Diaz
Ronald Drummond
Jerry L. Eckmann
Trudy V. Erickson
Antonia Esparra
Nathaniel J. Feldman
Leslie Cannon Fredette
Barbara L. Galison
Janet E. Gladish
Claire M. Hamill
Janice Hannaham
Delores Hawkins
David N. Hernandez
Vilma Hernandez
Kendall Jackman
Parastoo Jalali
Keating Johnson
Maria E. Jones
Harriet Kane
Manjit K. Kingra
Brenda Kinloch
Betty Lau
Lois M. Lazzarino
Robin Lee
Hope Leslie
Ralph Loder
Donna Long
Lynette MacLeod
Christa M. Mahar
Elena Makris

Isabelle Matteson
Barbara E. McCarthy
Annetta McKenzie
Martha B. Metzger
Paul Craig Miller
Beth R. Mollins
Marilyn A. Morgan
Joseph R. Navarre
Jane Nemiroff
Richard O'Brien
Evelyn O'Connor
Katherine Palmer
Miry Park
Diane I. Peck
Christopher Perry
Philip J. Pisano
Linda A. Pitre
Mildred Podwell
Brenda Ramirez
Blanca R. Ramos
Debra L. Rogers
Kris N. Rogers
George A. Sangster
Donna Schenk
Shirley Shay
Charlotte Sholod
Harriet Stettin
Elaine Stewart
Karl Sydney
Betty Tang
Deborah Thomas
Jasmine M. Thompson
Kathleen Thompson
Eric Uhlfelder
Jeffrey Joseph Vasquez
Donna Vicari
Karen G. Wachsman
Gary Scott Walsh
Barbara Wiegand
Janet Wiehe
Julia N. Wilfer
Albert G. Woodson, Jr.
Laurie E. Wulftange
Joanne Yea

PHOTOGRAPHY CREDITS

288 All photos are by Hardy Holzman Pfeiffer Associates except those listed below. Page numbers are followed by figure numbers in parentheses.

Peter Aaron/©ESTO Photographics: 154(6, 7), 264(3)

©Joe C. Aker: 227(1, 3)

©David Anderson: 94(1)

Don Apruzzese: back cover, 101

©Christopher Arend: 17(11), 168(1), 174, 266(4)

©Patricia Layman Bazelon: 29(14), 128(10)

©Robert Beckhard: 255(1)

©Hans L. Blohm: 237(1)

©Erik Borg: 25, 183, 185(6, 8), 186–87, 274(1, 2)

©Peter Brenner, Photographic Services Department, Los Angeles County Museum of Art: front cover, 22(24), 143(7)

Bridgemarket Associates: 270(2)

Brooklyn Academy of Music: 153(5)

©Louis Checkman: 199, 212(2), 213(3), 259(3), 270(3)

Courtesy of Cleveland Public Library: 216(2)

Community Redevelopment Agency of Los Angeles: 17(10)

Coral Gables/Biltmore Hotel: 262(4)

Courtesy of Cooper-Hewitt, National Museum of Design, Smithsonian Institution: 53(5)

©Whitney Cox: 126(7)

City of Eugene: 90(7)

©Enrico Ferorelli: 81

City of Fort Worth: 254(3)

©Jeff Heatly: 242(5)

©Carol Highsmith: 98(2)

©Wolfgang Hoyt: 267(3)

©Timothy Hursley: 16(8), 17(12), 89, 90(6), 95(5), 256(5)

©Elliot Kaufman: 29(8), 150(5), 157–59, 181, 262(3, 5), 266(2), 275(1)

©Balthazar Korab: 46(1)

©Alan Lincourt: 149

©Christopher Little: 18, 148(1), 150(6), 151, 161(2), 162–65, 169, 170, 171(5–8), 172–73, 175, 264(2), 266(1), 272(4), 285

Los Angeles County Museum of Art: 140(1), 145

©Christopher Lovi for Hardy Holzman Pfeiffer Associates: 19, 20(18, 19), 153(4), 202–3, 206–7, 217(1), 221, 223(4), 228(1), 229, 259(4), 268(1), 271(2, 5), 273(2, 3, 4), 274(4), 276(1, 4), 277(2, 3, 5), 278(1, 4), 279(2), 286

©Richard Mandlekorn: 131(4)

Peter Maus/©ESTO Photographics: 269(2)

Robert Mayer: 70(1)

©Norman McGrath: 14, 15(2, 4), 16(9), 20(16), 22(23, 27), 23(28), 27(3), 28(5), 29(15), 32(1, 2), 37, 39, 40(1), 41–43, 44(1), 45, 46(2), 47, 48(1, 2), 49, 50(1, 2), 51, 53(4), 54–55, 56(1, 2), 57–59, 65–69, 72(1), 73–79, 82–85, 86(1), 87, 88(1), 90(4, 5), 91–93, 94(2), 96, 97(8, 9, 10), 100(1), 102–5, 107–9, 111–14, 121–23, 131(5), 132–35, 136(1), 137–39, 236(3, 4), 237(2, 4, 5), 238(1, 2, 4, 5), 239(1, 2), 240(2, 5), 241(4, 5), 242(1, 2, 4), 243(1, 2, 4), 244(1, 3, 4, 5), 245(3, 5), 246(1, 3, 5), 248(2, 3), 249(3), 250(3), 251(3), 252(1, 2), 255(2, 3), 258(1, 2, 3, 5), 260(5), 261(1, 5), 262(2), 263(3), 267(5), 269(4)

©Jerry Morgenroth: 243(3)

©Grant Mudford: 142, 143(6, 8), 144, 146–47, 263(2)

National Capitol Planning Commission: 198(1)

New Haven Free Public Library: 15(3)

New York Central Terminal: 272(5)

©Milton Newman: 260(4)

©Zbigniew Orlewicz: 99(1), 225(6), 278(5)

Courtesy of The Punahou School: 223(3)

©Cervin Robinson: 15(5, 6), 16(7), 28(7), 29(11, 13), 60(1), 61–63, 71, 117–19, 125, 126(6), 127, 128(9), 129, 166–67, 177, 247(4), 254(2, 5), 256(2), 259(2), 260(3), 261(3), 272(3)

Courtesy of Rockefeller Center © The Rockefeller Group: 160(1)

©Laura Rosen: 52(1, 2), 254(4)

©Steve Rosenthal: 270(1)

©H. Durston Saylor: 28(6), 154(8, 9), 155

Security Pacific Photograph Collection, Los Angeles Public Library: 230(2)

Courtesy of State Historical Society of Wisconsin: 80(1)

Ezra Stoller/©ESTO Photographics: 249(1)

©Tim Street-Porter: 141

©Eric Sutherland: 244(2)

Courtesy of University of Nebraska at Omaha: 212(1)

Virginia Museum of Fine Arts Photo by Ron Jennings: 124(1)

©Paul Warchol: 178–79

©Bob Ware: 29(9), 232(4), 278(2)

Renderings
Brian Burr: 257(1)
Hugh Hardy: 197
Courtesy of Maguire Thomas Partners: 191
David Purceil: 200–201, 231(1), 272(2)

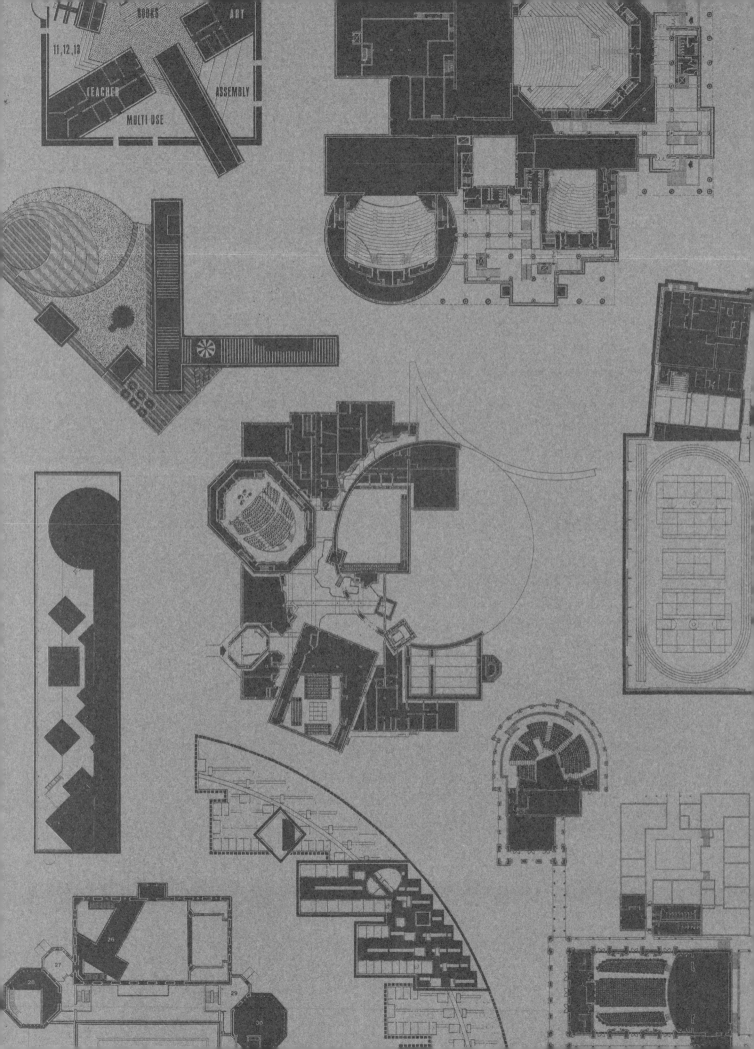